A Century of Spanish Art Abroad

Spanish Art at the Venice Biennale 1895-2003

A Century of Spanish Art Abroad

Spanish Art at the Venice Biennale 1895-2003

TURNER

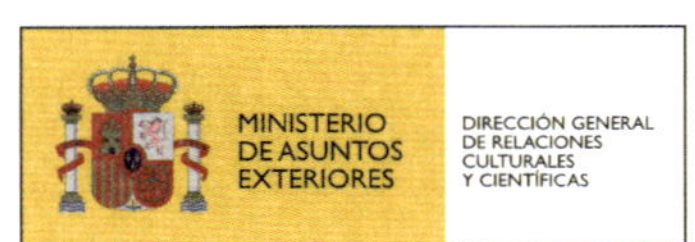

Fundación BBVA

Sponsored by:

Fundación BBVA

Photographs

Reina Sofía National Art Centre, Madrid, Photograph Archives

© MNAC (Calveras / Mérida / Sagristá)

Benlliure House/Museum

Manuel Benedito Foundation

Manuel Ramos Andrade Foundation

José María Yturralde

Art Nouveau and Art Deco Museum, Casa Lis

Chillida-Leku Museum

Asturias Fine Arts Museum

Castellón Fine Arts Museum

Seville Fine Arts Museum

Gustavo de Maeztu Museum

Prado National Museum

Pérez Comendador-Leroux Museum

Sorolla Museum

Toledo Royal Foundation

Photographers

Pedro Feria

Roberto Garver

Some images included in this book have been taken from the Italian catalogues published by "La Biennale di Venezia, Esposizione Internacionale d'Arte" as well as from the catalogues published by the Ministry of Foreign Affairs and other Spanish official bodies.

Published by:

© Ministry of Foreign Affairs. Directorate-General for Cultural and Scientific Relations / Turner

Co-ordination and Production

Silvia Domínguez

Blanca Reyero

© Text

Rosalía Torrent Escalpés

Jaume I. University, Castellón

Luis González Robles

Enriqueta Antolín

Translation

Ann Canosa

Jenny Dodman

Design

Manuel Fernández (MF)

Image Management

Juncal Caballero Guiral

Photocomposition

F. Principado

Printing

Gráficas Eujoa

ISBN 84-7506-611-9

Dep. Legal: AS 3.083/03

www.turnerlibros.com

Acknowledgments

Luis González Robles
Tomàs Llorens

Valencia City Council
Benlliure House/Museum
Manuel Benedito Foundation
Manuel Ramos Andrade Foundation
Regional Government of Andalusia
Ministry of Defence
Ministry of Education, Culture and Sport
Art Nouveau and Art Deco Museum, Casa Lis
Chillida-Leku Museum
Asturias Fine Arts Museum
Castellón Fine Arts Museum
Seville Fine Arts Museum
Army Museum
Gustavo de Maeztu Museum
Reina Sofía National Art Museum
Prado National Museum
Pérez Comendador-Leroux Museum
Sorolla Museum
Catalonia National Art Museum
Toledo Royal Foundation

Elvireta Escobio
Pascual Masiá
Vicenta Benedito

And all those who preferred to remain anonymous

It is an honour for the Ministry of Foreign Affairs to introduce this book, which gives an account of the history of Spanish participation in the Venice Biennale. A publication like this was necessary for several reasons; the first and most obvious is that the fiftieth Biennale will take place in 2003, so that the book will constitute a reminder and well-deserved congratulations on this anniversary. ▮ Over the course of the 50 occasions on which the Venice Biennale has been held, it has unquestionably become one of the pivotal centres of contemporary art. Whatever takes place in Venice is amplified, established and disseminated to such an extent that any review of the evolution of trends in art in the 20th century must necessarily discuss the Biennale. ▮ There is no doubt that the concept of art has changed since the first Biennale opened in 1895. It is no exaggeration to say that the Biennale has not only been the stage, but also the chief actor responsible for this change. The history of art shows that any significant mutation is associated at origin with controversy, scandal and debate. Precisely because the Biennale has not shied away from controversy, scandal or debate, it has promoted the appearance of new forms of expression, and therefore of understanding of the complex world in which we live. ▮ Spain has never distanced itself from this process, and that is the second reason for supporting the publication of this book. Our country has shown a firm commitment to the Venice Biennale, and to its spirit of renewal and modernism, from the outset. This commitment prevailed over the vicissitudes of our turbulent history of the past century, and permeated the Spanish participation even during those periods when our country appeared to be anchored in immobility. ▌Therefore, a look at the Spanish participation in the Biennale necessarily becomes a review of the evolution of contemporary Spanish art. Convincing evidence emerges from reading these pages that Spanish artists have adopted, without inhibitions, the most contemporary and avant-garde creative idioms, enriching them with new content and original interpretations of our artistic tradition. ▌For the Ministry of Foreign Affairs, which has been co-ordinating the Spanish presence at the Venice Biennale since 1950, this book symbolises the upholding and the projection towards the future of this commitment to the Biennale; but it also especially symbolises a resolute pledge to the promotion abroad of contemporary Spanish artists, who reflect the reality of a modern, dynamic and open country.

Page

The Mask and the Reality: Spanish Art at the Venice Biennale

The Venice Biennale:
Data for a Story

Anyone who has never been to the Venice Biennale would find it difficult to visualise how this exhibition is arranged and how art is shown here in a new and different way. This is because of the unusual organisation of space, which is structured round some singular buildings located in the *Giardini di Castello*. Although the constant growth of the Biennale has led it to expand beyond the limits of the Gardens and today the whole of Venice is involved in the exhibition, that area continues to be its basic reference –a place for walking and contemplation, of contrasting construction of its buildings (some traditional and others with a contemporary look), and of a multiplicity of exhibits housed in them.

The Gardens are the only large green area in Venice. The first Biennale was opened in 1895. Its venue –unique at that time– was an edifice planned by Enrico Trevisanato. In order to build it, it was necessary to demolish the old stables and the former stall that was the home of Toni the elephant, the much-loved and symbolic attraction for Venetian children. The design for the façade was entrusted to painter Marius De Maria, who erected a colonnade of plaster and synthetic marble crowned by a kind of Greek pediment on the apex of which there was a winged being. But nothing remains of that neo-classical (nowadays we would call it kitsch) façade, which has been remodelled on different occasions. In 1995 –the centenary year– the building underwent another transformation to adapt it to better meet modern expectations.

However, the special features of the area of the Gardens are not seen in this structure (which at the beginning housed all the works exhibited, both Italian and from abroad), but rather in the pavilions that were progressively built to accommodate the art representing the different countries. With that of Belgium in 1907, and Hungary in 1909, they initially constituted a triangle that was immediately challenged by the British and German pavilions –also built in 1909– placed opposite to those mentioned. The Spanish pavilion, for its part, was opened in 1922, still without some of its galleries and the decoration that would be added in time for the next exhibition. Thus, the Gardens were progressively filled with a number of structures that became embassies in miniature for the different countries. Each of them, with its particular formal characteristics, reflected the architectural ideas of the places that were promoting them. Done and redone on successive occasions, they also provided a record of their formal evolution.

And between the pavilions are the old trees. Many of them had to give way to bricks and cement, but those that remain still continue to offer passers-by a welcoming natural setting for reflection. This special form of exhibition presented to the spectator-traveller (traveller because visiting the Biennale is not only a matter of going to a *rendez-vous* with art, but also of a commitment to a wandering gaze by someone who loves to move around) has nevertheless incurred some costs. The greatest of these has been for the Venetians themselves, who have seen how a part of the Gardens, their Gardens, those where children, young people and old, used to go to relax, to play and to walk, were closed to the public –something that provoked a large number of protests.

But here Venice shows the face that, whether we like it or not, has contributed throughout the 20th century, to defining the city: it now lives essentially for those who come from elsewhere, in order to provide areas of cultural tourism for them during their days of transit through the city. The Venetians who have always lived there seldom stir beyond the confines of their respective *sestieri*: Cannareggio, Santa Croce, San Marco.... Castello –the traditional

The Gardens are the only large green area in Venice. The first Biennale was opened in 1895

sestiere of the Biennale and one of the *vaporetto's* last stops before going on to the Lido.

The Biennale was planned precisely in order to emphasize the cultural side of Venice. Venice at the close of the 19th century needed a project in order to open up to the outside world. A number of people got involved in it who could predict the future needs of the city and who, in little rooms at the Café Florian –whose decadent beauty continues to have an impact on travellers– held impassioned meetings for the purpose of setting up the Venice Biennale.

The cafés were commonly a place for discussion and debate on the most interesting topics of the moment –to such an extent, as Alessandro Stella tells us, that they came to be called "small parliaments or senates." The same author vividly describes how, at the cafés, the idea of a great art exhibition was conceived, one of whose aims would be to consolidate Italian unity and at the same time set up an area for contacts with the outside world. Indeed, the Biennale was planned from the beginning as an international art meeting. That is what the group of people meeting at the Café Florian with Riccardo Selvatico, mayor of the city, thought. He, together with other figures linked to a greater or lesser extent to art culture, wanted to make Venice a place for the future, although perhaps at the beginning they themselves were not fully aware of the magnitude of what they were proposing. The initial members of the group were joined by others who played a fundamental role in the development of the Biennale, as was the case of Antonio Fradeletto, an academic and an excellent organiser.

The idea of holding major national art exhibitions was not new in Italy. Indeed, the recent unification of the country needed all sorts of events to reaffirm the recently-acquired common identity. Art could be a strategic element to achieve these ends. Before Venice, Parma, Milan, Naples and Turin had tried out their own proposals, although the standard had not reached the level planned. Venice had also organised an exhibition in 1887, and with it had outdone those staged until that time. It took place in the *Giardini di Castello* themselves, and its success probably provided a driving force for the Biennale. Good organisational ability was shown at that time, and an ideal place had been found in the Gardens.

In 1893, Selvatico conveyed the proposal about the exhibition to the Corporation over which he presided, in order to commemorate, as was recorded at the council session, "the silver wedding of Their Majesties King Umberto and Queen Margarita." The idea of placing it under the protection of the sovereigns was excellent since in that way the consent of the municipal council was achieved and it was dissociated from the positioning of political parties. So it was not surprising that this fact was repeatedly referred to in official documents of the City Council and in the exhibition catalogue.

The success of the first Biennale contributed to its consolidation, although all the exhibitions that took place until the First World War remained complacently conservative, ignoring the creative effervescence of the close of the 19th and beginning of the 20th centuries. Only after the tenth exhibition in 1912, when Fradeletto, sensing the coming of new times, hit on the bright idea of assigning responsibility to Vittorio Pica, did a change begin to be felt, to which, however, the war –which surprised the exhibition in full activity– soon put an end.

But something else was moving in the Venice art world, unconnected with the Biennale –events that in the future would contribute to changing it. A significant episode was the taking over in 1907 of the management of the Venice Gallery of Modern Art by the very young Nino Barbantini. He took it upon himself to bring artists who used advanced idioms to Ca'Pesaro. For a time both institutions (the Biennale and the Gallery) were locked in confrontation, but the future would prove Barbantini right and he would have the last word. Another significant incident took place in connection with the Futurists. Their leader, Marinetti, expressed his anger in La Fenice, in his *Discorso contra i veneziani*. This was, in reality, a speech against a city that was asleep and dreaming a romantic dream, whereas he wanted it to be "industrial, commercial and military." In art, he would seek out the new against the exhausted discourse proper to the past.

When the war was over, the difficulties of a Europe in process of reconstruction were felt by the Biennale, but notwithstanding everything, the first exhibition in 1920 was perhaps the most attractive of all, since Vittorio Pica, the new secretary-general, introduced "by surprise" some innovations for which he was very soon reproached by the most conservative sectors. His management was curbed by municipal authorities who interfered directly in the affairs of the Biennale and attempted to impose their own criteria. Pica wanted to modernise an exhibition whose contents were seriously at odds with the trends of the times, but he was not strong enough to confront his powerful opponents. He had brought some of the most outstanding figures of the international scene to Venice, attracting those who are now classics of Modernism, but at the same time he allocated space to artists whom history has nowadays rightly forgotten. However, his management, consisting of lights and shadows, would in the future deserve the understanding of many people who were convinced of his positive intentions which,

> Those years were characterised by the expansion of the Biennale project. If at first it had come into being for the sole purpose of constituting an exhibition of visual and plastic art, the intention now was that another series of fields should be included

unfortunately, were not implemented. Tired and ill, Pica resigned from his duties after the 1926 Biennale and was replaced by Antonio Maraini. The latter, a man familiar with the latest trends in art, had defended Cézanne when the work of the French painter was the object of every kind of negative criticism in Venice. Maraini was able to win the confidence of the then president of the exhibition Pietro Orsi, and, feeling supported, he programmed the 1928 Biennale, which undoubtedly turned out to be the best of the period between the two wars. After some vicissitudes and changes of people in positions of responsibility, he succeeded in detaching the Biennale from the authority of the City Council and setting it up as an independent body with legal capacity. Giuseppe Volpi was called upon to assume the presidency, while Maraini remained in charge of the General Secretariat.

Volpi and Maraini were entrusted with furthering the new stage in the life of the institution until the Second World War once more interrupted the holding of the Biennales. This period was marked by two fundamental occurrences: in the first place Italian politics underwent a process of fascistisation from which the Venetian exhibition was unable to escape, with all the consequences that this implied. Secondly, those years were characterised by the expansion of the Biennale project. If at first it had come into being for the sole purpose of constituting an exhibition of visual and plastic art, the intention now was that another series of fields should be included, such as music, cinema and theatre, in response to Volpi's idea of making Venice a reference centre for the different spheres of the cultural universe. The aim was that tourists who went to stay only for the brief period of time that would enable them to tour the classic haunts in the city, would have a diversity of options open to them, beyond those strictly proposed by the Art Biennale. Volpi wanted Venice to always have a show prepared for visitors. Thus, the great project was put in motion and soon the Music Festival (which took place in 1930) was ready, as were the Poetry Meetings (of which only two were organised, one in 1932 and another in 1934), the Film Festival started in 1932 and over time has achieved the same impact as that of art, each, obviously, in its own specific field; moreover, the Theatre Festival began in 1934.

The organisation's wishes to expand did not end there: in 1931 exhibitions of Italian art began to be held abroad, the first of which took place in Athens and New York. Finally, the establishment in 1930 of the *Archivio Storico d'Arte Contemporanea*, under the aegis of an institute already set up two years previously, should be mentioned.

But together with this positive drive towards expansion in Italy, another, equally expansionist, but negatively all-consuming movement, had also started. This was Fascism. Many intellectuals, artists and men of literature allowed themselves to be taken in by an ideology that they believed could give back their "lost signs of identity." In the introduction to the catalogue of the 1930 Biennale (the eighth year of the Fascist era, in the words of the text itself), we read a message whose contents are clear: "The intensity of international changes has led in recent decades to the prevailing of a cosmopolitan aesthetic climate over the trends and traditions of different countries and races. This cosmopolitanism has mainly taken its laws from searches carried out in the convulsed and contrived environment of Parisian circles where true talent meets together with trickery, voracious interests and morbid ambitions. In order to please the stateless exclusiveness of these circles and cliques of initiates, the artists have

From the ashes of the war, a renewed Biennale arose. The appointment of Pallucchini as secretary-general, backed by the mayor, Ponti, resulted in one of the highlights of the Venetian exhibition

distanced themselves from the life of the people and have shut themselves up in the ivory tower of intransigent subjectivism." Very soon –in fact immediately– the trends and traditions of a country, "of a race," would be invoked on all fronts in order to reject those of neighbouring countries. Ultra-nationalist alarmism was already at the gates.

At the same time, equally serious was the silence imposed from on high on progressive criticism, as for example, on Nino Barbantini. In 1932 he had written an article on the Biennale of that year. He would say later, "The article of April 28, 1932, was the last that I wrote on art in my time. Many people liked it, but some did not. On the morning of the 30th the prefect summoned me to go and visit him as soon as possible, and he told me (an order from Rome) that I must not have anything more to do with contemporary art."

Volpi and Maraini found themselves caught up in this tide of events and responded, partly, by letting themselves be carried along on it, and partly by attempting to save some of their most cherished beliefs from the deluge. They had had a good artistic training and wanted the Biennale to reflect the current situation. But the process of fascistisation was unstoppable. Interference with the Biennale became increasingly brutal, being seen above all in the prizes that it had to award. The two most important, given by the National Fascist Party and the Ministry of National Education were, respectively: "For a picture inspired by people or events on the formation of the combat *Fascis* (the picture must show at least one life-size figure)" and "for a statue that exalts the physical and spiritual vigour of the race (the statue may not be less than life-size)."

If we had to take stock of these exhibitions of the Fascist era, we should have to say that they started out in correct mediocrity and ended up by being aesthetically and ethically distressing. To the contradictions and indecision of their directors, and to the Fascist impositions were soon added the reality of a war, which was already waging at the time of the 1942 exhibition. When the exhibition closed in September, it could already be foreseen that the conflict would be a long one, and that it would be difficult to meet the next date. The Gardens were closed to the Biennale and were invaded by the Fascist *Cinecittà*, who used them for nearly a year and a half as gigantic film studios. It is strange to see this *travestimento* of the *Giardini di Castello* in photos of the time. Men and women with diverse costumes, horse-drawn carriages, stage sets..., seemed to live cut off, in their imaginary world, from a war that was spewing out thousands of dead only a few kilometres away.

From the ashes of the war, a renewed Biennale arose. The appointment of Pallucchini as secretary-general, backed by the mayor, Ponti, resulted in one of the highlights of the Venetian exhibition. During the war Venice had never ceased to be a point of reference for Italian intellectuals who, independently of their respective ideologies, continued to consider the city as a focus of culture and a recipient of European concerns. When the war ended, the activities in Venice and the atmosphere it breathed would surprise us if it were not for the fact that it had never succumbed to events and had always attempted to preserve its cultural ties as much as possible.

During his period as secretary-general, Pallucchini wanted to link Venice definitively to modern art projects, but initially, above all (and this became obvious in 1948) he sought to display at the Biennale all those avant-garde movements that, since Impressionism, had arisen in Europe. He also aimed to fill the gaps that Fascism had imposed by sidelining the most significant contemporary trends being developed in other countries. In the opening speeches at the XXIVth Biennale, there was, moreover, a message of peace and a desire for reconciliation. Aware that some countries (such as Germany and Spain) did not wish to participate in it on account of the outcome of the war, Ponti clearly stated, "Art stimulates all men, beyond national borders, beyond ideological barriers, to speak a language that should unite them in humanistic understanding." Little by little normality returned to Venice, and during the following years the different countries recovered their pavilions and the exhibition progressively grew in prestige and in numbers of participants.

The high standard of the Biennales was not enough to obviate the problems. The old statutes, with their already-obsolete rules, made progress difficult. The complications and conflicts started. The Biennale's excessive dependence on the central authority made many initiatives unviable. The coming years would be stormy for the Venetian exhibition and would be the prelude to its own revolution.

The Pallucchini Biennales had borne witness to the emergence of Abstraction and to his controversial confrontation with the realisms. Still in 1958, already with Gian Alberto Dell'Acqua as secretary-general, abstraction (and specifically the informalist proposals) had a strong presence at the Biennale, specifically at the Spanish pavilion. But at the beginning of and throughout the sixties, and until the start of the seventies, other interests seemed to be shaking up the field of art. It was the time of Pop art, Op art, Kinetic art, Neogestaltism and *Povera*... all of which were formulas that, independently of their abstract or representative formulation, pursued interests linked to the basically perceptual or to referents of daily life.

The new Biennales provided excellent information on the latest developments in the sphere of art. They were even criticised for their excessive showing of the "latest thing" and of having relinquished the informative nature of the exhibitions prepared by Pallucchini. But the new secretary-general had opted for doing things differently, and already as of the first exhibition that he directed, had revealed his desire for artistic "emergence." Nevertheless, it was not Venice which first exhibited the alternative formulas to informalism. Paris, São Paulo and San Marino did so ahead of it. With all the more reason, there was now great interest in sanctioning the new trends –a fact that was observed above all at the 1964 Biennale, when the entry of Pop established this basically American phenomenon in Europe.

After having launched its Abstract, and post-Abstract, Expressionists into the world, and now Pop, the United States had already become an inevitable international artistic reference. In plain language, Alan R. Solomon said at the opening of the United States pavilion, "At the present time, Europeans have come to a realisation of the continuity of American influence in art, exercised in the first place by the generation of Abstract Expressionists and now furthered with renewed vitality by another generation of artists who are following multiple courses [...] Everybody recognises that the world centre of art has moved from Paris to New York."

A playful mood appeared to have invaded art and the Biennale in 1966. But perhaps this was only a mask for the underlying uneasiness that became apparent in May '68 with the events in Paris. The climate of action and protest was not only a Parisian occurrence. Many people in cities all over Europe had taken to the streets claiming their right to "question the social system." This climate was also rife in Italy, and as the date approached for the opening of the Biennale, a series of latent conflicts broke out that had now found an outlet for letting off steam. In the same way that reform of the statutes was insistently demanded, many artists in and outside Venice cast doubt on a Biennale modelled on "patterns." Venice lived through some days of agitation; its Academy had been taken over for some months by squatters and the protest demonstrations were repeated. One of them, organised by students and joined by the most committed artists, was dissolved by the police in St. Marks Square itself.... The Biennale opened its doors, then closed them and opened them again a few days later. The wish for reform was obvious, but it had to wait for a few years before being implemented.

´68 had passed by in Venice like a summer storm, but the causes that unleashed it remained practically intact. For this reason, and with a view to a possible resumption of hostilities, the problem of the reform of its statutes was brought up again –this time with the serious resolve to carry it out. However, the continuous reshuffles in the Italian government caused the project to be postponed time after time. In 1974 there was no Biennale, this being the first time in its history, not counting periods of war, that it had not been held. Although new statutes had already been envisaged in 1973, a reasonable time was necessary in order for the new provisions emanating from them to be put into practice.

Inspired by the spirit of '68, the "new Biennale" –whose first exhibition of visual arts would take place in 1976, but which two years previously was already programming multiple activities– took on a role that reflected the dissidence. The still recent May of '68 had forced the artists and their managers to position themselves politically. Ripa di Meana, the first president of the recently-opened "democratic Biennale" was not ambiguous in this connection. Among his first objectives was that of denouncing the oppression suffered by the Latin-American countries –specifically opposing the repression in Chile– as well as the consequences of the Spanish dictatorship. But the politicisation of the exhibition was not greeted by everybody with the same sympathy. Accusing it of "excesses," many expressed their wish to see it revert to its role as an art fair, and not degenerate into an international platform for denunciation. However, the public reacted positively and was moved by the Salvador Allende, or Quilapayun, Brigades.

Space was also allocated in the Biennale to feminist collectives especially invited by it, who through talks or exhibitions offered their view on the current problems of women. It was then that Cardinal Luciani, Patriarch of Venice (later John Paul I) issued a condemnation in St. Mark's Basilica of the "morally dirty" art programmed by the women's groups.

Ripa's management caused an uproar of criticism that naturally affected him given that even the trade unions challenged it, calling it "personalistic." But this criticism did not prevent him from working in successive years and presenting his dreams of Utopia. The theatre took to the streets in 1975 with the unforgettable performance of the new anarchists of the *Living Theatre*; in 1976 the *Giardini di Castello* again housed the exhibition of visual arts. One of its major projects concerned Spain, which presented a non-official art exhibition reviewing forty years of Spanish art from 1936 to 1976.

In general, however, this Biennale was not a showcase for ideology. It continued, above all, to be an art exhibition, where recent trends were displayed and where, at the same time, discourse on and interest in social and political issues were not neglected. It is in this context that the programming of the Spanish contribution must be understood. Words such as "artistic commitment" continued to resound. To Ripa di Meana's question about the type of requirement demanded from the intellectuals, in a civil or cultural sense, Alberto Moravia replied, "Cultural commitment. At the same time, cultural commitment can be no other than political commitment." Politics and terrorism were in the eye of the Italian hurricane when Aldo Moro was assassinated in 1978 –which occurrence was not omitted from the introduction to the catalogue for the Biennale that year.

The eighties dawned with new forms of doing art. Already since the close of the seventies a return to painting's traditional supports had been observed. Although the art-technology relationship would be progressively imposed, for some years there was a return to the use of classic supports and materials, and the "citationist" movement (references to the classics) became popular. Sculpture, for its part, acquired novel features and proved to be one of the best-received forms of art. The Biennales of those years reflected the elements mentioned, and particularly that of 1984, with an exhibition entitled "Art in the Mirror," became a clear exponent of those recurring formulas. But German Neo-Expressionists and post-modern taste also became a feature during a decade in which the new presidents of the Biennale focused their efforts on consolidating the Venetian institution, while at the same time different curators, reflecting different ideas and trends, would make their respective proposals.

The eighties, which were much more multifaceted than many people would like to acknowledge, marked a "return to order" which was translated into occurrences that seemed unimportant but were in fact very significant. An example was the restoration of the system of prizes, which had been abolished following the events of '68, when the favouritism, pressures and self-serving motivations that so often accompanied these recognitions were condemned. But prize-giving meant *glamour*, press releases and returning to the market system. '68, and with it its ideals, were now long gone.

The ideals had gone, but the problems remained. The disagreements recurred about who should direct the exhibition; the budgets were late in arriving; the reform of the statutes was urgently requested. In 1988 there were scarcely four working months to prepare an event of this magnitude; everyone was asking themselves about the chances of the Biennale competing with Kassel, whose Documenta was already considered the number one in contemporary art....

After the 1990 exhibition, the Biennale should have been held in 1992. However, it was postponed until the following year, 1993. It was a matter of giving it some leeway, a breathing space after so many management and financial difficulties. Above all, more time was needed to enable the new person in charge to organise the exhibition calmly. The controversial Achille Bonito Oliva was entrusted with this Biennale, which took place a century after the idea of the exhibition had taken shape at those meetings so long ago in the Café Florian.

Adopting the basic idea that contemporary art had developed through cultural nomadism and the co-existence of idioms, Achille Bonito structured an exhibition that was described as eclectic and personalistic. In any event, he had contributed to introducing the concept of multiculturalism, although it is fair to recall that this concept had already been seen in the seventies and that the nineties did no more than pluralise and redefine it. If this feature of multiple idioms and cultures belonged to the nineties, it would also be progressively true of the multimedia phenomenon, especially the videographic projects that became the protagonists of art galleries that had to remodel their space to adapt it to the new requirements of art that once more had minimised the impact of painting. Nowadays pictorial bidimensionalism has been taken over, in the media, by photography; and if sculpture has been preserved, it is only because it is increasingly less like the idea that we had about it. But nor is the language of the multimedia new; what has happened is that its moon now waxes high in the heavens. One day it will undoubtedly wane, and then it will rise again and we will find it different –in the same way as painting, sculpture and even forms of art about which we as yet have no intuition.

In Venice the different directors of the last decade of the 20th and the opening years of the 21st centuries have, as might be expected, developed very different projects. From the new interpretations of modern art by Clair to the "Platea dell'umanitá" by Szeemann, the Biennale has been determined –as is natural– by the personal options of its directors. For the current exhibition, which will be the fiftieth, Francesco Bonami proposes the title "Dreams and Conflicts: The Dictatorship of the Spectator." In this connection, it should be recalled that since the Biennales were established they have been held under generic titles that, at least ideally, should serve as points of departure not only for the general exhibition proposed by the Biennale, but also for the pavilions of the different countries. However, the latter's response has been very irregular.

The continuous growth of the Venice Biennale has meant that the *Giardini di Castello* no longer constitute the only nucleus –although they do continue to be the most representative– of the exhibition. Already in the eighties, the so-called Aperto was institutionalised in the *Corderie dell'Arsenale* (an area adjoining the Gardens), which is reserved for artists who have never exhibited before at the Biennale, and where it was planned to stage the most novel art productions of the moment –those which, as a result of the special design of the exhibition itself could not easily be a part of it– or at least in a massive or systematic way. Although the Aperto disappeared under a cloud of controversy, the aforementioned area, together with others that have progressively been added over the course of time, has gradually enlarged the Biennale's space for walking and viewing.

If this feature of multiple idioms and cultures belonged to the nineties, it would also be progressively true of the multimedia phenomenon

Spain at the Venice Biennale

Introduction

A long relationship links Spanish art to the Venice Biennale. Since the first exhibition in 1895 until today Spain has participated assiduously in the Italian exhibition, from which it has been absent on only a very few occasions. It has had an opportunity over the course of more than a hundred years to present its artistic production in the *Giardini di Castello*, and through it, to exhibit its lights and its shades, its mask and its reality. Mask and reality... the metaphorical play of Venetian resonances serves very well to express what Spanish art has been at the Biennale, the forms that it has taken there, the ideas that it has conveyed.. forms and ideas that at times have lighted up –and at others masked– its most outstanding achievements.

For a long time Spain had turned its back on new international ideas, and therefore it also turned its back on the artists who dabbled in them. At Venice it would display, as signs of identity, art anchored in a tradition considered to be the immutable truth and pride of a people. Simultaneously, however, there were entries by Spanish artists imbued superficially and late with the trends of Modernism. In any event we can say that, at the first Biennales, Spain reflected at Venice a country whose 20th century, artistically (not counting artists such as Picasso), had been inaugurated on the basis of 19th century *fin-de-siècle* art, capable of including entirely opposing emotional and formal nuances, although only exceptionally linked to the emerging trends. From the every-day to the exotic, from the truculent to the candid.. all these features competed in painting and sculpture. Spain's initial entry at the Biennale, in keeping with the reality of the country, looked old fashioned and would appear antiquated to us, especially in comparison with the works and the idioms that were then being developed in other parts of Europe. But it did not fail to reflect the current reality in art and, at the same time, did not conflict with a Biennale that was a paradigm of academicist habits and trends.

As the 20th century progressed and until the start of the Civil War, it could be observed how the achievements of Spanish art were masked at Venice: although experiencing moments of great interest –at least abroad– it was unable to establish a meaningful foothold at the exhibition. The discoveries of artists linked to the new trends were minimised. Although some of them were represented at the Biennale, only an insignificant sampling of their work was shown, discriminated against by a policy that rewarded eclecticism and numbers as against formal argument and individualisation.

During the war and the post-war period, the compulsion to impose images of national identity would result in the exhibition of pro-Franco art in the exceptional showcase of the Biennales. A duel result was thus achieved: the imposition of figurativism and the exaltation of the nascent regime. A thick veil covered the other side of Spanish art –that which was developing in exile, but also that which was beginning to germinate in the country itself.

Recovery came in the fifties, responding to the emergence of creativity in the shape of Informalism, although also in new forms of realism far-removed from academies and decorativism. It seemed as if art and artists had suddenly taken off the masks of prescribed history and decided to show their art bare, divested of the burden of years of inertia. Franco's Spain –or perhaps a curator of proven intuition– decided to take these representatives of what was new to the Biennale. The latter, however, would soon ask themselves about their role within the dictatorship's art policy and would question their own presence at exhibitions

The period of Spanish democracy (or rather, the period of transition) opened in Venice with an exhibition organised by non-official sources

programmed by the State, debating on whether to show the reality of art or the mask of a country.

The period of Spanish democracy (or rather, the period of transition) opened in Venice with an exhibition organised by non-official sources. It was a matter of synthesising everything that for forty years, theoretically, was unable to be shown either on the national or the international circuits. And, indeed, many things could be seen that either on account of their content or the ideology of their creator, had not been allowed until then. "Social reality" –the key concept at this exhibition– came into its own at the Biennale, although another part of reality –especially informalist reality– had already been exhibited in previous years. At the same time, the word "avant-garde" –another pivotal element– was strongly in evidence.

Almost thirty years have elapsed since Spain won its democracy. During this time it could be thought (given the new determinants) that there was no longer any need to talk about masking in its exhibition policy at the Biennale since, with varying success, attempts had been made to show significant formulas in current art. But our country had still not renounced its Venetian trait, in the sense that it continued to toy with a possibilist mask. Thus, on occasions its programming was done in the interests of what could seem plausible abroad rather than of adherence to vehicular criteria of emerging art. It is in this connection that reproaches have been levelled at the Spanish pavilion, from within and without, for certain absences. But this is a modern fair, and this is surely the price that has to be paid for hiring the stand.

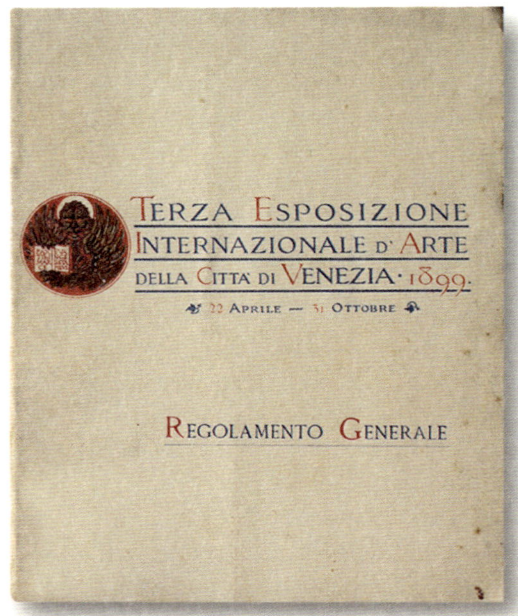

Title page of Italian catalogue, 1899

The First Biennales: 1895–1914

Now we shall review Spanish art at Venice from 1895 –the year that the exhibition was inaugurated– to 1914. The war, which put a brake on so many activities, also affected the Biennale. The start of great wars is usually a date on which history puts a full-stop to no matter what activity. In the specific case of Spain, in so far as art was concerned, an unpredictable variable was introduced since, as a result of the conflict, the first major influx of art and artists took place, artists who for a while found refuge in a country not involved in the war.

Spain would participate in the first Biennales with a strong showing of eclecticism. At that time, academicist painters of history lived together with painters of local customs (*costumbristas*) and regional customs of different kinds, who in turn rubbed shoulders with orientalists or "Realists" with an expressive streak. At the same time, Catalonia's contacts with Europe had resulted in the echoing of experiences such as Impressionism and movements such as Modernism in the projects of some artists, especially in those of that region. At the same time, we cannot fail to be aware (a little later) of some timid traces of the nascent avant-gardes, such as the Expressionist, Fauvist and Cubist.

However, the contacts with Modernism were few during the years of transition from the 19th to the 20th centuries. In painting and sculpture, historic themes still persisted, being one of the mainstays of art of the time. The new historicism –as Valeriano Bozal pointed out– was unrelated to the one so much esteemed by the Romantic movement. As opposed to the sincerity of the Romantics' search, history according to the ideals of the new bourgeoisie was only of interest as a decorative framework for the present. The last third of the 19th century produced two waves of historic painting. Of the two, only the second managed to send its representatives to the

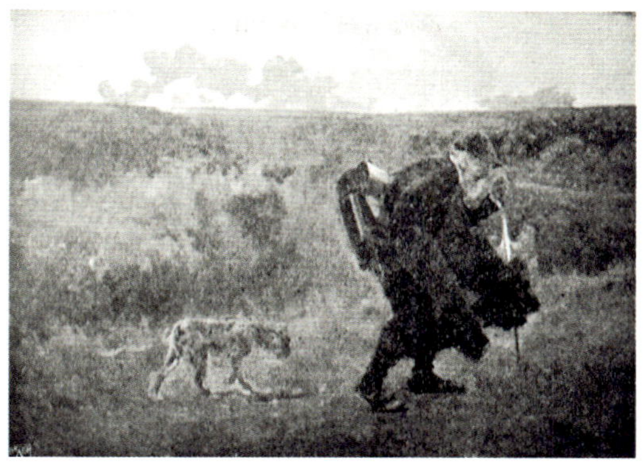

Biennales. The first –consisting, among others, of Casado del Alisal, Palmaroli, Gisbert and Rosales– was much esteemed, but the second comprised artists of lesser interest. Gaya Nuño, who was implacable, referred as follows to the new craze for these pseudo-historic themes: "The genre had had its day; but the mediocre artists had not yet come to this realisation and continued to afflict the national exhibitions with pictures that were increasingly enormous, increasingly melancholic, bitter, truculent and bloody. Neither the attractive colouring of Casado del Alisal nor the portentous drawing of Rosales...."

Among the second wave of painters of history were some who took their work to Venice. This was the case of Emilio Sala from Ascoy and Muñoz Degrain from Valencia. In any case they do not seem to fully deserve Gaya's criticisms, given that Muñoz Degrain was an esteemed painter with dramatic and fantastic touches who broke with the Valencian tradition of *costumbrismo* (the depiction of local customs), although effectism proved to be his weak point. The first time that he exhibited at the Biennale was in 1924, the year of his death. At the 1932 Biennale, an individual retrospective exhibition was dedicated to him which included some pictures with historic themes. Emilio Sala, for his part, was at the first Biennale.

Emilio Sala
"Ocaso" (Sunset)
Italian Catalogue, 1895

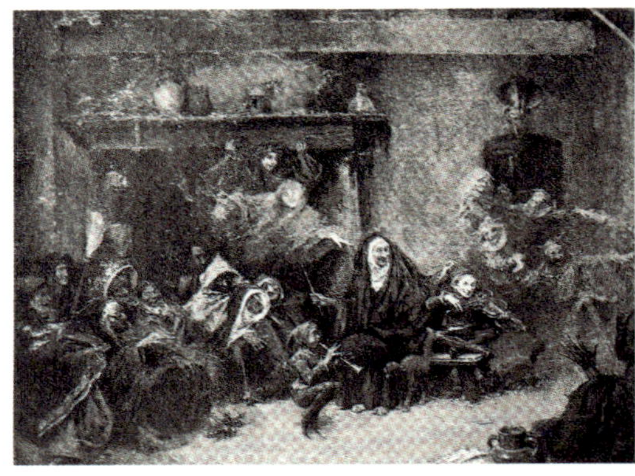

Professionally, he divided his time between painting and the theory of painting. As of 1890, he dropped history in order to devote himself to genre themes and illustration, when it was discovered that he was very adept in the use of colour. We could also mention, among other painters linked to history, José Villegas and José Benlliure, both of whom had an early presence at the Biennale. But although those mentioned were interested in history, it doesn't mean that they participated in the exhibition with works of this type.

Historic painting in our country was transformed into social painting when current subjects were dealt with. Some painters wished to reflect the Spain of that time, which was undergoing a period of great tensions in the form of the confrontation between the industrial proletariat and the bourgeoisie –tensions that were repeated among the Andalusian peasants and the miners in the north, who were aroused to fury about their inhuman living conditions. This was a period of key dates: between 1898 (the definitive dismantling of a hypothetical empire which had effectively come to an end centuries before) and 1909 (the year of the shameful and ferocious repression of the workers and a crucial year for the Moroccan issue). There was no place for artists who depicted these dramatic moments at the Biennale –an institution that upheld "order."

The so-called regional and national painting (two sides of the same coin) shared the stage with the painting of history. They highlighted aspects of climate or landscape (the case of Sorolla), or –through the most disadvantaged classes– extolled the purported essences of a people (the impression we get from the work of the Zubiaurre brothers). Only at times did this painting convey the feeling of sincerity (we could cite Castelao, much later). But for most of the time its meaning was something else. If the examples quoted were to be framed within a specific geographical area, the "national" painting could be that of Zuloaga, intent on the pursuit of the "soul" or on characterising the Spaniard or things Spanish, which was so well-received at Venice. This artist had already exhibited at the 1903 Biennale, at which point he started a long relationship with Venice in the same way as the Zubiaurre brothers after 1910.

But apart from these "autochthonous" tastes, a relationship with Europe started to become apparent in the Spain of the close of the 19th century and beginning of the 20th, which would lead to important innovations. In the first place, the influence of Impressionism was noted; it had its exponents in our country, especially in the region of Valencia and in Catalonia. Martí Alsina had already made incursions into the movement, although he was not the only precursor of this trend which had already been perceived in so many Romantic works, including that of Rosales. But it was Francisco Oller, from Puerto Rico, who –after his stay in Paris– gathered together his French experiences and decisively introduced the new practices related to light and colour. Regoyos, was also an Impressionist at one time, and even a Divisionist. The general consensus is

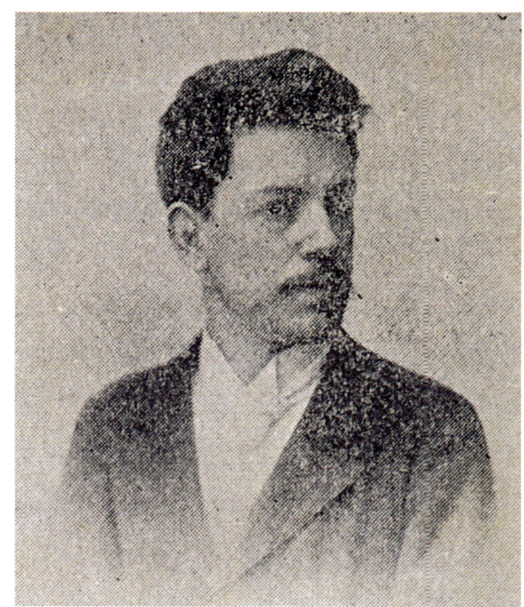

José Benlliure
"Entretenimiento musical" (Musical Entertainment)
Italian Catalogue, 1897

Portrait of Joaquín Sorolla

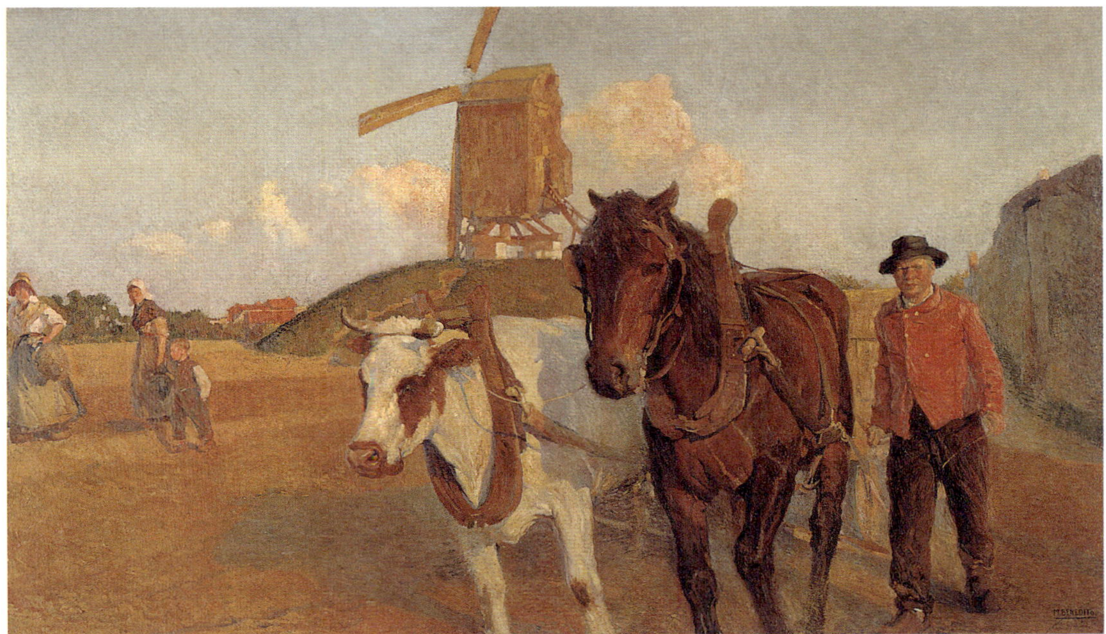

that the best Spanish Impressionist was Aureliano de Beruete (whose work was only seen at the Biennale in 1942, thirty years after his death); with him, and representing different points of view, there were Ignacio Pinazo and Joaquín Sorolla. Many other artists were occasionally caught up in the movement: Nonell, Casas, Eliseo Meifrén, etc. The Spanish Impressionists, above all Sorolla, were well received at Venice. Their luminous style contributed a degree of lightheartedness and a false Modernism to that Biennale which, although it systematically ignored the existence of the French Impressionists, made no objection to welcoming the production of some of their epigones.

Some significant facts would show that in Spain –specifically in Catalonia– there was starting to be some preoccupation with art unrelated to the academies. Here we refer to the groups that were formed at that time, such as the one in the café Els quatre gats (The Four Cats), which started in 1897 and was defunct six years later. Open to novelties in art and a centre for debate, it was promoted by Ramón Casas, Rusiñol and Miguel Utrillo (art critic and writer), who were joined by other artists.

Catalonia was always the reception centre for Modernism, one of the leading trends in the Spain that bridged the centuries. It developed around painters such as Anglada Camarasa, Lluís Masriera, Rusiñol, Ramón Casas and Isidro Nonell, and among sculptors such as Josep Llimona and Miguel Blay. We shall see that some of these names have already been mentioned in connection with other trends, but it is not surprising that in the ebullient Barcelona of the start of the century, the influences from Europe should follow each other in quick succession, mixing with their autochthonous counterparts. We cannot fail to allude to the *noucentisme* in Catalonia after 1906. This was a project that brought together politics and culture and whose outcome was the definitive raising of the awareness of the Catalonian bourgeoisie. Although the artists linked to this trend came from different places, their art was characterised by a sobriety unknown to Modernist and post-Modernist principles. Care must be taken not to link *noucentisme* to the avant-garde since it markedly supported a "return to order," but it contributed a qualified adoption of certain linguistic terms used by the latter, and above all helped to invigorate the Catalonian art scene –especially that of literature.

Several artists who livened up the close of the century in Barcelona went to the Venice Biennales –before or after the world war– but their presence was not so frequent as that of others who, time after time, exhibited at the exhibition. The sixth exhibition brought together the greatest number of members of the group, since –apart from Casas and Rusiñol– Canals and Joaquín Mir were also there. It is true that there were painters and sculptors who added a decadent note, although the 1905 Biennale was attended by Anglada Camarasa and Iturrino, noted representatives of the new ideas on art that were beginning to develop in Spain. It would perhaps be the most interesting Biennale during the pre-war period.

However, neither Impressionism nor Modernism are considered purely avant-garde movements –the first on account of its lack of a social aspect and the second because of its undeniable element of decorativism. With regard to the "historic avant-garde," echoes of Fauvism reached the Spain of that time and succeeded in interesting different Spanish painters. Among them was Iturrino, who at times so strongly reminds us of Matisse, whose close friend he was. Another painter from the north, Echevarría, also succumbed to the influence of the brilliant hues of the Fauves, although he replaced the large surfaces of flat colour with more Impressionistic touches. Iturrino

Manuel Benedito
"La vuelta del trabajo" (The Return from Work)/ 1905 Biennale
Asturias Fine Arts Museum

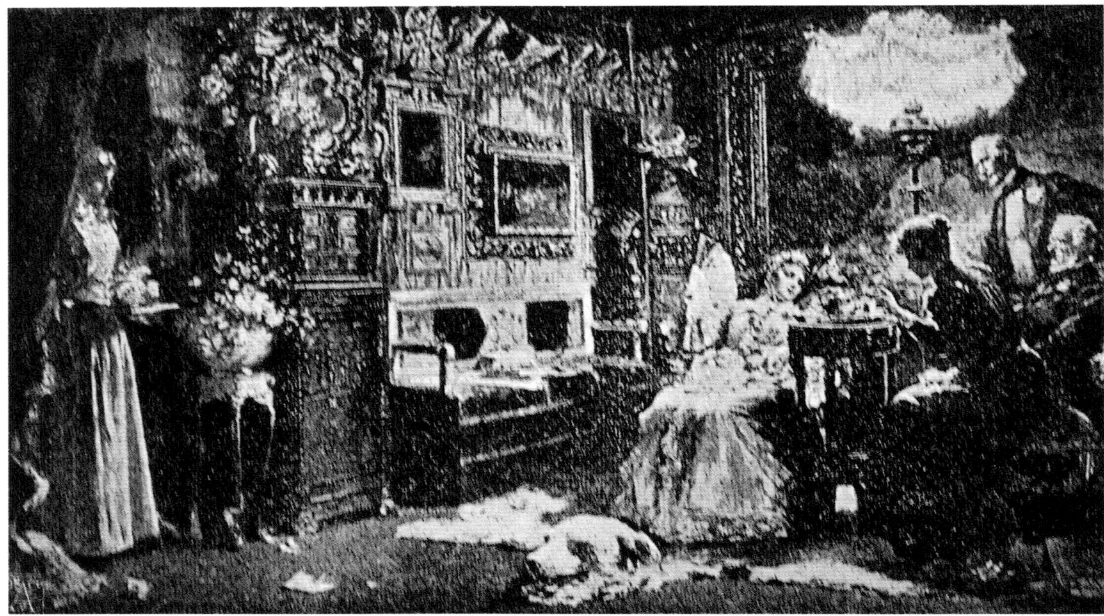

was at the 1905 Biennale, but Juan de Echevarría would have to wait until 1956 until a retrospective was held on him.

Our country's contact with another of the European avant-gardes –Futurism– was likewise seen. Its first manifesto was published in the journal *Prometeo*, the same year (1909) that it saw the light in France and Italy. But this movement had a greater echo in literature. It arrived through Ramón Gómez de la Serna, friend of Marinetti and director of the above-mentioned journal, and died out shortly afterwards, without leaving any significant traces. Nothing of it, of course, would reach Venice, but nor would the experiences of different Spanish artists in Paris, where they not only made contact with the avant-garde, but also created an avant-garde –in other words, Cubism. However, the paintings of Picasso, Gris, and so many others who did a large part of their work there, did not gain entry to the Biennale which, when it came to selecting participants, always turned to more "typical" Spanish production.

We cannot, in this synthesis of the art scene of the final years of the 19th century and beginning of the 20th, omit a reference to the peculiarities and contributions of the different Spanish regions, which presented differentiating traits that would be definitive in some initial Biennales monopolised by Valencians and Andalusians. In Valencia, the figure of Sorolla had attained proportions of such magnitude that it dimmed the star of Pinazo, who subsequently recovered. His painting aligned itself with Impressionism, although its peculiarities have led to his production being labelled only as "Sorollist." Sorolla's "effectism" –and a good dose of anecdotism– have incurred what undoubtedly is unfair criticism against him, given that he certainly evolved a novel manner of painting; perhaps if history at that time had recognised that the splendid Pinazo was up to his level, we should not find ourselves in the position today of having to minimise Sorolla's achievements in order to vindicate those of his colleague. In any event, Sorolla was the point of reference for a whole series of Valencian painters who made light their constant experimental resource.

Andalusia did not have a Sorolla, but it did have a Romero de Torres, who was never at the Biennale and who at times seemed to practise an Andalusian pre-Raphaelism, converting women, suffused with eroticism, into his main theme. He was not such a special referent in Andalusian art as Sorolla was in Valencian art. Nevertheless, they shared regionalist topics.

The first Biennale, as we said, was attended by a large number of painters from Valencia and Andalusia. We know that there were two ways to get entry to the exhibition: by direct invitation or by having one's paintings selected by a panel from among the works submitted. However, most of the foreign artists went to Venice after being summoned by the Biennale itself, while the panel mostly sifted through the works of the Italian artists. It can be assumed –and this is corroborated by fact– that in the choice of artists to represent Spain, the Spaniards who were members of the Sponsorship committe through which Riccardo Selvatico, mayor of Venice, aimed to offer a select and international image of the exhibition, would play a crucial role. The Spaniards who formed part of this committee were José Villegas, José Jiménez Aranda, José Benlliure and Joaquín Sorolla. They all boasted a common feature: that of having lived in Rome –some for several years. For this reason they were well known in Italy, and it was they who were called upon when the Biennale was being planned. José Villegas was born in Seville in 1848, but in 1868 he moved to Rome, where he remained for thirty years, returning to Spain with the explicit mission of directing the Prado

Salvador Sánchez Barbudo
"La convaleciente" (The Convalescent)
Italian Catalogue, 1895

Museum. He was one of the history painters, and was known above all for his paintings of bullfighting scenes. Jiménez Aranda was also from Seville. He was the oldest of the group, having been born in 1837. He also lived for a while in Rome, although he then moved to Paris. He became a teacher at the Fine Art School in his home city, Seville, forming part of the school of preciosity of which Mariano Fortuny was the main representative. They were friends, having coincided in Rome.

As well as the Andalusians, there were two Valencians on this committee. The first was José Benlliure (born in 1855), who soon gave up Paris –where he had gone under the influence of his maestro Francisco Domingo– for Rome, whose environment undoubtedly suited him much better from the standpoints both of his work and of his character. He lived there for a good part of his life. Like Villegas, he devoted himself to painting history, although he was strongly attached to sentimental *costumbrismo*. The second Valencian was Joaquín Sorolla, the youngest of the group (he was born in 1863), who had also been a scholarship-holder in Rome. When he was invited to the Biennale his style had not yet taken definitive shape, and there was still a touch of Realism in his canvases.

Apart from being members of the Sponsorship Committee, all those mentioned went to Venice as exhibitors, whereby they became judge and judged. At that first Biennale, Benlliure presented titles such as *Viejo en oración* (Old Man in Prayer) and *Sopa en el convento* (Soup at the Convent), along the lines of his intimate-*costumbrista* style; Jiménez Aranda with *Gentilezas* (Kindnesses) –an appropriate name for his mode of work– and *La onomástica* (The Saint's Day) returned to his preciosist style; Sorolla only presented one work: *Constructor de barcas* (Shipbuilder), which was still within the orbit of Realism. Finally, José Villegas entered a portrait and above all his *Coronación de la dogaressa Foscari* (Coronation of the Doge's Wife), a picture in his usual historic style, on which he had spent many years of work.

Apart from these artists, the list of those who accompanied them to Venice for that first exhibition was very significant. In the first place there were Gonzalo Bilbao and Salvador Sánchez Barbudo, both disciples of Villegas in Seville. The latter took not only his own works to the Biennale but also those of the artists who followed in his footsteps, thereby confirming the partiality of the results obtained. He was not, however, the only one who did so, as it was very probably Jiménez Aranda who invited José García y Ramos, who had started learning to paint with him in Seville. The latter artist did genre paintings on Andalusian themes: *La sevillana* (Woman from Seville) was the title of the work that he presented at the Biennale.

The other artists at this exhibition were Valencians, surely because the other members of the committee were likewise from there. First of all we find Garnelo Alda, of Sorolla's generation. He had also spent time in Rome and did anecdotic painting. Furthermore there was Emilio Sala. The last Valencian –and the only sculptor of the group– was the indefatigable worker Mariano Benlliure, the brother of José, who already from his early youth had received all the distinctions imaginable in Spain with his bulls and bullfighters, gypsy women and assorted portraits, apart from having done a multitude of commemorative monuments. He took *La Marina* (Seascape) and *Bacanal* (Wild Party) to Venice.

At the second Biennale a fifth Spanish member, the Aragonese history painter, Francisco Pradilla, joined the Sponsorship Committee. As for the exhibiting artists, they were once more the

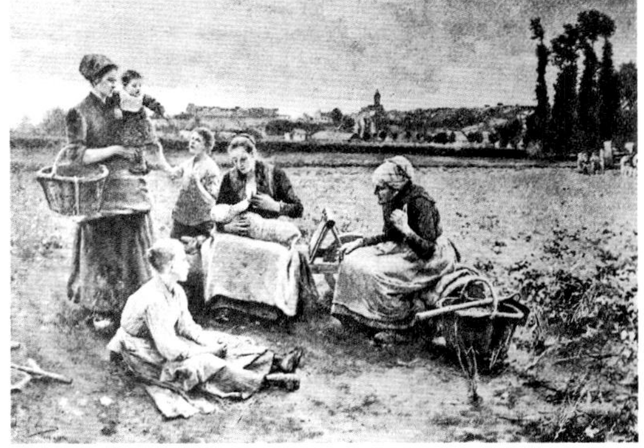

Luis Jiménez Aranda
"Charlas del pueblo" (Village Chats)
Italian Catalogue, 1897

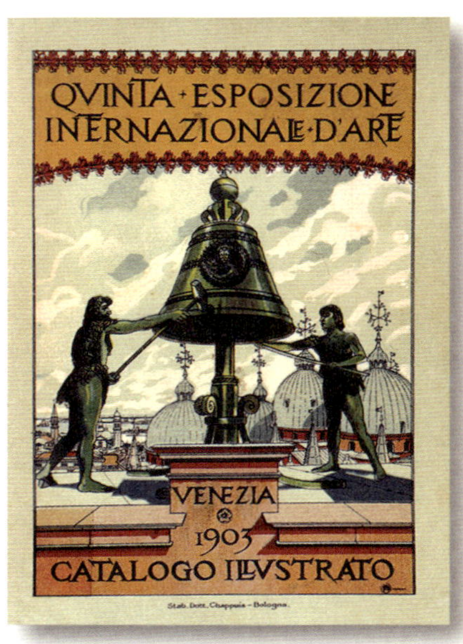

members of the committee themselves (except for Pradilla), as well as Garnelo Alda and Sánchez Barbudo. They were joined by a number of artists such as Ramón Tusquets who, in addition to the usual history painting, had a more interesting facet consisting of Italian *costumbrismo*. Antonio Fabres, likewise a *costumbrist* who, as well as oils, did watercolours and drawing, also participated. Luis Jiménez Aranda, brother of José and at times a good colourist, and Ricardo de los Ríos, who is chiefly remembered as an engraver, completed the list of artists at this second Biennale that contributed little to the first. Nevertheless, one of the most important prizes of the exhibition –that of the Province of Venice, was awarded to Spain; specifically for Sorolla's work– *La bendición de la barca* (The Blessing of the Boat).

There were very few Spanish representatives at the third Biennale in 1899 –only Sorolla, José Benlliure and Mariano Fortuny, who were joined by Gustavo Bacarisas. The scanty Spanish participation was not unnoticed in Italy, where the absence of Villegas was regretted. At the fourth Biennale (1901), there were even fewer artists from Spain, perhaps as a direct consequence of the demise of the Sponsorship Committee: only Sorolla and Mariano Benlliure appeared. At the fifth, in 1903, apart from Sorolla there were José Benlliure, Ignacio Zuloaga, Hermenegildo Anglada Camarasa and Antonio de la Gándara. New names, and success for Zuloaga who, despite taking only one picture to Venice, *Bailarinas españolas* (Spanish Dancers), was the subject of a long article in the catalogue and was awarded the gold medal. Notwithstanding his youth (he was born in 1870), this painter stood out from among the exponents of easy *costumbrismo*, the plague of our art. Only later was it possible to judge Zuloaga's work objectively, restoring its certainly conservative meaning; but at that time his tough and realistic way of looking at things was admired. Anglada Camarasa, who would be well received at future Biennales, was also there, as was Antonio de la Gándara, who aroused interest on account of his very elegant portrait painting. Having a Spanish father and an English mother, he had been born in Paris. His relationship with Spain was very tenuous. In all, five artists and only ten works.

The 1905 Biennale (the sixth) had a larger number of participating artists and a higher standard of painting. Largely responsible for this was Ignacio Zuloaga, who formed part of the Organising Committee of the International Salons. For the first time a connection was made with the Modernism that had arrived in our country via Catalonia. Thus we see Anglada Camarasa who presented no fewer than ten works, when on average each artist used to exhibit one or two. His emblematic *Las flores del mal* (Les fleurs du mal), reminiscent of Baudelaire, his *Muro cerámico* (The Ceramic Wall), *Los Campos Elíseos* (Les Champs-Elysées), etc., won the gold medal for him –a great success for this artist who now clearly leaned towards brightly-coloured folk themes and Modernistic decorativism. With him, Ricardo Canals, Ramón Casas, Rusiñol and Mir Frinxet provided –to a greater or lesser extent– the connection with Europe. The presence of Iturrino and Darío de Regoyos must also be deemed positive. Moreover, there were others like him, including the assiduous Manuel Benedito, with an academic Realism and an Impressionist touch proper to the Valencians; Gonzalo Bilbao, who took his *Salida de las cigarreras de la fábrica de Sevilla* (Exit of the Cigar-Makers from the Seville Factory) and also Enrique Paternina with his *Declaración de amor* (Declaration of Love). With this last painter –as well as others of relative importance– we refer the reader to the lists of artists at the different Biennales.

1903 Biennale Title Page

Zuloaga, however, suffered a hard blow at this Biennale. He had officially invited Picasso and the latter took probably two of his works to Venice, but they were removed –possibly even after they had been hung– at the request of the Biennale management, with the excuse that they could have offended the public's taste. A long time would go by before Picasso returned to Venice. This episode, documented by Jean François Rodríguez, reminds us that the Venice exhibition was tremendously conservative and that it not only ignored but also openly rejected the new developments that were taking place in European art. Only in the light of this are we better able to understand Spain's participation in this exhibition.

After the seventh exhibition, held in 1907 with only a small number of Spanish participants and few novelties, Spain was absent for the first time, since the eighth exhibition in 1909. Zuloaga's departure in 1905 had provoked a crisis that nobody knew how to solve. However, the Biennale management intervened in this matter and strived to ensure that at the next exhibition, which was held a year early in 1910, Spain would once again be well represented. But the opening that had been planned years earlier did not materialise and conspicuous representatives of the most traditional style of painting monopolised the space. In any event, it was in Italy, from the pen of Lancellotti, that we had one of the few commentaries on the Spanish entries during those years: "Spain has an environment in which Zuloaga, Zárraga, Benlliure, Zaragoza, Chicharro, etc. predominate. All –or nearly all– of its artists are chips off the same block. They are precise, and strong on drawing, rigorous students of form, they have long brushstrokes and their colours, although almost always false, harmonise so well that they appear true to life and make themselves accepted...." Apart from the above–mentioned artists, the appearance of the brothers Valentín and Ramón de Zubiaurre, of the so-called Basque School, is significant. They exalted the characteristics and culture of their homeland on the basis of a degree of moralising. From that time onwards they attended the Biennales assiduously. Valentín continued to participate, and was at the 1950 Biennale.

In 1912, a sole painter –the Mexican Ángel Zárraga– with only two paintings, represented Spain. He had worked at Sorolla's studio and his pictures are melodramatic in a cloyingly sweet way. In 1914, the last Biennale before the war, the solo exhibitions of Anglada Camarasa and Joaquín Sorolla were worthy of note. The latter left Valencia at this time and travelled all over Spain in order to offer us his personal view of Seville, Granada, Toledo and Burgos. Apart from this there was nothing new. In the second decade of the century modernity and coherence continued to be lacking.

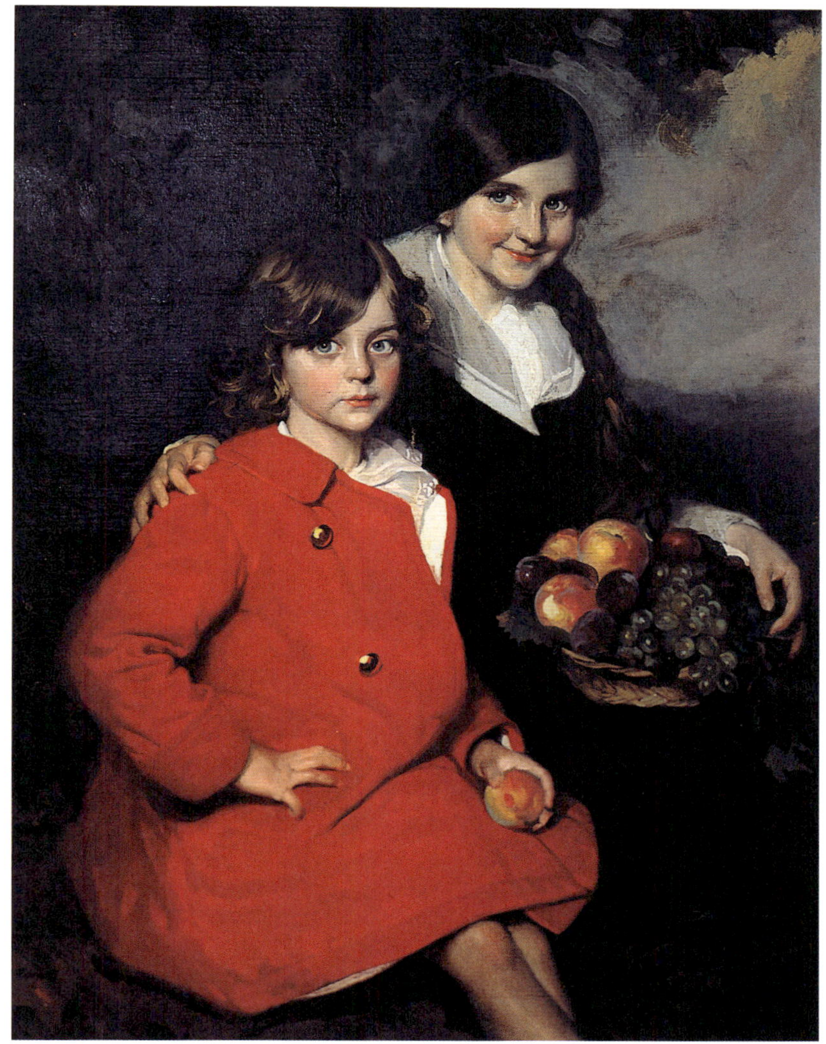

Manuel Benedito
"Mis sobrinas" (My Nieces) / 1914 Biennale
Manuel Benedito Foundation

From the Post-War Period to Wartime: 1920-1936

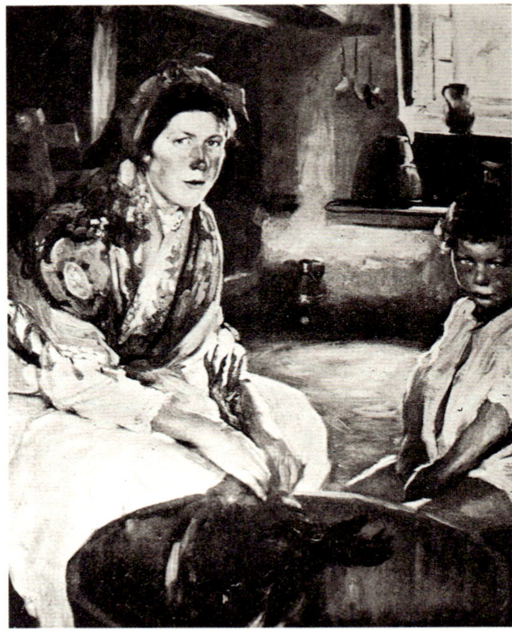

Fernando Álvarez de Sotomayor
"Interior"
Italian Catalogue, 1924

The First World War interrupted the usual cadence of the Biennales, which was not resumed until 1920. The next world conflict shut it down again, although not immediately –in 1942. Meanwhile, Spain had experienced its own war, but not for that reason did it lock up its pavilion, which was now under the aegis of the "nacionales" (Franco's side).

From the standpoint of art, from the First World War until the Civil War there were extremely interesting developments in Spain, which would be reflected only marginally at the Biennale. Catalonia increasingly stood out as the spearhead in the connection with Europe. There was no innovative explosion there, but some sufficiently firm steps were taken to enable it to be consolidated as the most interesting art centre in the country. Through its exhibitions at Dalmau it attempted to recover the time lost in the assimilation of new trends. The arrival in the town of a group of artists who were fleeing from the war –Picabia, Gleizes, Marie Laurencin and Arthur Cravan, meant an important injection of creativity into the timid and expectant art scene. In 1917 an initiative arose from this group of refugees to publish the journal *391*, which had a clearly Dadaist orientation and only managed to publish four issues. Together with it, *Un enemic del poble, fulla de subversió espiritual*, (An Enemy of the People, News-Sheet of Spiritual Subversion) directed by Salvat Papasseit and Troços, by Junoy, undertook the task of disseminating the new trends through articles and drawings. This was also done by some specific exhibitions, like the one held in 1918 at Dalmau in order to make French art known to Catalans. At the same time new art groups appeared, such as Els evolucionistes (The Evolutionists) and the Courbet Group, which was related to *noucentisme*.

Although by the time the war ended it had not been possible to consolidate a single specifically avant-garde nucleus, Neo-Cubism had been established and Surrealism would soon come. These two trends were the most significant in the country. Among those who, to a greater or lesser extent, used Neo-Cubist formulas, were Daniel Vázquez Díaz, García Maroto, Emiliano Barral, Ángel Ferrant, Ramón Gaya, Mateo Hernández, Manuel Ángeles Ortiz, Alberto Sánchez, etc. Vázquez Díaz –who exhibited so lavishly at Venice– was one of the painters who recreated Cubism in a more personal way. For him it was linked more to the solidity of the original construction than to any analytical stage thereof. Neo-Cubism signified a habit of seriousness, a desire for conciseness and the pursuit of agreement with the international avant-garde. Although he had nothing to do with strict Neo-Cubism, Victorio Macho should be remembered. He was a paradoxical artist who mixed renovation and the style of the academies.

Perhaps for that reason he was well received at the Biennale, at which he was present in 1924, and a solo exhibition was held for him in 1932. However, Manuel Ángeles Ortiz was never there. Nor was Alberto Sánchez. It was about these generations that, much later, the 1976 Venice Biennale would talk.

The influence of Surrealism was immediately observed; after all, some of the best Surrealists would be Spaniards. 1925 was the year in which expectations were crystallised as a result of Breton's *Manifesto of Surrealism*. The one with the greatest ties to the international concept of Surrealism was Salvador Dalí. Miró, who only arrived in Venice in 1954, had a very special way of conceiving it. Remedios Varo, Maruja Mallo, Moreno Villa and Pablo Sebastián, formed their own views of the movement. The interest in exploring the subconsciousness was no longer so obvious, having shifted to certain magical or fantastic elements to be found in nature.

In the thirties the Spanish art scene started to become extremely lively, sanctioned by the advent of the Republic which favoured a cultural opening-up –always pursued until then on the fringes of officialdom. In any case, the true avant-garde of Spanish art would develop in Paris: Picasso, Juan Gris, Óscar Domínguez, Julio González, Gargallo and so many others would do the greater part of their work –and the best– in that city. Spain lived with its back turned to them: practically unknown in their own country, they would also be ignored by the Biennale which, with some exceptions, sought Spain inside Spain, although it was not always able to elucidate in it the positive from the negative.

Together with avant-gardism, trends were evolving in Spain linked to the different regions. In Galicia, Castelao denounced the situation of the Galician peasants. The risk of melodrama in representing them was replaced by the specific contrast between exploiters and exploited. Apart from Castelao, Asorey and Maside would be the best representatives of this Galician school. In the Basque Country, the powerful work of Aurelio Arteta acted as a counterpoint to that of the Zubiaurre brothers. This great Muralist, who attained his true dimensions in the times of the Republic, depicted the labourer in the harshness of his daily work, without sentimentality and without morbid fascination. He would die in exile in 1940. Together with him, Tellaeche and Elías Salaverría likewise attempted to divest of rhetoric the world of these lower classes, whom they continually portrayed. In Asturias, the work of Evaristo Valle, above all, is remarkable. He was a painter of coal mines and fishermen –exploited beings who struggled in order to escape their misery. His work has something of the nature of exhortation, distanced from that of the other artists of his generation.

The Biennale paid no attention to them and on very few occasions showed any interest in the new Basque painting. Elías Salaverría went to Venice in 1930 and 1940 (on both occasions with just one picture), and Aurelio Arteta went in 1934, also with only one picture. This was a very scanty presence in comparison with the great importance in every sense of the work of these artists. Someone who was a habitué of the biennales, notwithstanding the quality and courage of his painting, was José Gutiérrez Solana, who exhibited on about ten occasions. Spain was very given to inventing sentimental and expressive myths and saw in Solana an acceptable referent. An excellent painter, with comprehensible themes, but also a rebel, he could be related to that dark Spain which Spanish art never wished to throw off entirely, that art which admires Goya's black paintings and the

In any case, the true avant-garde of Spanish art would develop in Paris: Picasso, Juan Gris, Óscar Domínguez, Julio González, Gargallo and so many others

most brutal works of Picasso. Solana was the acceptable myth.

It is interesting to observe the artistic evolution in Spain in order to ascertain to what extent its innovations were absorbed by the Biennale. We can say, however, that of the fertile generation of Spanish avant-gardists, only a few went to Venice on one occasion or another. Under Fortuny's wing, the exhibition of the period between the wars continued to prefer the academicism of the old schools and would only infrequently show a different face. Not a single Picasso, Miró, Gris or Gargallo, to mention only some of the best known, set foot in the Biennale during these years. The Costumbrists and those who exalted regional habits continued in the breach, together with the sentimental artists who continued to be the favourites in Venice.

Of the fertile generation of Spanish avant-gardists, only a few went to Venice on one occasion or another

In Venice during the twenties, the Spanish participation had a lot to do with the preferences of Mariano Fortuny y Madrazo. This artist from Granada, son of the esteemed painter Fortuny Marsal, had found the city of his dreams in Venice. He made his home there, in a house that now contains a museum destined to house the exultant photographs of Robert Mapplethorpe. Fortuny y Madrazo was a painter, set designer and, above all, the creator of some fantastic fabrics that are still produced in Venice. The aesthetic volubility of this artist meant that, at the exhibitions that he programmed (he was behind practically all the Spanish exhibits at the Biennales in the twenties), there was much eclecticism, but of course very little or nothing of the avant-garde.

As a surprise move at the first post-war exhibition, that of 1920, Fortuny programmed, together with Vittorio Pica, secretary-general of the Biennale, a single artist –Federico Beltrán Masses, who was born in Cuba en 1885 and died in Barcelona in 1949. Although we would certainly not agree with the extraordinarily harsh judgment of Nino Barbantini who was of the opinion that only one picture by this painter would be enough to dishonour any display of art (given that questions of honour cannot appropriately be applied in this case), he was by no means a satisfactory option for the Biennale. Among other reasons because what is expected of the Biennale is a presentation of current art, and in this sense Beltrán Masses was not a suitable choice. Although he was a good colourist (his greatest quality), he was guilty of great effectism. Today the art history books remember him for his literary roots and Symbolist decadentism.

Curiously enough, of all the artists whom we have reviewed until now, he is the one who has provoked most comments. Lancellotti explained as follows the impression that he got from his pictures, “Here we are, in a gallery which has given rise to much scandal both from the moral and artistic points of view [...] Is Beltrán Masses a painter worthy of special consideration, a new genius who has appeared on the horizon? He must be convinced that he is, given that he walks around the exhibition and through the gardens with a broad satisfied smile under the small shadow of his blonde moustache. Unfortunately other people are not so sure./ What could at first sight appear to be [...] a certain elegance of lines, is dispelled by a calmer and more attentive look. Beltrán is a lecherous creature, and his canvases, considered from this standpoint, show a perverse materialism. But at the same time they are badly painted and badly drawn.”

Not that we should let ourselves be over-influenced by these comments by Lancellotti to whom, moreover, are attributable other unfortunate remarks about very important artists of our century. Furthermore, they unleash a number of moral prejudices that can invalidate other assessments. Nevertheless, this constitutes an example of coinciding opinions from entirely different critical ambits on the not-very-sound choice of the late-Symbolist painter. And –strangely enough– these descriptions arouse our curiosity about the artist himself and a wish to go to the Lis Museum in Salamanca, where part of his work is kept.

The other Spanish participation in the Biennales, from 1922 to 1936, was frankly discouraging: it is not that good artists were lacking, but they were isolated and reduced to insignificance by the reigning mediocrity. There was no planned approach for the Spanish pavilion at Venice; year

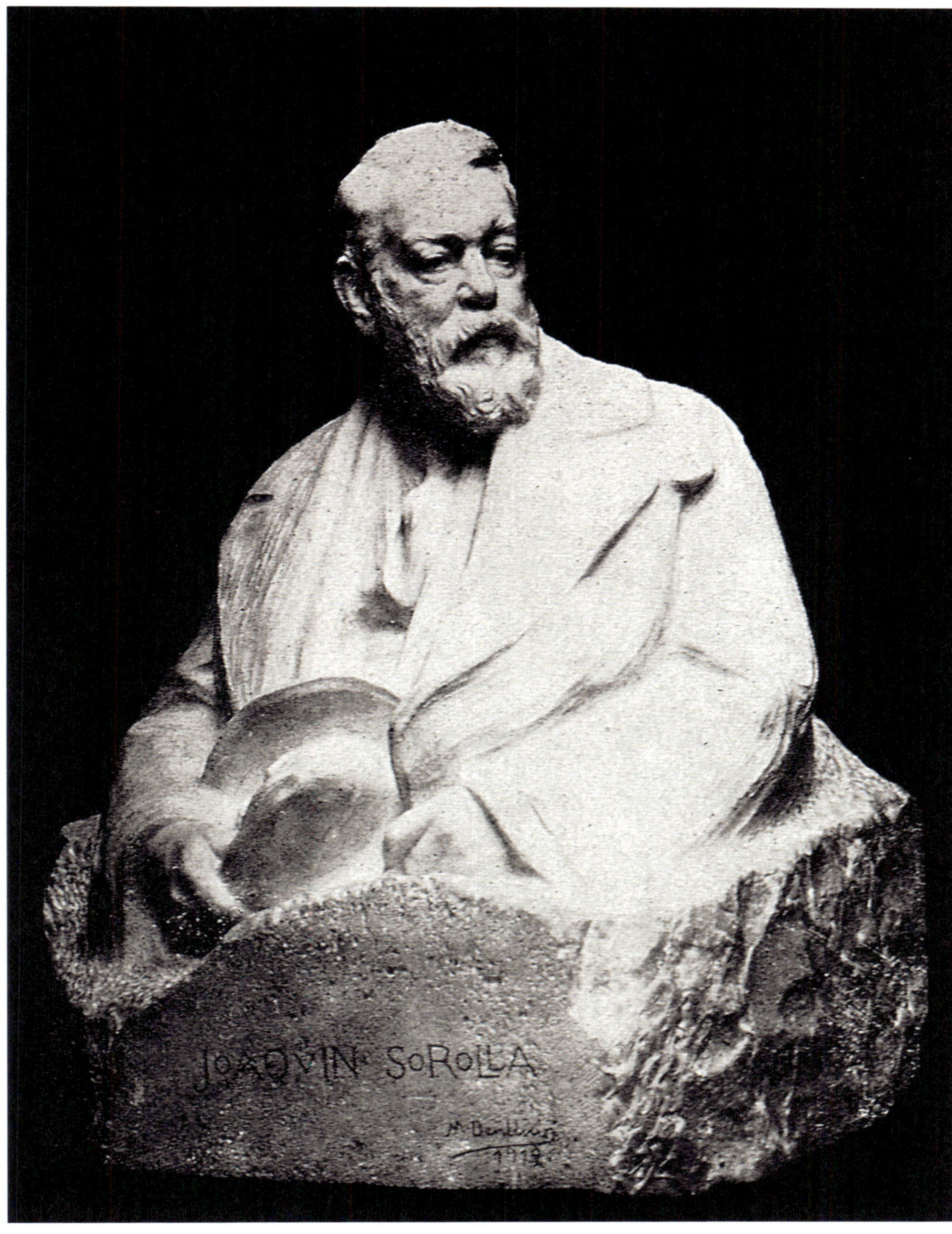

In Venice during the twenties, the Spanish participation had a lot to do with the preferences of Mariano Fortuny y Madrazo

Mariano Benlliure
"Retrato del Pintor Joaquín Sorolla" (Portrait of Painter Joaquín Sorolla) / 1924 Biennale
City Museum, Valencia City Council. Photograph made available by the Benlliure House/Museum

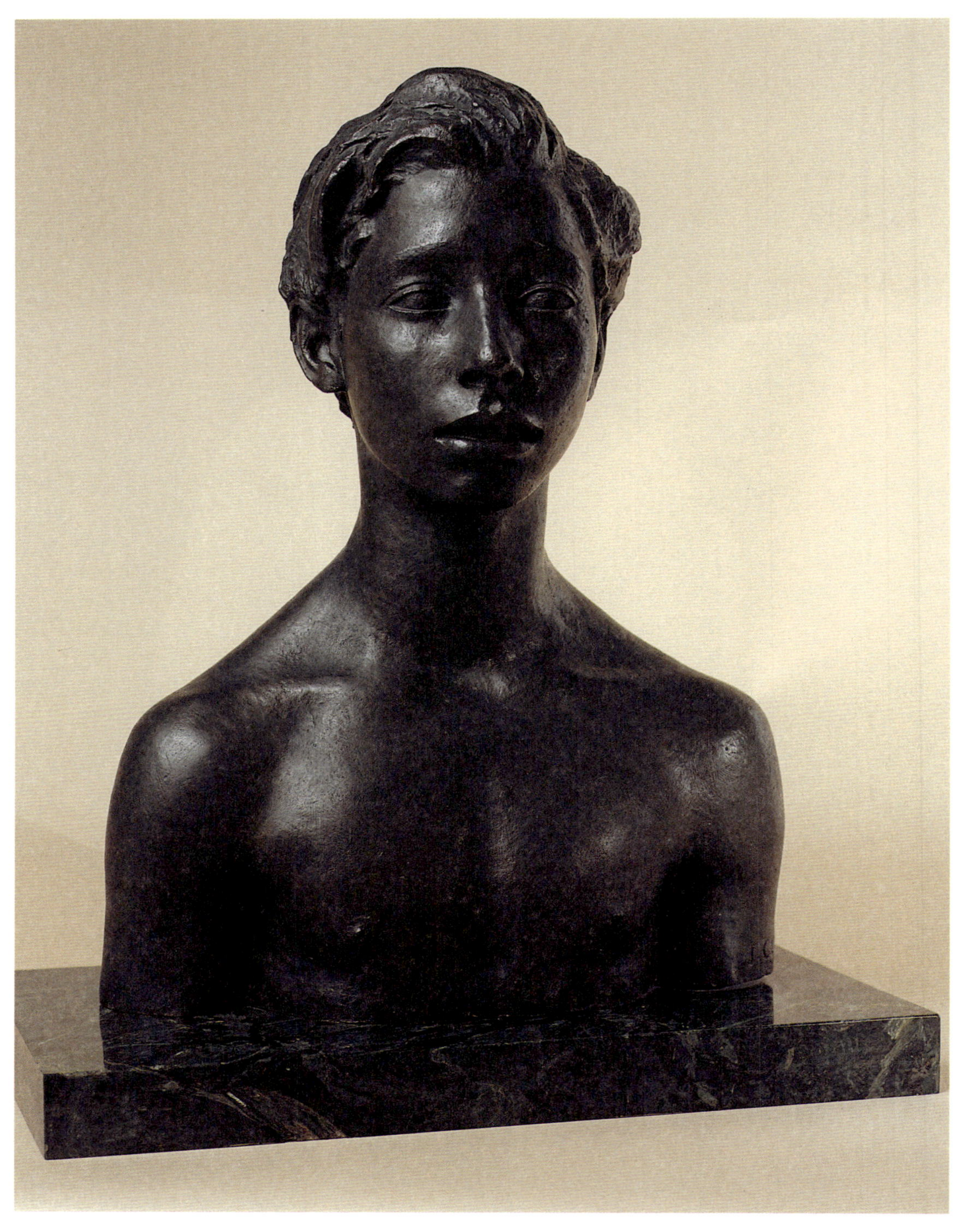

José Clará
"Gitanet" / 1936 Biennale
National Art Museum of Catalonia

after year it merely comprised an assorted group of totally unconnected artists, each of whom only exhibited one or two pictures, making it impossible to gain an overall understanding of their work. This trend towards an enormous dispersion of artists and works seemed to recede to the extent that the curators became more interested in showing a considerable number of works by specific artists rather than one or two by many. However, the number of artists represented was always excessive.

The starting up of the Spanish pavilion contributed to this proliferation since it led to the enlargement of the space for the exhibition of works. Opened in 1922 –still without all its galleries and without the decoration on the façade– its building had been promoted by Mariano Benlliure, as we are told by Marco Mulazzani. The design was done by architect Javier de Luque, although it was initially assigned to Antonio Flores. The distribution consisted of a central gallery flanked by lateral galleries and it "did not depart from the national vocation, offering an image inspired by the Baroque of the late 17th century." 1922 was a year of considerable Spanish representation (twenty-four artists) but it was greatly surpassed by the following exhibition, at which more than sixty exhibited their work. However, there were no surprises.

Eclecticism is the best word to describe the exhibits of those years. Together with the usual figures, who seemed immortal for Venice (Benlliure, López Mezquita, Sorolla), there were many others (Pons Arnau, Ricardo Verdugo, Gabriel Morcillo) who adhered to academicist or post-Sorollist canons and who made up the exhibition. Apart from them, artists who would in the future be associated with the Franco regime, started to appear; their clearest exponent was José Aguiar, Franco's portrait-painter and a glorifier of the "crusade." Álvarez de Sotomayor, who became the personal friend of the Head of State, also participated frequently at Venice. The most positive thing about the Biennales of that period was the presence of Solana –which, moreover, was backed up by a relatively large number of pictures– as well as that of Pinazo, Casas, and, exceptionally, Ángel Ferrant at the fifteenth exhibition. The sculptors were also significantly represented –Adsuara, Capuz; in other words, those who would successfully continue their artistic career during the Franco era, now enjoyed their first opportunity to go abroad.

There is little more to be said about the Biennales of that time. In 1926 emphasis was put on a large number of artists, in 1928 there were two solo exhibitions –by Gustavo Bacarisas and Antonio Ortiz Echagüe, who are scarcely remembered nowadays. The first, from Seville, did colouristic *costumbrismo*; the second, from Castile, took one of his best–known pictures to Venice: *Jacobo van Amstel en su casa* (Jacob van Amstel at Home). This was an optimistic interior reminiscent of the Dutch painters. Both at this and at the following exhibition in 1930, there was a large number of sculptors, among whom was the artist from Castellón, Adsuara, a lover of scenes depicting maternity.

We are now on the threshold of the Republic. It is true that this was a stage in Spain when some of the avant-garde groups that had germinated during previous years, were consolidated. But not much of this was noticed at Venice. Perhaps it was the 1932 Biennale, the first held under the new political system, which was the most interesting of the Republican Biennales, although the choice for the three solo exhibitions: Victorio Macho, Solana and Muñoz Degrain did not amount to anything new. But at least the usual piling up of pictures and sculptures had stopped, to enable a coherent view of the work of the sculptor and the two painters to be offered. Evaristo Valle and Arturo Souto, to introduce two divergent artists, also attended this Biennale. The first, an Asturian absorbed by topics and landscapes of his native countryside, would have a future very different from that of Souto, a painter and engraver who would die in exile in Mexico.

The Spanish participation that year was not proposed by Fortuny, but by a large committee chaired by Ricardo de Orueta, director general of Fine Art, and seconded by José Francés, of the San Fernando Academy of Fine Art. Francés, who was involved in the organisation of the pavilion during this 1932 exhibition and the two following ones, was a historian and art critic, one of the most influential of his time. He was interested above all in caricatures. He was awarded all honours both before and after the Civil War, in which he was on Franco's side, and even requested that art should be subject to political control. In any event, the war had not yet come, and these Biennales were held in times of peace.

As a significant event we shall mention that a woman, the very young Rosario de Velasco, represented Spain for the first time at the 1932 Biennale. She would do so again on successive occasions, becoming a regular exhibitor at Venice. Born in Madrid, she studied with Álvarez de Sotomayor and then practised poetic figuration. She was the first of not very many women artists at the Biennale; only in recent years have the numbers increased.

The committee that organised the 19th Biennale in 1934 comprised a very conservative group. Its delegate was once again Mariano Fortuny and

The presence of women was significant since, together with Velasco and Mallo there were Margarita de Frau and the first woman sculptor, Eva Aggerholm

with him, among others, were Eduardo Chicharro, José Francés and López Mezquita (who acted as curator). Frankly it is difficult to understand the cultural policy of the government of the Republic in respect of the Biennale, in that it was unwilling to offer a renovated view of Spanish visual art. The Spanish presence was accompanied by an introduction signed by José Francés in which we are told that this committee "has attempted to emphasize values that are significantly Spanish in nature, and to strengthen the deep and indestructible Spanish individuality that re-unites the best exponents of our art with the past: respect for the classical tradition and formal perfection, triumphant to day in a world of assimilations of little sincerity, of foreign and opportunistic influences [...]. Little by little the 20th century renovates the 19th; we see that today without the prejudices of the contemporaries. [...] Overriding the improvised criticisms and the contempt of impatient arrivistes we are now starting to rebuild, while seeking a base." The customary chauvinism by which so many defects are hidden, attempted to justify not only the survival of Sorollism, but also the most radical academicism.

The solo exhibitions programmed for this Biennale were those of Valencian sculptor José Capuz, influenced by Victorio Macho, with work of robust features, and that of Catalan painter Joaquín Mir, the landscape painter with the extravagant palette, whose star has gradually dimmed with time. Together with them, and in Sorolla's circle, were Eduardo Chicharro, Solana, Martínez Cubells, López Mezquita, the Zubiaurre brothers, Santa María, Gonzalo Bilbao, Aguiar, Julio Moisés, etc.; all of them (except Solana) within the ambit of conservative and academic painting. Among the sculptors were: Adsuara, Pérez Comendador, Ortells and Ballester; and also Manolo Hugué, with his relative Modernism linked to *noucentisme*.

At the 1936 Biennale, José Francés was in charge of the Organising Committee. José López Rey y Arrojo acted as curator. They performed their tasks by presenting an eclectic exhibition aimed at confronting novelty and tradition, although counting on both terms being complementary given that, as López Rey said in an article resonant of Baudelaire, although with very different intentions, "...novelty cannot be measured without referring to tradition, nor can the latter be determined if not in permanence through mutable novelties." With this explanation, an attempt was made to justify the continued existence of art that was already outmoded in Europe, and even in Spain it could only be sustained in official redoubts.

A solo exhibition by José Clará, in which the sculptor again displayed his serene realism, was the *pièce de résistance* of this Biennale. Around him there was a large number of artists, ranging from Maruja Mallo and Manuel Hugué to Álvarez de Sotomayor and Eduardo Chicharro. The presence of women was significant since, together with Velasco and Mallo there were Margarita de Frau and the first woman sculptor, Eva Aggerholm, an exponent of traditional figuration. But independently of their formal attachments, this relatively large number of women indicated that in art, as of then, women would also have to be taken into account.

This would be the last Biennale of the Spain of the Republic. In 1938 Mussolini handed over the pavilion to Franco's Government.

The Wartime Biennales: 1938-1942

The Biennales of war..., Spain, in the midst of its Civil War, went to Venice. It was 1938 and Antonio Maraini, chairman of the Biennale, greeted "...the presence of Spain victorious, in the pavilion that had become `Nationalist´ (i.e., attached to Franco's side)...." Italian Fascism wasted no time in confiscating the Republican government's mini art embassy in the *Giardini*. Italy was experiencing a rapid process of Fascistisation, which would soon involve it in the confrontation of the Second World War. For Italy, Spain was like a mirror in which it could see its image reflected. When, in turn, the Second World War broke out, the intention was that the Biennale should continue its activities. However, in the midst of the conflict, the situation became untenable and it was forcibly closed for a few years.

The "two Spains" referred to by Antonio Machado came into evidence during these difficult times in every sphere of the life of the country, including that of art. They were reflected in both great international exhibitions in which Spain participated during the Civil War: the International Exhibition in Paris in 1937 and the Venice Biennale in 1938. In Paris, on the Republican side, an exceptional exhibition was programmed in which the anti-Fascists protested against the war. This exhibition, on which we shall have an opportunity to comment when we talk about the 1976 Biennale (when every possible effort was made to rebuild the Spanish pavilion) was the complete opposite to what could be seen at Venice –not only, and obviously, on account of its revolutionary contents, but also because these contents were expressed in forms that were also revolutionary. It suffices to here to recall the *Guernica* by Picasso.

The thirties had provided a driving force for the process of renewal of Spanish art. The war put the best poster designers at the service of the Republicans and involved painters and sculptors…, the majority, and the best, were in Paris that year. But the other Spain could also been seen in the city where, thanks to the efforts of Cardinal Gomá, it surreptitiously obtained a place in the Pontifical pavilion, where José María Sert did an altarpiece dedicated to the intervention of Saint Teresa of Jesus in the Spanish Civil War. The painting was flanked by columns that at first displayed the colours of the "Nationalists", but the protests of the French government obliged them to be draped in black.

During the war, the artists of both sides became actively involved in propaganda activities, especially that of designing posters. But they did not stop painting or doing sculpture. Indeed, it was then that some of the most significant works of the 20th century were done, by artists faithful to the Republic. However, in Venice the ones seen were those of the "Nationalists." The art of Franco's supporters in wartime consisted of exaltation of the *caudillo* (leader, i.e., Franco) and apologetic descriptions of the events of the conflict, as well as the expression of anger against an enemy that was not only military but also, as it seemed to them, an annihilator of any essence of Spanish personality, of all traces of ecclesiasticism, and of any feeling of tradition or "good manners."

It was the Falangists who drew up a Fascist system of aesthetics for times of war, and they did so in particular through *Vértice*, a magazine that started to be published in 1937 by the National Art and Propaganda Delegation and in which men of literature collaborated, such as Agustín de Foxá, Edgar Neville, Luis Rosales, Laín Entralgo, Dionisio Ridruejo..., in other words, the intellectual elite of Franco's supporters. There was no quarter in this magazine for avant-garde art, while at the same time a clear preference was shown for Solana, Vázquez Díaz, Zuloaga and Palencia. But what interests us is the artists who illustrated it, among whom were Teodoro and Álvaro Delgado, Acha, Olasagasti, and above all, José Caballero and Carlos Sáenz de Tejada. The works of these last two, the most interesting in formal terms, could be seen at Venice on different occasions.

The case of José Caballero was exceptional. He had formed part of the intellectual avant-garde of the thirties, sharing with García Lorca interest in the experience of "La Barraca" (the theatre group founded by Lorca) and had illustrated some of his works. He was the most original and creative of the artists who were collaborating with the Fascist publications at that time. There was not in his work that overwhelming monumentality, that moralising intention of other painters within the Nationalist orbit. Rather, he resorted to Surrealism in order to create images that, on account of their very nature, were not unanimously applauded from within the Nationalist ranks. Many years later, when the 1976 Biennale was convened, at which Spanish art of the past forty years was reviewed, Caballero was not invited. This provoked an emotional letter from the painter, alleging the lack of choice that had been open to him. For his part, Carlos Sáenz de Tejada introduced a disturbing theatrical sense into his work. He had not entirely forgotten the lessons learned from the avant-garde, but the themes and the grandiloquent manner of treating them remind us of the aesthetic approaches of Fascism. A portrait-painter of courageous and handsome combatants who, one knee on the ground await their death, he was also the illustrator of violent battles in which the action is recounted in meticulous detail, without thereby undermining the grandeur of the picture as a whole. Possessing Mannerist resources, such as the diagonal arrangement of his large figures, he was almost always a virtuoso of description, constantly appealing to the emotions of the viewer.

Together with these names, there were many others: Pedro Pruna, Haffner, Balrich, etc., completed the catalogue of famous 'Nationalist' illustrators.... Pruna was at the Biennale of our Civil War in 1938; Sáenz de Tejada at that of the World War in 1940. Several years later Caballero was there. But let us now focus on 1938, when the Spanish pavilion at Venice, in the midst of the conflict, opened its doors. There was not a single reference to the war in the introduction to the catalogue written by Eugenio d'Ors, curator of the exhibition. His mission was theoretically shared with the president of the Lisbon Academy of Fine Art and with a sculptor, but the organisation was basically his responsibility. Converted into one of the chief intellectuals of the Franco regime, this Catalan who forswore his language following some murky incidents, would develop his aesthetic philosophy in Madrid. Many people recognise a positive role in the artistic recovery of postwar Spain, although others minimise its contributions, asserting that in no case was it the avant-garde that was recovered. In any event, he was one of the few intellectuals of stature on whom the regime was able to count, and it has to be admitted that his Venice Biennale served the interests of the new system very well.

The pavilion of Spain at the 1938 Biennale was a wartime pavilion, in a war that even had pretensions to being "holy" (we must not forget the constant references by the victorious side to their "crusade"). From this are derived the dual aspects of pathos and spiritualism seen in it by Alexandre Cirici when he talks to us about its "moving theme [...], through works such as *Madre española* (the Spanish Mother) by Pérez Comendador" and its spiritualism, created from a kind of "exacerbated Mannerism which greatly elongated the figures in a very conventional way, as if they were El Greco's translated into the style of fashion mannequins." This was the rhetoric with which Pedro Pruna "used to present his angels and a symbolic scene of the *Expulsión del Paraíso* (The Casting out from Paradise) in which youth and feminine beauty were punished by an ambiguous angel armed with a sword." Apart from these two notes, a third appeared with José Aguiar: the exaltation of the Chief, the *Caudillo* who would guide Spain on its new path. Aguiar, with a single picture, the *Generalísimo Franco*, introduced himself as one of the most conspicuous representatives of the new order.

But there was more at this emergency Biennale. Eleven artists in all participated, Ignacio Zuloaga being the one to exhibit the greatest number of pictures (twenty-eight). Zuloaga did not displease the regime. On the contrary, the asceticism with which he portrayed the Spain of always, the country of musicians and bullfighters, and also of peasants and aristocrats proud of their past, was well received. With him, Mariano Fortuny y Madrazo, with a frieze of sixteen paintings of Egypt, cultivated Escapism, another of the favourite genres of the time. For his part, Álvarez de Sotomayor (who had been and would again be the director of the Prado Museum) was one of the most influential people in "official" art circles. That was undoubtedly one of the main reasons for his presence at this Biennale, with pictures on different topics in which his zeal for portraits of the aristocracy blended with his more *costumbrist* themes. He contributed nine paintings. Gustavo de Maetzu, brother of Ramiro also a writer and an over-descriptive painter who focused on *costumbrismo* and landscapes, exhibited five. José Aguiar, with the above-mentioned portrait of Franco, José de Togores with a nude (although with her back turned), and finally Pedro Pruna (described above by Cirici) completed the list of Spanish painters at the Biennale. Pruna, a Picasso protegé during his time in Paris, and with an interesting past, joined the rebels during the war. In any event, history, the academic world, spirituality, the apology of the new order..., such were the features of that 1938 pavilion. And above all shame, a great deal of shame.

There were three sculptors chosen for the exhibition: the Spaniards Quintín de Torre Verastegui and Enrique Pérez Comendador, together with the Argentine Pablo Manes. The first of these –a portrait-painter and painter of religious images– took to Venice, among other exhibits, a fragment of Christ's Passion and a study of Nicodemus. Enrique Pérez Comendador, who enlisted in the Nationalist movement during the war, was a sculptor who mastered different materials. Formal Realism and idealisation co-existed in his work –mainly portraits, nudes, processional images and public monuments. Finally, we find the works in plaster and bronze by Pablo Manes, which were infinitely more interesting than those of his fellow sculptors.

Eugenio d'Ors himself had to do a veritable balancing act in order to justify the presence at Venice of some of these artists. If we read the introduction to the catalogue carefully, some things catch our eye. In the first place, we find a brief description of the contributions of the artists or of their significance relative to the current time, without any value judgments: Mariano Fortuny pointed out a transition between Rococo virtuosity and Impressionism; Álvarez de Sotomayor achieved great success with his portraits of Madrid society figures; Quintín de Torre carved magnificent figures out of wood...; of Pérez Comendador he said that he appeared "as one of the most typical representatives of the concerns that have recently shaken up official art."

Eugenio d´Ors himself had to do a veritable balancing act in order to justify the presence at Venice of some of these artists

Commitment was required from the artists at this Biennale. The alliance between the Falange and the Franco regime gave this commitment a special nature since it was not only a matter of illustrating totalitarian concepts proper to Fascism, but also others deriving from the confused requirements of Christian morality, family and educational values, the vindication of traditions...; therefore the art postulated was not only that of immediate rousing speech, but one which would also leave the traces of ideology. In view of these conventions the artist was forced to bend his paintbrush, his pen or his chisel. The following demand was made of painters in *Vértice* by Luis Felipe Vivanco: "Painter, you must also render to the spirit the growing pride of the craftsman's hand. Acknowledge, however hard this may be, human realities of an order higher than that which can be attained by the brilliant exercise of your brushes [...] May your sight have real content in this world, and may it be decidedly Christian in the exaltation of all creatures! [...] We are interested in the blazing trail of your personality in the service of the subjects that raise the level of your existence."

As we have said, in the initial years of the Second World War, Venice, which was far from the epicentre of the conflict, kept up the usual cadence of its exhibitions by holding two Biennales. With its Civil War over, and remaining neutral in the war that was devastating Europe, Spain did not fail to attend the exhibitions, being one of the few countries that –given its sympathy for the Italian political regime– did not boycott them. Thus, in 1940 and 1942, with full autarchy, the new government re-opened its pavilion in Venice, and only left it temporarily in 1948, when the war that had defeated Fascism was already over. In 1950 the Spanish State started to organise its exhibitions again.

A large number of artists went to Venice, to these two solitary Biennales in the forties. During the years marked inside the country by repression and guerrilla warfare, an effort was made to confer an air of normality on the Biennales. Obviously, it was not possible to complete a project for laying the foundations of artistic recovery during the short period of time that we are describing. Moreover, no-one was interested in doing so. During those years, the same illustrators of *Vértice*, who were responsible for the wartime drawings, strived to devise an iconography for peace, but it was always related to experiences of the recent past. It was the deceptive peace of the victors. During this stage of military predominance, attempts were made to consolidate the iconographic clichés of the new era, and the popular images were determined by the ideas of the Falange. Outside Spain, the great majority of artists and intellectuals were welcomed by the exiles, and this was decisive for post-war culture. These clichés were constructed around the idea of an avenging Catholicism that preferred punishment to mercy, and a disciplined political hierarchy with austere and ascetic features.

The illustrators were the most active artists in the Spain of those years, given that their propaganda activity was very effective for the system. With them, the painters and sculptors also started to channel their work into an apology for the regime –directly (through magnified portraits of Franco) or indirectly (by depicting soldiers' mothers, religious images, etc.). Nevertheless, not even by combining the efforts of draftsmen, painters and sculptors, would it have been possible to put together even minimally acceptable exhibitions, since the quality of these artists was fairly mediocre. Therefore, when first of all the Marqués de Lozoya and Enrique Pérez Comendador (in 1940) and later Francisco Íñiguez and Enrique Lafuente Ferrari (in 1942), had to organise the Spanish participation in the Biennale, they were forced to resort to the artists already established during the pre-war period and who if possible had a past unconnected with Republicanism, or who at least were politically neutral. There was also the possibility of turning to the already-vanished maestros of the end of the 19th and start of the 20th centuries, and this was the course that was chosen in 1940, when, as the *pièce de résistance* of the pavilion, Darío de Regoyos, who had died in 1913, was programmed with twenty-three pictures. He was introduced in the catalogue as practically the only Impressionist who had succeeded in crossing the frontiers. Mention of him enabled the Marqués de Lozoya –the author of the catalogue– to refer to Impressionism as far back as Goya. Beside the works of Regoyos, there was a wide selection of paintings by Eugenio Hermoso, who although at one time had approached the avant-garde, outdid him in the hackneyed depiction of peasants of his native Extremadura. He exhibited pictures with titles such as *Regionalism and Catholicism* and *Peasant Piety*.

There were no more solo exhibitions. The rest of the pavilion was taken up by a large number of artists who brought only a few works; of course José Aguiar and Mariano Fortuny Madrazo were there, as well as Solana, Vázquez Díaz, Benjamín Palencia and Genaro Lahuerta.... Very direct allusions to the past conflict were not lacking. Carlos Sáenz de Tejada, with his usual powerful style, showed suggestive titles such as: *Trinchera* (The Trenches), *La carta del héroe* (The Hero's Letter), *Interior de un carro blindado* (Inside a Tank), *Barbarie roja* (Red Barbarity), etc. Joaquín Valverde did a portrait of Franco and Mariano Benlliure presented a bronze statue of General Millán Astray. All this, together with the most varied genealogy of all things Spanish, was seen in an exhibition whose eclecticism was justified by Juan

With its Civil War over, and remaining neutral in the war that was devastating Europe, Spain did not fail to attend the exhibitions

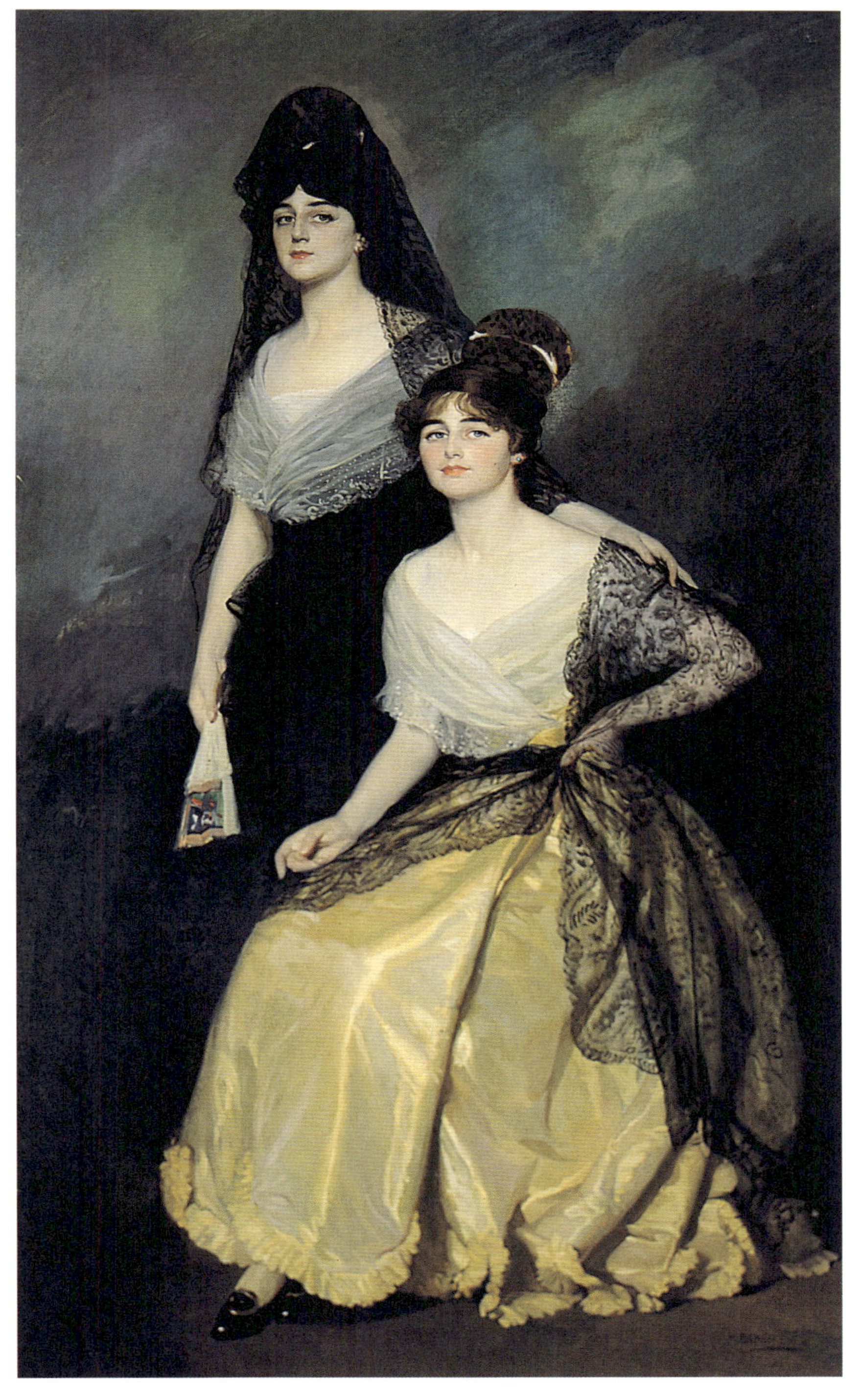

Manuel Benedito
"Señoras de Cárcer" (Ladies of Cárcer) / 1942 Biennale
Manuel Benedito Foundation

An attempt was made to encourage new artists to become part of the Spanish exhibition scene, undoubtedly in the pursuit of a renewal of names

de Contreras y López de Ayala, Marqués de Lozoya, as follows: "The post-war circumstances have made it impossible to show other exhibits because Spanish artists have not been in a position in recent years to produce a large number of works. At any rate the chief trends of present-day Spain are represented, from the robust traditionalism of Zuloaga and Zubiaurre to the elegant modernity of the group from the Levant."

There are no references in Juan de Contreras's article to the Spanish art that was being produced abroad. It seemed not to exist. For the Marqués de Lozoya the latest, together with the previous Biennale, was "perhaps" the most suggestive that Spain had ever organised. He noted the difficulties experienced in preparing it, especially in connection with the works of the sculptors, and expressed his satisfaction about the result and above all the spiritual strengths of a country in which "heroic soldiers and sculptors of exquisite sensitivity have never been lacking, even in the moments of greatest depression."

In 1942 Francisco Íñiguez, director-general of the National Artistic Heritage was the president of the exhibition, while Enrique Lafuente Ferrari was the curator. But behind them the influence of the Marqués de Lozoya could be felt, given that this Biennale to a large extent comprised the work that he had chosen for the exhibitions in Madrid, Barcelona and Berlin.

An attempt was made to secure the presence of new artists on the Spanish exhibition scene together with some of the already traditional participants in the Biennale, undoubtedly seeking the restoration of names such as those of the Zubiaurre brothers, Zuloaga and Vázquez Díaz who –still–, were programmed on this occasion in Venice. But the alternatives do not seem to have been very valid options. Rafael Durancamps was introduced as a novelty; he had started his art activities with Joaquín Mir, but had subsequently left for Paris. After giving up Mir's chromatic heritage, his painting acquired greater formal structuring. At the same time, there was the intimist painter Julia Minguillón (who with Rosario de Velasco –once again at Venice– were the most modern of the Biennale); also the landscape artist Núñez Losada y Suárez Peregrín. All of them had won the Madrid National Prize, although this fact, with the passing of time, was no longer considered particularly meritorious. And Sáenz de Tejada still continued in the breach, sticking to titles such as *Episodio de los rojos en Cuenca* (Episode Involving the Reds in Cuenca).

But the exhibition was once again structured round an artist who had died in 1912, Aureliano de Beruete, linked, as we have seen to Impressionism. Beruete fulfilled the role assigned in the previous Biennale to Regoyos: that of offering an appearance of Modernism which could not be found in the Spain of that time. The strange thing is that this idea of Modernism was sought in artists who had died many years previously, who at one time had been in contact with the European avant-garde. The Impressionists were already deemed classical, Expressionism was almost considered an autochthonous trait.... The idea of these Biennales consisted of placing a series of artists with, at times, moderate formal style and an aseptic message, and on other occasions artists who were explicit bearers of ideas promoted by the Franco regime, around a well-known figure who would provide certain guarantees of quality.

Years in the Wilderness: 1948-1956

Spain did not attend the 1948 Biennale –the first after the war. But Pablo Picasso did go, directly invited by the organisers. Rodolfo Pallucchini, secretary-general of the Biennale, contacted the artist personally and succeeded in having some of his pictures seen at Venice. More than forty years after his work had been rejected at the Biennale, and taken down from the walls in the Spanish pavilion, the undeniable maestro of the 20th century was finally recognised. Twenty-two works dating from 1907 to 1942 provided a cursory review of some of his most characteristic facets. Still-lifes, a painter and his model, a fight between a bull and a horse, and *Pesca nocturna en Antibes* (Night Fishing in Antibes)..., these and other subjects could be seen at the recently-reinstated Biennale.

Already on previous occasions –and after the *affaire* of 1905– efforts had been made to persuade the artist to exhibit at Venice. These took place in 1926, 1928 and 1932; but at first no reply was received from Picasso, who was no doubt annoyed about the initial abortive attempt. In 1932 there were financial problems that prevented his participation. It is very significant that it should have been the 1948 Biennale, which was not attended by Spain, at which the artist should finally have been recognised. Renato Guttuso wrote a militant introduction for the artist, acknowledging him as the maestro of the century, the painter who had had the most influence during it, and who had an infinite number of imitators –but very few continuers, because, he said, "Picasso's teaching consists precisely of what cannot be imitated."

Meanwhile, the Spanish pavilion remained closed. The autarchic stage was still in its last throes, and only in 1950 did the foundations start to be laid for leaving behind the paradoxically voluntary, and at the same time obligatory, isolation. In 1946 the UN had ostracised Franco and this was only revoked four years later; coinciding with this opening-up, Spain returned to the Biennale. It did so under the management of Carlos Cañal, director-general of Cultural Relations, attached to the Ministry of Foreign Affairs. Cañal was backed up by the Marqués de Lozoya, who would play a role in this and the three following Biennales.

We cannot say that the results of the exhibitions of this period were satisfactory, notwithstanding the many interesting names that were connected with it. Eclecticism, lack of criteria, and above all absence of risk, were its main features. The artistic recovery of the country was taking place –although extremely slowly– but the most progressive groups scarcely received attention. Art was still burdened by the legacy of official culture, with its ultra–conservative and formally anachronistic message. On the other hand, the "extra-official" culture would seek references in

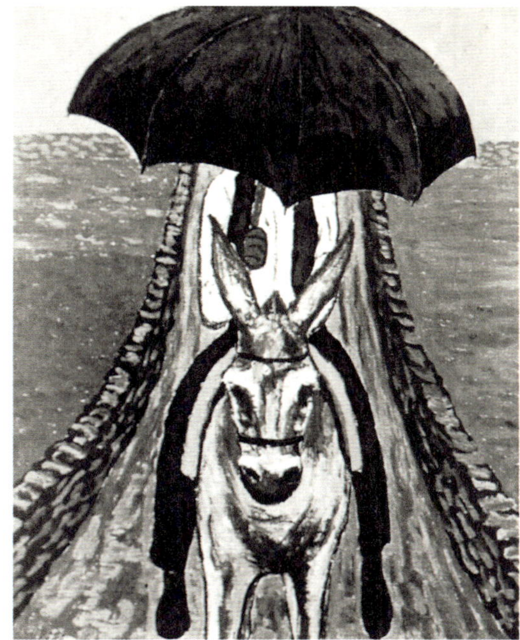

Godofredo Ortega Muñoz
"Hombre con burro y paraguas"
(Man with Donkey and Umbrella)
Spanish Catalogue, 1954

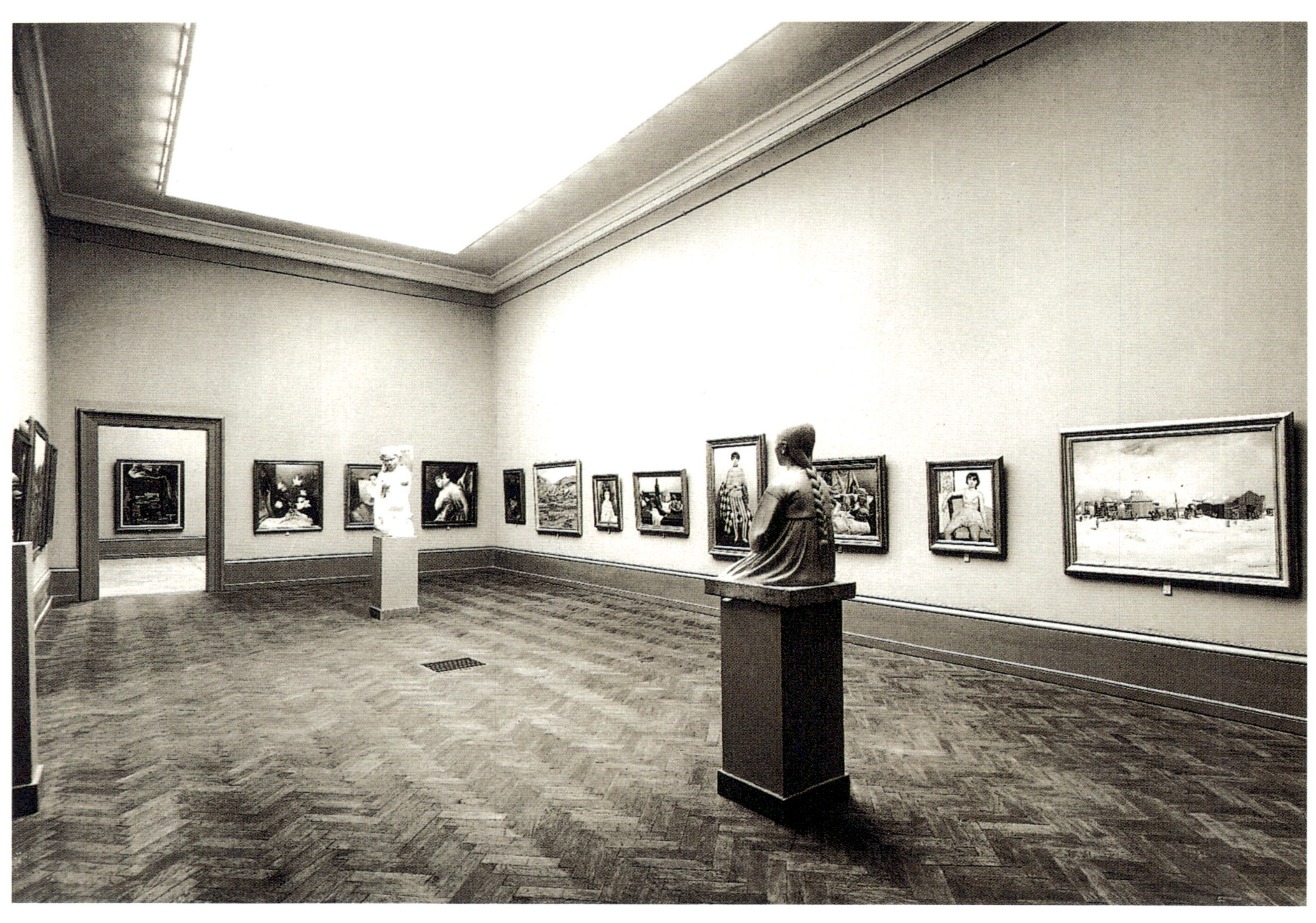

 View of the Spanish exhibition at the 1950 Biennale

pre-war achievements and would strive to renew contacts abroad –a difficult undertaking in a Spain that still considered everything foreign as a source of contamination. It is true that the first period of the Franco regime, when there was only room for the "official culture," could be considered over, but the recovery in art was not immediately echoed in Venice.

We have to remember the difficult forties, when the "official culture" could only be relieved in the field of art by some isolated name or other, such as that of Ángel Ferrant, or some event such as the foundation by Eugenio d'Ors in 1941 of the *Academia Breve de Crítica de Arte*, which promoted the *Salones de los Once* –the first of which was held in 1943. At them we find once more some of the names that before the war were linked to progressive trends. Furthermore, a commitment was made to artists of the future. Notwithstanding his Fascist connections, D'Ors contributed during the post-war period to creating an atmosphere of good sense in the field of art. The Salons did not "discover" new artists, but their eclectic and measured nature signified a step forward in a rarefied artistic atmosphere that continued –especially in architecture– to pursue imperialistic dreams.

In sculpture, the old maestro Mariano Benlliure, who would die in 1947, was still admired, although the sculptor *par excellence* was Juan de Ávalos, whose liking for the colossal was much in keeping with the new tastes. Other sculptors who practised classicist figuration such as Capuz, Orduña, Pérez Comendador and Adsuara, continued to be well received. They were all present at the Biennales. In Catalonia, Marés, Monjo and Josep Clarà were very well considered, although the latter could not be measured by the same yardstick as the others: even though he had nothing in common with Modernism, his immutable Classicism evidenced great sincerity. As for painting, that preferred by the institutions around 1950 was likewise hardly innovative. The situation facing the country was not very encouraging: for instance, ration cards were still in force. There had been no time to prepare the future. The pro-government artists were no longer directly inspired by partisan themes, but did have sentimental roots and moralising intentions. Academicism continued to be in vogue, and López Mezquita, Valentín Zubiaurre and above all Álvarez de Sotomayor, were recognised to be among the best. They imposed their portraits, *costumbrismo* and traditionalism; some tried their hand at landscape painting, in an austere style that idealised the people.

Apart from these artists, there was a clear preference in the post-war period for Solana, Zuloaga and Vázquez Díaz. Although the last two (openly Zuloaga and tangentially Vázquez Díaz), were close to the system, this was not the case with Solana, and it remains a mystery why he was so well treated by those in high places of artistic officialdom. It is obvious that painting in the Franco era could not be justified exclusively through the mysticism of Pruna or the images of Sáenz de Tejada, and therefore more solid foundations were sought on which to establish it. But Solana soon died (in 1945), as did Zuloaga, and only Vázquez Díaz was "used" by the regime, although painter and officialdom ended up on not very good terms.

A large number of the artists mentioned were still exhibiting in 1950. Then a change was observed that we could consider more generational than a matter of taste. The figure of reference at the exhibitions of 1950 to 1956 was Juan de Contreras y López de Ayala, Marqués de Lozoya, whose artistic preferences were for Realism and morals within the Catholic religion. The Spanish

"Official culture" could only be relieved in the field of art by some isolated name or other, such as that of Ángel Ferrant

But the critical year for the artistic regeneration was 1948, to such a degree that Areán talked about the possibility of a "Generation of '48" in art

ambience at these Biennales was anti–modern, especially if we compare it with that of other countries. However, all this notwithstanding, some figures appeared whose presence signalled the end of the "Franco culture," whose aesthetic aspects were described as follows by Alexandre Cirici: "Talking about Franco aesthetics is the same as talking about the adaptations that the visual artists and critics (those of monumental art with aspirations to exhibit in museums, and those of commercial art and propaganda) made in order to be compatible with the different stages of its development and to obtain the lucrative official prizes, or at least immunity from repression."

Benjamín Palencia, who in 1945 had founded the Madrid School, also talks about this period. The School, at which, among others, Álvaro Delgado, Carlos Pascual de Lara, Francisco San José and Gregorio del Olmo were trained, would have great repercussions on the Spanish pavilion in Venice, which would prove to have an extraordinary centralist vocation. Together with Palencia, who was the most outstanding landscape painter in Castile at that time, we should mention Zabaleta, with his striking Andalusian peasants, and Ortega Muñoz, who portrayed the aridity and mystery of Extremadura. Landscape painting was, during these years, one of the most-practised genres. More contemplative and less interpretive than in previous years, its best exponents were the Valencians Genaro Lahuerta, Francisco Lozano and Pedro de Valencia –and also some Catalans.

Despite the situation of political isolation, the first attempts were made after 1947 to renew contacts with other European countries. For Cirici, it was precisely the centralist, cultural narrow-mindedness, which supported all things traditional and academic, that stimulated a rebellion whose first focal points would necessarily be outside Madrid –far away, both geographically and politically, from the centre of the State. Of these, we should remember first of all the "Indalianos" in Almería –a group founded half-way through the forties, with Classicist and Surrealistic influences– but especially noteworthy were the components of the "Pórtico" of Saragossa, which appeared in 1947, originating a real stir in the city by suddenly introducing abstraction.

But the critical year for the artistic regeneration was 1948, to such a degree that Areán talked about the possibility of a "Generation of '48" in art. The most important events to mention, apart from the appearance of Dau al Set, were the founding in the same city of the October Salons, the start of the activities of the experimental cycles of Art Nouveau; and finally, the founding of the School of Altamira. Dau al Set was the group that contributed the most important elements.

Made up of painters Cuixart, Tàpies, Tharrats and Ponç and of writers Arnau Puig, Joan Brossa and Cirlot, it practised a Surrealism of strange leanings. They were not so much an epigonal formation as the bearers of new and special views. Apart from these groups, a number of positive individual experiences should be mentioned: the beginnings of Millares, the motives of Ángel Ferrant, and Sempere and his Abstract exhibition in Valencia. All this provided encouragement for the desolate visual arts scene in Spain. They conducted the first avant-garde experiments and their development depended entirely on their own efforts. Neither the State nor the bourgeoisie wished to be identified with them.

The fifties, however, would bring interesting expectations, coinciding with the opening-up on the political plane. The first event deserving of mention at the start of the decade was the 1951 Hispano-American Biennale, which was called upon to play the innovative role denied to its

Venetian counterpart. The gap between real culture and official culture began to be filled. This first Hispano-American Biennale was followed by two more, supported by the Hispanic Institute of Culture. There was an intense penetration of modern trends by artists who would subsequently evolve in different ways, but who already stood out on account of their different investigative methods: Mampaso, Ponç, Rivera, Manolo Gil, José María de Labra, Jorge Oteiza..., and many others. Apart from the progress achieved by the Hispano-American Biennales, the decade was enriched by occurrences such as the founding in 1951 of the Canary Islands group LADAC (The Archers of Contemporary Art), sponsored by Eduardo Westerdahl, in which abstraction was defended.

These activities, together with the first imports of exhibitions from abroad, as well as the appearance of the new generations of young critics such as Moreno Galván and Aguilera Cerni, and the appearance on the scene of rationalist formulas in architecture, helped to dust off the atmosphere. Everything was ready for 1957, a crucial year in contemporary Spanish art.

In Venice, of all these developments, it was the figurative ones, or those which did not show very obvious signs of formal rupture, which were accepted. The painters of the time who made the greatest impression in the 1950 Spanish pavilion were, among others, Vázquez Díaz, Palencia, Gutiérrez Cossío, José Benet and Zabaleta, as well as the landscape-painters Lahuerta, Lozano and Pedro de Valencia. Specifically, Francisco Lozano was at the four exhibitions of the period to which we now refer, whereas Lahuerta and Valencia only went to that of 1950. Together with them, a group of artists of much lower standing was similarly represented. But at the following Biennales we find some names representative of the links with the avant-garde. Miró was there in

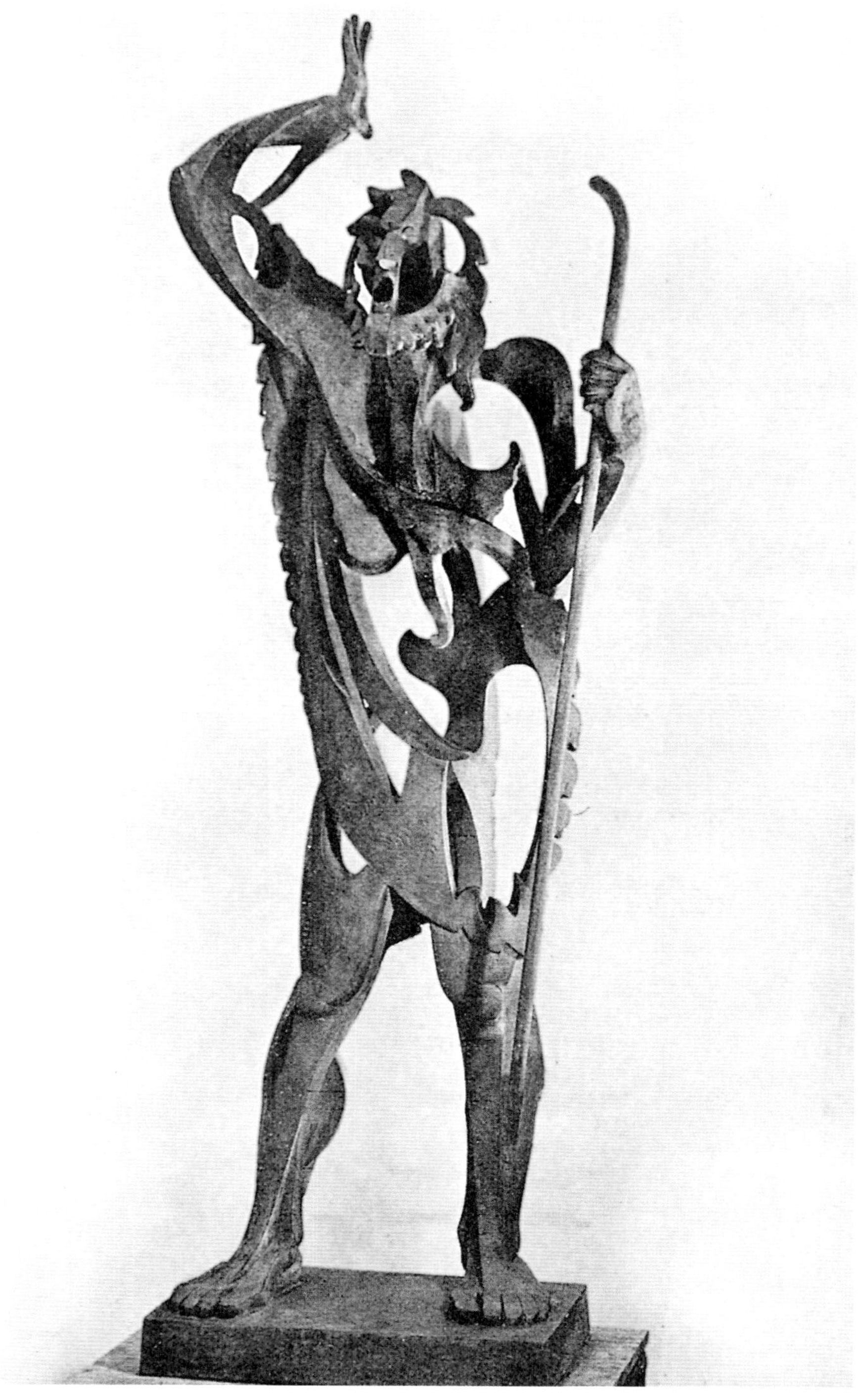

Pablo Gargallo
"El profeta" (The Prophet)
Spanish Catalogue, 1956

1954, and other important figures were at the 1956 Biennale, in which the poet Luis Felipe Vivanco, the pro-Franco intellectual, participated. Long gone were the melodramatic harangues published in *Vértice*; he now played a role in the recovery of art.

Although the Franco guidelines were already greatly enfeebled at the 1950 Biennale, the close links with academic art and its corresponding messages were an indication of the art that was preferred. Preventing acceptance at the Biennale of works such as *Barbarie roja* (Red Barbarity) was not enough in order for the Spanish pavilion to lose its regressive look. But it did contrast deeply with a Biennale that, continuing Pallucchini's policy, revised the historic avant-gardes and at this exhibition programmed Picasso again, as well as Juan Gris –both in the international pavilion.

The latter painter was precisely taken up again by Carlos Cañal, director-general of Cultural Relations and chairman of the committee entrusted with organising the Spanish pavilion, who said in the introduction to the catalogue, "The avant-garde trends in the art of our times that is now in crisis are full of Spanish names; the international pavilion is holding a retrospective on the work of Juan Gris, a Spaniard whose true name was González, to which Spain is contributing the portrait that our Vázquez Díaz did of him in the days of their common apprenticeship in Paris." The reference to the first surname –which was so Spanish– of Gris, treated with a degree of coldness in comparison with the warm allusion to Vázquez Díaz, "our" Vázquez Díaz, was significant.

On the one hand, in Canal's introduction the existence of very important sectors of avant-garde artists was being recognised; and on the other, the reality of the exhibition was that the latter had not been invited to Venice. If, for example, the presence of Gargallo, who died in 1934, offers a touch of Modernism, that of Sánchez Cid, Cruz Collado, Juan de Ávalos and Capuz, tells us that the official preferences had not changed. However, it has to be admitted that Cañal had an artistically progressive outlook that led him to confront Enrique Pérez Comendador, curator of the pavilion for that year, in a controversy related by Delfín Colomé and Ángel Llorente. As a miscellaneous collection of pictures had arrived in Venice, Pérez Comendador only wanted to hang the most classicist. Cañal intervened convincingly and constrained him to exhibit all the works. Comendador accused him of conducting a "mistaken policy" and, in an eloquent report to the Ministry he asked, "Why should not the admirable policy followed by Spain, which will prove it to be right and will bring it success in the future, not also be followed in the field of art?" Cañal wrote a report in rebuttal in which he elaborated on his decision that today's art could not be absent from the pavilion. Cañal won a power struggle that ended in the dismissal of Comendador.

As for the rest, the Spanish pavilion at this XXVth Biennale returned to the visual arts tradition of the 19th century, and the central exhibition was based on the Madrazos, ranging from the paintings of their greatest exponent, Federico, court painter at the court of Isabel II (1815 to 1894, who was one of the most important Romanticists in Spanish art), to the canvases of his sons Ricardo and Raimundo. Mariano Fortuny (1838-1874) shared the space with them. His work delighted his contemporaries and also, it seems, the academics of the mid-20th century. Together with him was his son Mariano Fortuny y Madrazo, who died in Venice –the city that he made his own– the year prior to the holding of this Biennale. As we see, the choice veered towards the past. But in this case there was a special reason for it: the scanty funding for the Biennale meant that many of these works, which were already in Venice and belonged to the last painter mentioned, constituted an economic and classic solution. Solana, once more, provided the hard, bitter counterpoint to the painting of the aforementioned painters, but he also belonged to the past. And the approach of the Venice exhibition would increasingly resemble a platform for the future.

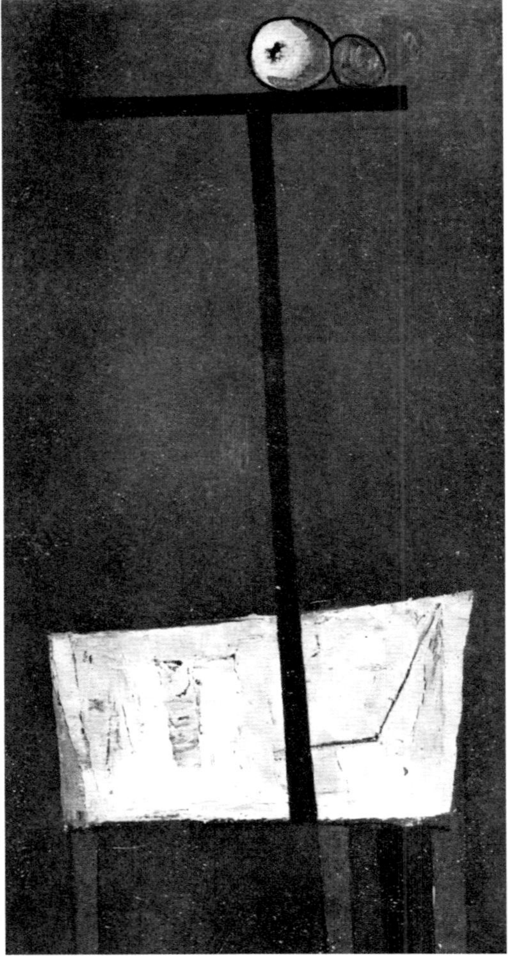

José Caballero
"Mueble con objetos"(Piece of Furniture with Objects)
Spanish Catalogue, 1956

All this in the midst of works that in general were anodyne. Floral and *costumbrista* works alternated with some of the good landscapes of the post-war period, among which special attention should be paid to the Castilian scenes by Benjamín Palencia. Most of the artists participated with only one work. This was the case of Dalí, who exhibited *Muchacha en la ventana* (Girl at the Window), of 1925.

The curator of the XXVIth Biennale (1952), Enrique Lafuente Ferrari, negotiated with Pallucchini the exhibition of a small number of works by Goya –which was suggested by the Biennale itself on considering the painter to be a precursor of the Modernist movement, from many different standpoints. Together with him about thirty artists completed the pavilion. Some of the most consistent artists of recent generations had an effective presence, since Lafuente Ferrari, in view of the success of the Hispano-American Biennale of the previous year, invited many of those who had been prominent at it to take part in Venice.

The new curator, who had a wide culture and a good critical sense, was full of good intentions. A professor of History of Art at the San Fernando Fine Art School, he would also be the director of the National Museum of Modern Art. Although his interests lay more in history, he also paid attention to contemporary art. He wanted to bring Salvador Dalí and Joan Miró to Venice. But it seems that prior commitments on the part of the former, and the fact that the latter was unable to collect his works together, made it impossible to implement this plan. The habitual Benjamín Palencia and artists like Caballero, Guinovart, Tàpies and Eudaldo Serra were indeed there. Lafuente Ferrari summarised his intentions as follows: ".. the Committee wanted, in so far as possible, to present an ensemble chosen on the basis of liberal and wide-ranging criteria –the only one that would be able to reflect fairly exactly the complexity of Spanish art and the variety of its trends. Nothing was excluded *a priori* by the Committee."

In spite of everything, this was not a progressive Biennale, as we can see from the list of artists –especially if we bear in mind those who were "forgotten." But a new style became apparent –or at least the need for one. In painting, Antonio Vila Arrufat was prominent on account of the number of works that he exhibited. He was a classicist linked to *noucentisme*, who showed pictures covering a thirty-year period (from 1921 to 1950). In sculpture, Mateo Hernández, who practised idealised realism, predominated; he died three years ago.

The Marqués de Lozoya, again curator at the 1954 Biennale, was a witness of how the exhibition's grand prize for engraving was awarded to Joan Miró, who this time had been able to collect his work together for Venice. It was a great success and undoubtedly a reason for reflection for Juan de Contreras y López de Ayala, who basically had modelled the pavilion on the work of Isidro Nonell, in the usual policy of recovery of historic works that was the norm at the Spanish pavilion during this period.

At the same time, the inclination felt by the curator for Realist painting was undeniable; in this connection he put together an exhibition that attempted to link all the work chosen that year at Venice to this artistic genre, contrasting it with Abstraction, which had already seen the light in our country and had started to make great strides. On introducing the catalogue, José Camón Aznar, reinforced these theses: "The Spanish contribution to the Venice Biennale faithfully narrates the main routes of current Spanish art.

The exhibition's grand prize for engraving was awarded to Joan Miró, who this time had been able to collect his work together for Venice. It was a great success and undoubtedly a reason for reflection

And the first thing ascertained in the light of these canvases is that it is rooted in the most elementary reality of the earth and of men, thereby preventing access to those mental abstractions that are the indication of modernity of other schools." He acknowledged that works such as those of Miró were perhaps not subject to strict mimetic relationships, but insisted that, even then, it was possible to speak about "... that last portion of reality that in the most evasive Spanish pictures always exists."

As a result of the personal preferences of the Marqués de Lozoya, this Biennale moved strictly within the orbit of classic figuration (except for one or two isolated cases). But it was, moreover, a special figuration in that the subject was mainly landscapes. It was mostly painters from the Madrid School (Francisco Arias, Eduardo Vicente, Martínez Novillo, etc.) who were invited to the Biennale. The centralism responsible for this selection of artists was seen in the discovery that, of the thirty-one living and participating artists, twenty-two lived in the capital of Spain, whereas, as we have already observed, the first outbreaks of reaction against academic and official art took place in areas far from Madrid. This fact indicates the interests connected with the exhibition, at which there were artists who were respectable but far removed, in their immense majority, from contemporary exploration. Artists such as Dalí, Tàpies and Caballero were the counterpoint. Furthermore, others such as Néstor Basterretxea, Juana Francés and Francisco Farreras, were at that time at an interesting point of inflection.

Together with the Marqués de Lozoya, Luis Felipe Vivanco was to be seen at the 1956 Biennale, contributing to the catalogue. Lozoya's introduction stressed the collective nature of Spanish art, a nature whose essence was difficult to explain: perhaps it was its ferocious individualism, perhaps the vivacity of its strength of expression, the rejection of ephemeral influences..., again Lozoya, who had started to notice the lack of national qualities in current art and who described artistic formalism as a new academicism, found in Spanish art a refuge against everything foreign. In his judgment, the Spanish pavilion had been able to highlight the collective quality of its art, and he talked about –without mentioning any names– the landscape-artists, the still-life painters and the painters of religious pictures. Nevertheless, he warned that Spanish distinguishing marks were more difficult to identify in the sculptors at the pavilion, who had paid no attention to their own traditions, preferring to follow the universal trends. He was undoubtedly referring to Pablo Gargallo (the sculptor exhibiting the most works), but also to Eudaldo Serra, with his Surrealist studies, or to Cristino Mallo, with his expressive small-format pieces. Other sculptors presented classic works; some, like Gabino, were at the start of an interesting evolution.

Vivanco's introduction spoke about the contribution made by the Spanish sculptors to the extension of figurative limits. Abstraction had already been accepted as an established fact, even in painting. For the first time, he said, Spain was presenting a group of Abstract painters, such as Tàpies and Caballero, painters who, together with others such as Millares, Canogar and Feito, he described as "a-formists." Now we have come to Informalism. The Spanish pavilion in 1956, seemed to be planning new concepts in art, and noticing hitherto unknown ideas. But if we look closely at the artists to whom most space was allotted in the exhibition, we can see that things had not changed very much. In the section of reviews, the work of Juan de Echevarría, deceased in 1931, was given a very prominent place, enabling the organisers to consider themselves promoters of Modernism on account of the Fauve and Impressionist features of the artist. The habitual Benjamín Palencia; and Joaquín Vaquero Palacios –the polyfacetic artist who took to Venice a series of anthropomorphic landscapes done by him that same year, 1956– also exhibited a large number of pictures. His best argument was mystery; the most problematical, theatricality. Apart from them, Eduardo Vicente and Zabaleta, were significantly well represented.

The "González Robles Era" and Ceferino Moreno's Participation: 1958-1972

A few years ago I had an opportunity to meet Luis González Robles, the curator of the Spanish pavilion at the Venice Biennale from 1958 to 1970 and then on two more occasions, in 1982 and 1984.

During the conversation we reminisced about something that I now find especially moving: he was also the curator for a remarkable exhibition staged to commemorate the twenty-five years of Franco's bitter "peace." And my father, painter Raúl Torrent took part in that exhibition. An Informalist with a fighting spirit, his vulnerable temperament and compulsion to swim against the tide prevented him from promoting his production and obtaining recognition for his splendid work. And I say this based on conviction and not on the memory of my dead father. Informalist painters used to frequent our house in those days, among whom I remember Cruz de Castro, who was once at the Biennale.

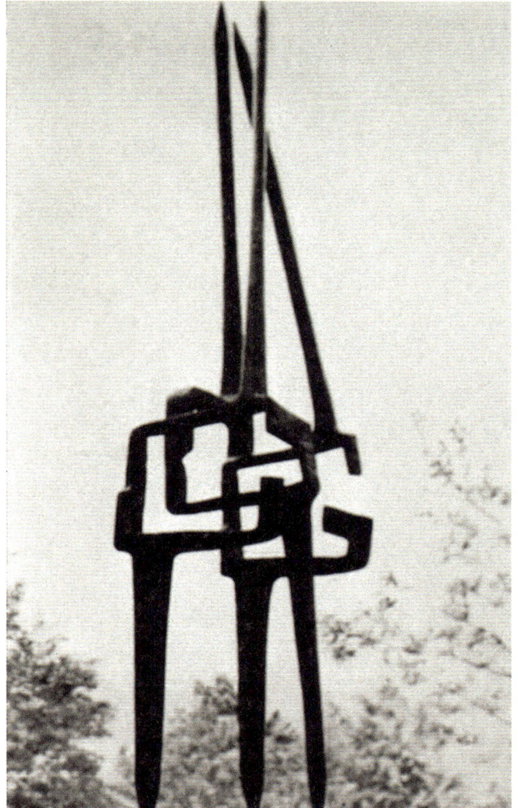

Eduardo Chillida
"Elogio del Aire" (In Praise of Air)
Spanish Catalogue, 1958

My father, a contradictory character if ever there was one, was a soldier under Franco: an atypical civil servant of Franco, just as González Robles was a "sensitive civil servant under Franco," as someone has recently described him. Luis González lived and worked under a regime for which the word "culture" meant order, academia and apology for traditional values. Satisfied with this regime, he nevertheless introduced some touches of artistic culture into it that denoted intelligence and good taste.

Did González Robles try through these exhibitions to "whitewash" Franco's regime and give the system an image of modernity? It can be assumed that they were indeed exploited in this sense, but the more likely explanation is that "insensitive Franco officials," on perceiving the success not only of the Venice Biennales, but also of other previous exhibitions, chose to support the new values and the new formulations in visual art. González Robles made room for –he didn't discover– artists who were struggling to make their way out of a confined space for self-expression. That was greatly to his credit, and he played a part in Spain (as was also said recently) similar to that played by Leo Castelli in the international sphere.

However that may be, when Luis González Robles took over the management of the Spanish pavilion at the Venice Biennale in 1958, an exceptional qualitative change took place. There had been outstanding artists at the 1956 exhibition but it lacked a coherent approach. At this Biennale, on the other hand, there were

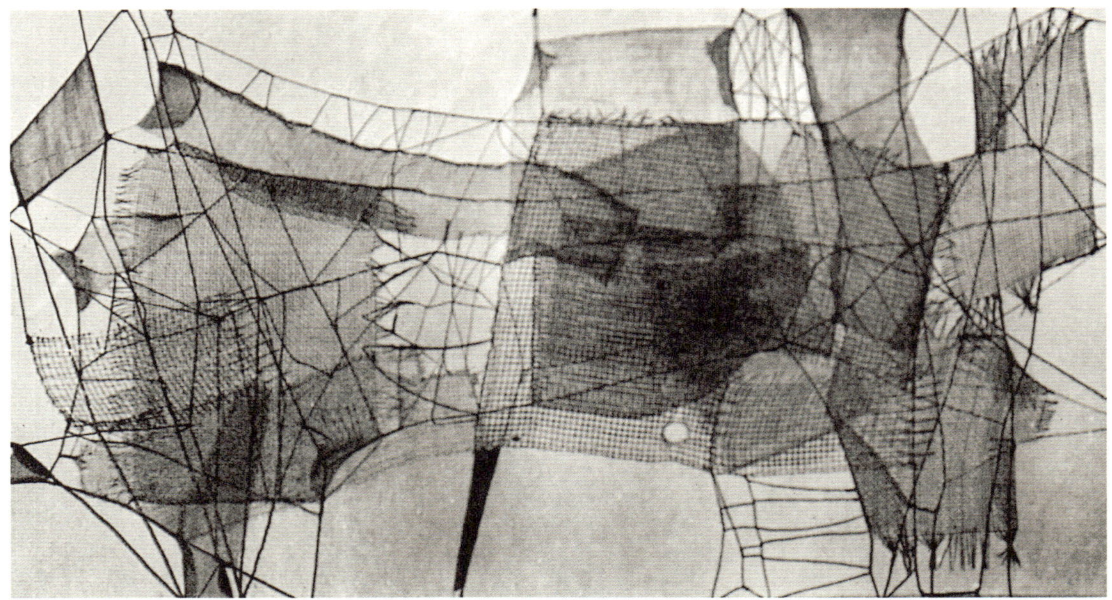

already a defined programme and solid intentions. If in previous years the exhibitions had often been organised in accordance with personal tastes, without bearing in mind the emergence of creativity, the intention now was to provide a view of new developments in the country, and these new developments in Spain came from Informalism. But not only from Informalism. González Robles's mission consisted of making enquiries about who was formulating new idioms, what these idioms consisted of, and bringing them before the public gaze. Nevertheless, he neglected interesting emerging trends, as we shall see.

González Robles's mission consisted of making enquiries about who was formulating new idioms, what these idioms consisted of, and bringing them before the public gaze

It was by no means his first experience as an organiser. He had played a role, with greater or lesser degrees of responsibility, in the Latin-American Biennales and that of Alexandria. He did outstanding work as curator of the 4th Biennale of São Paulo in 1957, at which Jorge Oteiza –who died in 2003– obtained the grand prize for sculpture. He was also head of exhibitions at the Madrid Museum of Contemporary Art, of which he would be the director from 1968 to 1974. His latest public activities are focused on the starting up of the museum that bears his name, in which he has housed his valuable art collection.

The major problem faced by González Robles during his years as director of the Spanish pavilion at Venice was the position of the artists themselves who attended the first Biennales organised by him and who later refused to repeat the experience, persuading many others in their train to boycott the exhibitions. Emphasis has been placed by different circles on the advantage taken of the new Informalist trends in Spain in an attempt to present an image of opening-up to the outside world. For this reason many artists deserted the exhibitions programmed by the

Manuel Rivera
"Dirección diversa" (Different Direction)
Spanish Catalogue, 1958

State, feeling that they were merely pawns in a game at the service of spurious interests. However, if the regime's aim was to offer an image of political opening-up, it failed to do so, and the only thing that seems to have been deduced abroad was that dictatorships were also capable of accepting abstract and revolutionary artistic formulas. After all, as Virgilio Guzzi said, "... the fact that Spain has also exhibited abstraction this year could go to show [...] it's not true that abstract art is exclusive to free and democratic countries, as has often been repeated."

As confirmed by Tomàs Llorens (who personally knew many artists compelled to adopt a position in respect of this situation), until 1966 artists linked to the left were allowed to go to the state, national, and above all international, exhibitions, as was the case of that of Venice. The measure was accepted because it was considered professionally necessary for artists to go abroad in order to make themselves known. But as of that date, Llorens continued, the Spanish pavilion at Venice was discredited. In his opinion, from then on the regime no longer limited itself to using art as a weapon for projecting itself abroad, but at the same time, through the international exhibitions, set out to, "... make a discriminatory selection, politically directed at ideological neutralisation within the avant-garde themselves. Thus, for example, it cut the ground from under the feet of the youngest artists who held the most advanced views regarding the alternative to "Spanish Informalism"; and sowed confusion among the new realist ideas and the old figuration...."

At any rate, until anti-system feeling crystallised, González Robles was able to organise the exhibitions that he considered most appropriate at that time. He had in his favour the artistic effervescence prevalent in Spain during the closing years of the fifties and, of course, his wish to take this effervescence to the Venice pavilion.

A number of very significant events took place on the art scene during the period under review. The most important was the Associationist movement, whose point of reference was 1957, the year before the first exhibition organised by Luis González in Venice. During that year the following groups made their appearance: Parpalló of Valencia, El Paso of Madrid and Equipo 57 of Córdoba. The first of these had the fewest repercussions state-wide, since it was mainly concerned with self-training. Its mentor was art critic Vicente Aguilera Cerni, who took on a structuring role following the early demise of painter Manolo Gil. Many of its components participated in the Venice Biennales, while some, like Sempere and Soria, did so as early as 1960.

The other two groups, El Paso and Equipo 57, represented the irrationality/rationality dichotomy in Spanish art. The first signified the emergence in our country of the Informalist movement, highly charged with romanticism. As opposed to this profile, the second advocated specificity and exactitude. Whereas the members of El Paso became incontrovertible figures at Venice, the same thing did not happen with those of Equipo 57. It was easier for good taste to become linked with the expressive gestures of the Informalists than with the formal sobriety of the Rationalists.

This was understood by González Robles, who gave priority to the expressive facet as opposed to that of the contained image. Although the Madrid group El Paso had a short life span because it was dissolved in 1960, its influence was definitive and its shadow very long. Especially involved with it were artists Millares, Saura, Canogar and Feito, although Juana Francés, Pablo Serrano, Manuel Rivera and Antonio Suárez moved within its orbit at the beginning, and Viola and Martín Chirino participated later on. Moreover, it was completed by critics José Ayllón and Manuel Conde. For its part, Equipo 57 of Córdoba –which had, however, been set up in Paris– was organised around, among others, Ángel Duarte, José Duarte, Juan Cuenca and Agustín Ibarrola. Its research was conducted on the subject of space and form, and its aim was to achieve art that, given its preciseness, could be translated into useful objects.

Simultaneously with the setting up of these groups, some painters such as José Ortega and Ricardo Zamorano were already championing committed painting, of testimony and denunciation, which would coincide with the "realist generation" in literature and in a way be a prelude to the social concerns of the next decade. Only one year after the formation of aforesaid

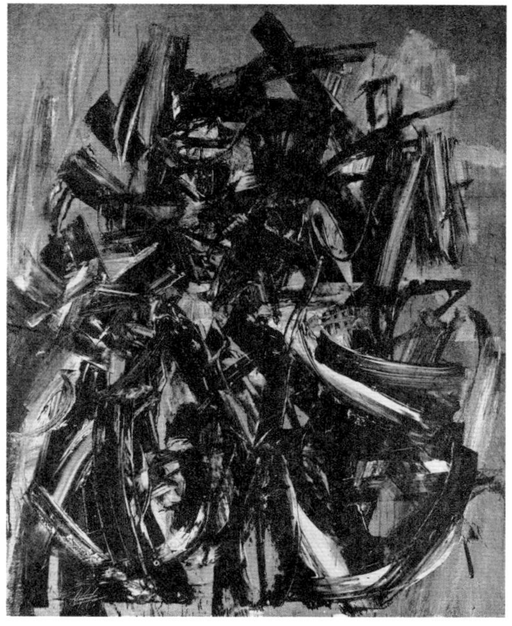

Antonio Saura
"Salvatierra"
Spanish Catalogue, 1958

groups, the 19th Venice Biennale took place. The Spanish pavilion was greeted by the Italian press as *la più bella sorpresa della Biennale* (the most beautiful surprise of the Biennale). A number of unusual circumstances came together to produce an unequalled exhibition. First of all, in Spain, the artists of El Paso had coincided in developing some abstract propositions that proved to be an authentic revolution in the pavilion. Secondly, there was someone interested in collecting them and exhibiting them; and finally, these trends were intelligently contrasted with forms of Realism. González Robles was aware that the pavilion's orientation had to change, and that the "urgent contemporaneousness" factor had not been "sufficiently valued in previous Spanish participation at the Venice Biennale."

Abstraction was law at Venice that year, not only on account of the Informalism of El Paso, but also on that of geometry. Together with the representatives of abstraction, who constituted the immense majority, there were only three of figurative painting, all of whom were within the orbit of what was called "Spanish Realism": Francisco Gutiérrez Cossío, Godofredo Ortega Muñoz and José Guinovart. The three had participated before in the Biennale but their presence there now became paradigmatic, providing the counterpoint to Abstraction and the exemplification –through their work– of a broader aspect of Spanish post-war painting of which they constituted spearheads in one way or another. Gutiérrez Cossío, who was sixty, was the veteran of the group. Most of the pictures that he exhibited (still-lifes, vases of flowers...) were recent, but there was also the important *Retrato de la madre del artista* (Portrait of the Artist's Mother), which would mark a point of inflection in his work. Ortega Muñoz also took very recent works –especially his *Veranos* (summers). José Guinovart, for his part, showed two types of pictures, all dated 1958 and yet very different from each other: some clung to Expressionism; others chose a different form of figuration in which the subject was diminished to a certain extent by the importance acquired in relation to it by the treatment of matter.

The abstract works were divided into three sections: "dramatic," "romantic" and "geometric abstraction." In the first, González Robles included Canogar, Millares, Saura, Suárez, Tàpies and Vela, recognising in all of them "a shock value, a rhythmic flight and an austerity that unified their expression in a constant theme that did not exclude the singularity of idiom of each one." Romantic abstraction was illustrated by the works of Cuixart, Feito, Planasdurá, Tharrats and Vaquero Turcios: "... painters who, with the most disparate expressive resources, were able to establish a lyrical balance between what was contingent on form and the permanence of content." Finally, geometric abstraction was defined in painters such as Farreras, Mampaso, Povedano and Rivera, who: "... although with their own characteristics [...] use the geometric diagrams of the school with a freedom which shows their Spanishness."

A critic of González Robles's requirements writes about a matter that was repeatedly referred to in many articles about the Spanish presence at Venice: in other words, the hypothetical "Spanishness" of our artists. There is a reference in the catalogue to the problems of the artists represented, "all of whom have clear Iberian leanings which are based on a strictly ethical concept of the world." But it was not only him; for example another critic, Vicente Aguilera Cerni, referring to the same exhibition (and specifically to the "Spanish Abstract School"), talked about the "existence of a nucleus with strong and different individualities between themselves, but

A number of unusual circumstances came together to produce an unequalled exhibition

brought together by the common denominator of a radical Spanishness that strengthens their adherence to the international vocabulary of today's painting." It was certainly not made very clear what this Spanishness consisted of, unless the thread of Iberianism is sought in the dramaticism whose reference is Goya's Black Paintings, to which Spanish art always appears to have felt itself the heir.

In any event –and independently of these issues– the very well informed Vicente Aguilera Cerni, who took a great interest in Informalism, was distinguished at this Biennale with the prize for criticism, precisely for a series of articles published in the magazine *Índice*, in which he discussed Spanish Abstraction and in particular El Paso.

The success of the pavilion brought with it rewards until then unthinkable. Eduardo Chillida, the maestro who completed the splendid exhibition of that year, won the grand prize for sculpture. He had taken seventeen sculptures to Venice, dated from 1951 to 1958, among which were *Elogio del aire* (In Praise of the Air) which speaks so much to us about his aspiration to achieve an understanding with nature. In turn –and going back to the prizes– Antoni Tàpies received the second prize for painting (the first prize went to Mark Tobey). Furthermore, UNESCO awarded another prize to the pavilion as a whole, taking into account all the works as well as their arrangement.

So the members of El Paso shone at this exhibition, but so did three of the founding members of Dau al Set from Barcelona: Tàpies, Cuixart and Tharrats. Their common research into visual art, together with their training as a team, had borne fruit, and it had been demonstrated that the individual, personal qualities of each artist had been safeguarded in the group as a whole.

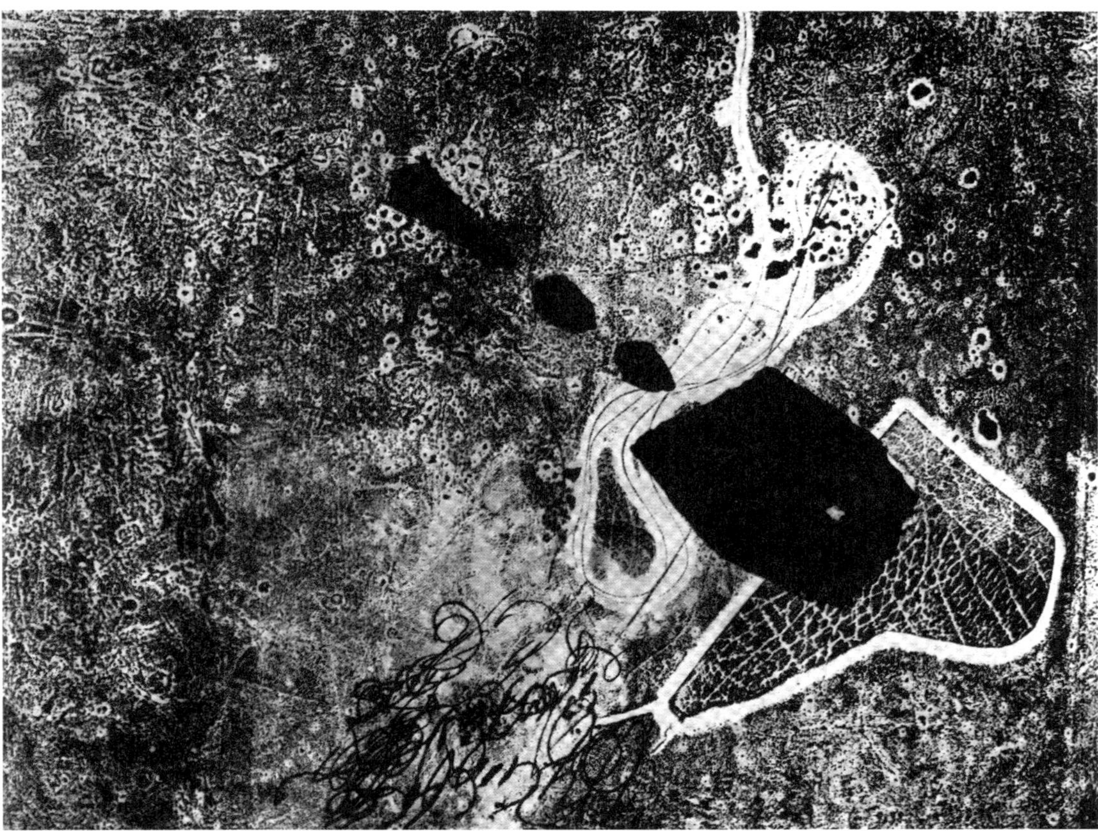

The expressive violence of Millares and Saura, the metal-filament constructions by Rivera, Cuixart's dense materials and the refined materials of Feito all attracted attention, but perhaps Tàpies's already completely-defined work did so more than that of the others. The work by Vaquero Turcios, Povedano and Vela, etc., was on a different plane. Recognising "Picasso's true grandchildren" in the Spanish artists, the Italian critics were enthusiastic about the pavilion. So were the French and U.S. critics. The Spaniards for their part, and in particular Aguilera Cerni, praised an exhibition in which could be found: "From the admirable mysticism of the material offered by Antoni Tàpies, to the heartrending cry of Manolo Millares, [...] the sumptuousness of Juan José Tharrats, the mystery of Modesto Cuixart, the dramatic energy of Antonio Saura, the poetics of Luis Feito, the intensity of Rafael Canogar and the experimental lyricism of Rivera. Of course, without forgetting the enormous Eduardo Chillida and the others...." Other critics linked to daily newspapers such as *Arriba*, which in no way could be suspected of being progressive, also showed their interest in the results obtained at Venice.

The entire Biennale of that year emanated abstraction, but the most powerful abstraction

Juan José Tharrats
"Maculaturas" (Blemished Pages)
Spanish Catalogue, 1960

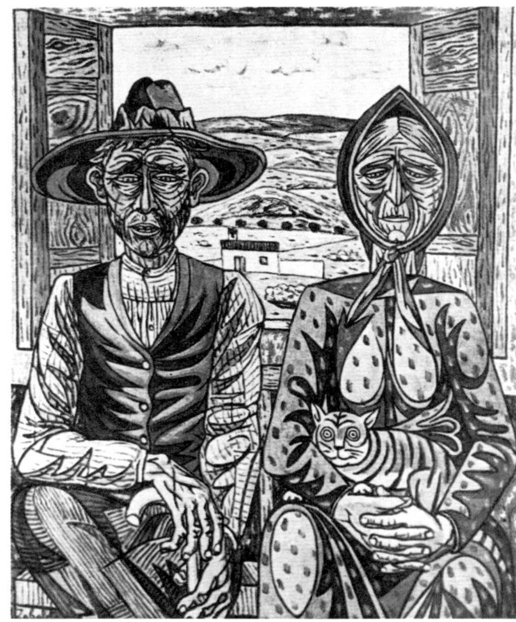

was seen in the Spanish Informalists, with all due respect for the American Abstract Expressionists. Significantly, Rivera recalled that when the guests at the *vernissage* cocktail party entered the pavilion, "... there was a striking silence. It was as if the pictures had magnetic force."

Following that Biennale some artists began to question their presence in the visual arts activities organised by the State. An event consisting of the exhibition to be staged in 1959 at the Paris Museum of Decorative Arts, divided their opinions. In principle, the members of El Paso, together with Antoni Tàpies, refused to participate in it, given that quantity, in their opinion, was taking precedence over quality with regard to selection. Later on they agreed to take part, except for Tàpies. But it was not only the aforementioned problem concerning the number of works that was of concern to the artists. Painters and sculptors asked themselves about their own social responsibility. For the time being, however, the interest in disseminating their work proved stronger than their personal doubts. But the members of El Paso and other artists progressively stayed away from the exhibitions prepared in Madrid.

At the 1960 Biennale these new circumstances were not yet observed. On the whole, the artists who exhibited were not such decisive figures as those of the previous exhibition, but González Robles proposed to introduce new names in order to emphasize and recognize the creative (and also quantitative) power of those years in Spain.

The formula followed was practically the same as that for the previous exhibition, given that there was a large number of abstract artists as against a much smaller one of figurative artists. The plan was completed with the work of a single sculptor, Ángel Ferrant, and of an engraver, Tharrats. The thread that on this occasion united the artists was, in the words of González Robles, their "rigorous devotion to Matter," towards which Spanish artists, throughout their history, had shown themselves particularly predisposed.

The figurative painters on this occasion were Rafael Zabaleta, Marc Aleu, José Vento and Juan Fluvià. Zabaleta, who died while the Biennale was under way, did not fit in with the new trends and seemed like a stranger at a Venice associated with another type of idiom. Nor was Marc Aleu's certainly interesting painting appreciated. The one who best responded to this enthusiasm for the treatment of matter that had guided the selection of artists was José Vento, in whose characters great qualities could be sensed. Juan Fluvià took up the divisionist theory once again and, breaking down his themes into large patches of colour, left to the viewer the task of reconstructing the objects.

As against these artists, there was a long series of abstract artists, the immense majority of whom were linked to matter: Eduardo Alcoy, María Droc, Francisco Farreras, Luis Feito, Juana Francés, José Luis García, Juan Hernández Pijuán, Antonio Lago, César Manrique, Alfonso Mier, Monjalés, Lucio Muñoz, Francisco Nieva, Carlos Planell, Julio Ramis, Joaquín Ramo, Gerardo Rueda, Salvador Soria, Salvador Victoria and Juan Vila Casas. They did not, as a group, include names as resounding as those who made up the 1958 pavilion, but quite a lot of them were well known. Some, such as Feito and Juana Francés, had belonged to El Paso; that same year, Lucio Muñoz had been chosen at an exhibition held at the MOMA in New York. Monjalés, Salvador Soria and Eusebio Sempere should be mentioned on account of their connection with the Parpalló group from Valencia, whose members were thus able to achieve projection abroad. Monjalés started to devote himself vigorously to his work. A metamorphic process was observed in Salvador Soria, involving new materials and the desire for unusual textures. Eusebio Sempere introduced kinetic trends –something that had been neglected in our exhibitions at the Biennale. He only showed three works, but they were very special in that they illustrated his experiences not just with movement, but also with light. The contribution by Ángel Ferrant, on the other hand, consisted of numerous works in iron, along the lines of his "infinite sculpture" (unfinished objects, almost mobile, which at that time absorbed his interest). The sculptures were all dated 1960, as were, for that matter, most of the works of the Spanish pavilion for that year, giving rise to the positive sensation of artistic emergence.

After that year, when this latest Biennale was held, the crisis in Informalism could be observed in Spain. Experiments in it continued throughout

Rafael Zabaleta
"Campesinos de los montes de Granada"
(Peasants of the Granada Mountains)
Spanish Catalogue, 1960

the decade, but in the same way that the international art scene was changing and moving away from Abstraction, Spain likewise started to develop other kinds of artistic approaches. Our history, however, was not the same as that of other countries. We continued to live under a dictatorship, and the playful quality of movements such as Pop, which was crucial in the sixties –or the pre-conceptual activities of the Zaj group– did not have sufficient impact at that time. Informalism, notwithstanding its apparent semantic innocuousness, had opened the floodgates of protest because in the end the strength of its works was interpreted as the modern propaganda of the new era. But the artists, with growing political awareness, embarked on art with a much more direct message. This was already the beginning of social realisms.

An initial significant event was the appearance of what has been called "new figuration," a complex movement that returned to figures but which took from Informalism the value of gesture. Juan Barjola and the Genovés of the Hondo group were two of its most outstanding representatives. The Hondo had been formed in 1961. Apart from Genovés, it comprised, among others, Paredes Jardiel, Mignoni and Gastón Orellana. Informalism started to be placed in doubt, accused of lack of determination, and certain figurative references started to be accepted within its own ranks, if the message so required.

However, the true artistic alternative arrived with critical or social realism, which had been developing at all levels for several years. Art, as another mirror of social concern, tolerated a high level of militancy. Some intellectuals started to demand it, such as Alfonso Sastre, who in 1957 wrote, "Social concerns belong to a higher category than those of art. We would prefer to live in a just world, in which there were no works of art than in an unjust one decorated with excellent artistic works."

The message was clear and reached the artists. Within a short space of time an authentic cultural front arose which, from the most diverse ambits of creation, clamoured for committed art. In the field of visual arts, the response to the appeal had a name: Estampa Popular (Popular Images). The first Estampa group was set up in Madrid at the close of 1959; afterwards came those of Barcelona, Bilbao, Seville, Córdoba and Valencia. Very significant artists joined these groups: Ricardo Zamorano that of Madrid, Guinovart that of Barcelona, Ibarrola that of Bilbao, Francisco Cortijo that of Seville, José Duarte that of Córdoba, Toledo that of Valencia....

Vicente Aguilera Cerni baptised this series of groups with social and denunciatory interests as Crónica de la realidad (Chronicle of Reality). Apart from the Estampas, teams such as the Crónica de la Realidad, or painters such as Genovés, expressed this compulsion for denunciation.

As might be imagined, the Spanish pavilion was not so attuned to reflecting these trends as it had been with the Informalists. In any event, it was as unthinkable that González Robles would have taken the most explicit dissidents of the regime to Venice as it was that they would have agreed to go. Certainly some painters such as Genovés (at the 1966 Biennale) and some others such as Canogar (definitively leaning towards the trends of "social reporting" as of 1963), were invited to the exhibition, although obviously with a "contained" work. But those who could read the signs understood.

Of course, the exhibitions programmed by González Robles were determined by these

A group of artists drew up a document in Madrid, which other groups from different regions adopted. In it they refused to participate in any exhibition staged on the initiative of the Franco Goverment

circumstances and by the aversion that began to be felt for the State exhibitions. Finally, at the end of the decade, in 1969, a group of artists drew up a document in Madrid, which other groups from different regions adopted. In it they refused to participate in any exhibition staged on the initiative of the Franco Government. Not all the artists were in agreement with this boycott. The most representative case was that of Canogar, who considered that his painting did not represent Franco's regime, but rather Spaniards. Nor was Feito (who received the David Bright prize at the 30th Biennale) in favour of the boycott, since he did not consider it appropriate to mix art and politics. But there were only a few cases, and González Robles was obliged, as of 1968, to dispense with several artists and select others, many of whom were first-rate but did not constitute homogeneous groups. The unity seen in his initial offerings, always based on mature observation of the Spanish reality in visual arts, receded with the passage of time. We cannot lay the blame for the loss of vigour of the pavilion on the boycott alone, but also on the choices of González Robles himself who, perhaps wishing to be conciliatory, settled for eclecticism.

The irreversible crisis affecting the many types of abstraction, of which the Spanish version was Informalism, could be widely observed at the 1962 Biennale

The irreversible crisis affecting the many types of abstraction, of which the Spanish version was Informalism, could be widely observed at the 1962 Biennale. The most interesting feature that year was the participation by Pablo Serrano. He exhibited more than twenty bronze sculptures under the generic title of *Bóvedas del hombre* (The Vaults of Man) –which, in the words of the curator, were "vaults in which to shelter the orphanhood and intimacy of human beings" and which continued to explore spatial issues. González Robles was always effective in the field of sculpture; he programmed only a few indisputable artists, who thus had an opportunity to exhibit a large number of works.

With regard to painting, the curator had once more decided on a contrast between the abstract and the figurative. This option had started to be questioned; it seemed to be an excessively simplistic way of presenting Spanish art since it left out artistic formulas that did not lend themselves to this type of comparison. Moreover, the so-called figurative artists had for some time been shedding specific references while the abstract artists were simultaneously resorting to referents. In any event, among the artists included in the Biennale under the label of "Figure" painters were Albalat, who took to Venice his reality transfigured by geometry of free outlines; Genovés, who wished to recover the human link; Medina, who was perhaps the most related to classic Expressionism; Hernández Mompó who, notwithstanding his abstract appearance drank at referential springs; and finally, Cristino de Vera, the most intimist. "Pure" Informalism had passed its peak; now other

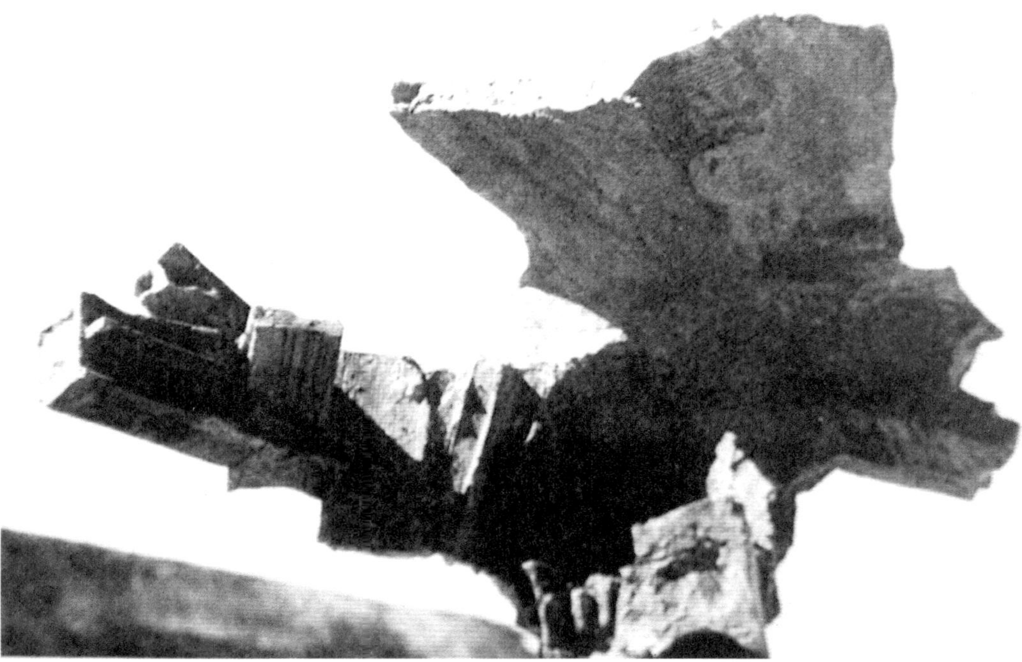

works attracted attention at this Biennale. Apart from Serrano's sculptures, we can mention a group of artists who, experimenting with unusual materials with great daring, made sculptural-pictorial art objects: this was the case of Arcadio Blasco, with his ceramic pictures; Guinovart with the use of wood; Martín de Vidales with his compositions of oil on leather; and finally Torner y Ubiña who had a personal way of employing metal. Far removed from these experiments, we have to mention Zobel with his very polished lines, and of course Canogar's oils, together with the work of Federico de Echevarría, Vicente Vela, Eduardo Sanz, Antonio Suárez, Enrique Gran, José Guevara and the etchings by Cuni and Jesús Núñez.

At the 32nd Biennale in 1964, González Robles caused surprise by reverting to history. Juan Ainaud de Lasarte, director-general of Art Museums of Catalonia, provided an introduction in the form of drawings by Ramón Casas, the Catalan painter who died more than thirty years ago. A series of charcoal drawings by him, with touches of colour, were exhibited, in which different figures of artistic and literary circles of his time were evoked. This was viewed with slight astonishment.

A second change consisted of the number of sculptors invited; this time there were three: Miguel Berrocal, Martín Chirino and Marcelo Martí. But with regard to painting, Luis González insisted on his already classic approach for the exhibition, confronting figuration with abstraction. Luis González introduced the artists to us as follows: "Among those who consider the Figure to be the motive for their artistic idiom are: Álvaro Delgado, Juan Barjola, José Jardiel, María Victoria de la Fuente, Nadia Werba and Francisco Peinado. Then, Eugenio Granell is like a link between the romantic memory of figuration and the attractive and varied field of abstraction; those who continue to compose phrases in a very personal and well-defined way are: José Caballero, Manuel Viola, Juan José Tharrats, Juana Francés, Antonio Lorenzo, Juan Vilacasas, José Orús, César Olmos, Dimitri Perdikidis and José María Iglesias."

Vicente Aguilera Cerni, one of the habitual critics on issues connected with the Biennales, had started to perceive confusion in the curator's proposals, and complained about an absence of criteria in respect of the pavilion. Although he had greeted the 1958 Biennale with enthusiasm, he now talked about a lack of coherence, and criticised the fact that some works, such as those

Pablo Serrano
Serie "Bóvedas del hombre" (The Vaults of Man)
Spanish Catalogue, 1962

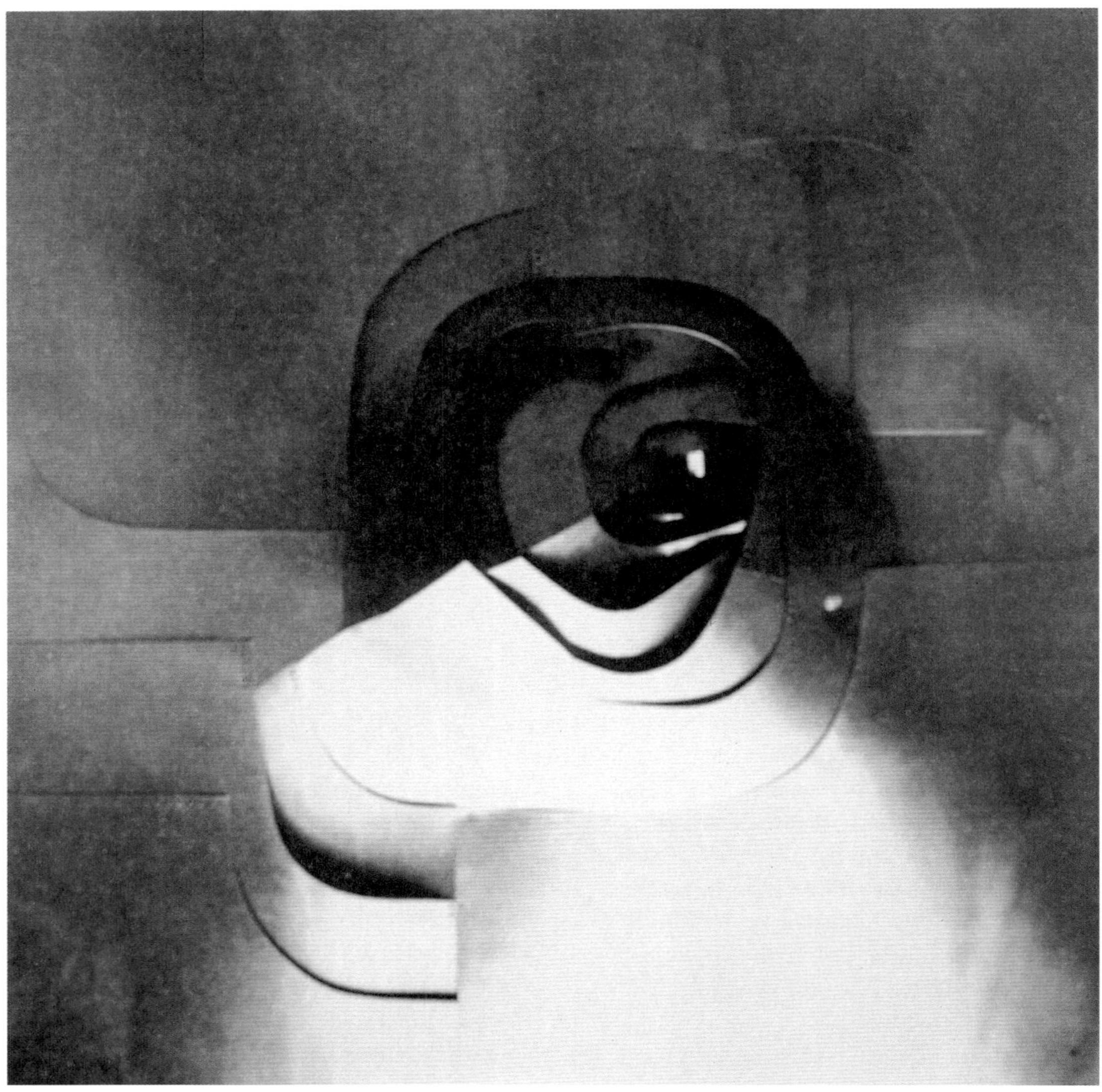

of Jardiel, a founder member of the Hondo group, had been mixed into the general confusion. Luis González's star no longer shone in the same way as before.

At the 1966 Biennale, artists such as Genovés gave way to Crónica de la realidad, which, as we have seen, had scarcely had a presence before at Venice. In the exhibition catalogue the painter said, "I consider that the main aim of Art is to bear witness to the age in which the artist lives." Denunciation of injustices should be a duty for the human being. Works such as *Avance y retroceso* (Progress and Regression) –on display at this Biennale– fell within this context. In the picture, a group of people is running, undoubtedly pursued by others bent on depriving them of their freedom. On another plane they are fleeing to the other side, while continually being attacked and subjected. It was clearly an indictment against Franco, but although this could not have failed to be noticed by González Robles, it was not sufficiently explicit to worry the Franco censorship.

González Robles tried at the exhibition not to favour some artists relative to others, but rather to aim for a homogeneous whole. In the introduction he outlined his conviction that at this type of exhibition it was important to give preferential treatment to the latest generations of artists instead of concentrating on the work of those who were already established. Therefore a mission was proposed which –in his own words– would be "informative," and would reflect the experiences of a Spain that not only had art centers in Madrid and Barcelona, but also in other cities and provinces. On this occasion he accepted all the offerings submitted: Abstract Expressionism, re-interpretation of the figure, Neo-Constructivism and considered that *el buen hacer* (a high standard) should be the only requirement common to them all. This was

Amadeo Gabino
Spanish Catalogue, 1966

ambiguous to say the least and in any case should have been taken for granted. Among the artists were Alfaro, with his pursuit of dynamic spaces; María Droc, who sought vindication for the autonomy of *collage*; Gabino, with his polished surfaces and optical sensations; Federico de Echevarría and Perdikidis, more subject to the initial versions of Informalism; Mendiburu with his wood sculptures based on nature..., and other different artists for an exhibition with multiple nuances.

The year of protest, 1968, arrived impetuously at Venice and the opening of the Biennale took place in gardens overrun by the police. The Italian Communists staged different demonstrations in front of some of the pavilions, including the Spanish pavilion, demanding freedom for the country and letting off steam with shouts against the dictator. Delfín Colomé tells how, when the storm had died down, "... the wily González Robles hung up a manifesto at the entrance to the pavilion signed by the Spanish artists whose work was on display –Vilacasas, Subirachs, Hernández Mompó and Feito– and some foreigners: `We are against any form of coercion or violence. We believe it is urgent to conscientiously and audaciously review and rejuvenate the outdated structures in our world. Let us do away with the *art* and *criticism* that are no good for anything.´ That was a way of saying everything without saying anything: an example of sublimated cultural diplomacy."

In any case the Biennale, in general, was more the setting for extraneous protest than for grievances concerning art itself. What it did have –both at this exhibition and above all at the next one in 1970– was an air of entertainment. Venice was losing in programmatic approaches what it was gaining in visual experimentation and ideas –through perceptiveness, *Arte Povera*, conceptual art and, of course, "happenings."

The Spanish pavilion did not allow itself to be influenced by the general atmosphere and presented a "serious" image. During those years the boycott was real, and those who agreed to go to the Biennale were assailed by doubts. González Robles resolved the situation in connection with the 1968 exhibition by inviting artists of the new generations, but also some from previous ones. The bond that would unite them on this occasion, according to the curator, would be their human interest; moreover, everyone would speak "the language of the most vigorous Expressionism, which has been and is still the constant feature of Spanish art of all times." In his opinion, it could be thought that the way was being opened up to a new rational being, immersed in social affairs, thereby gaining in humanism and a return to the Renaissance. Following this interest, a figurative option would be the natural state of things, without a trace of Informalism. Abstraction, for its part, had been geometrised or, in other words, "rationalised."

However, not all the artists who went to this Biennale were really concerned with the human condition. At times Luis González indulged in a risky game of interpretation. Anzo's presence, for example, could be fully justified within the curator's overall plan, but not that of Feliciano Hernández; or many others. The connection was growing weaker, in the same way as the alleged Expressionist link was already weak. At the same time, not all the artists were new. Canogar and Feito, among others, were returning to Venice in a role that contradicted the positions of the curator himself; however, those who were going for the first time were the most numerous, such as Antonio Bueno, Agustín de Celis; and, funnily enough, the one who would soon replace Luis González as curator of the Spanish pavilion at Venice, Ceferino Moreno. Sixteen artists participated in 1970 in the last of the Biennales

The year of protest, 1968, arrived impetuously at Venice and the opening of the Biennale took place in gardens overrun by the police

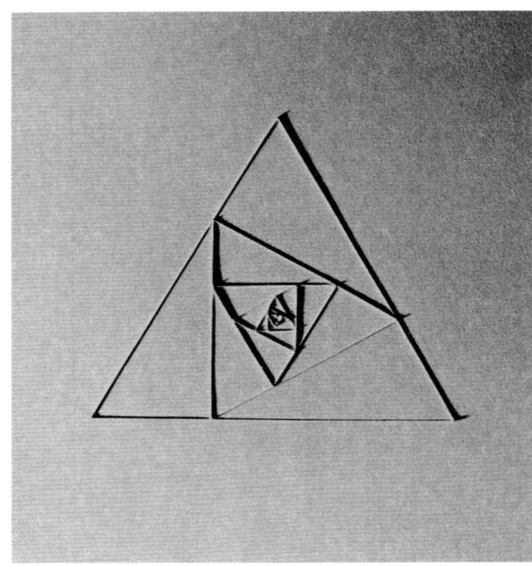

that, for the time being, would be directed by González Robles (twelve years later, he once more took charge of the Spanish pavilion). "The new image of man" was the theme that united the exhibitors. If two years earlier an attempt had been made in the selection to reflect human problems, the same topic was taken up again this time, but with references to the relationships that the individual establishes with his environment. It was a matter of linking them to time and space. González Robles perhaps wished to connect his discourse to that which was a basic approach of the age: the human being relative to his historic situation. But the curator was unable to count on those on whom he should have been able to count: the artists involved in "social reporting." Moreover, many of them had already started to give way to the new trends that were becoming established in the art of our country. The appearance of engravings or ink sketches was not unusual at this exhibition, although mixed techniques, oils, and already acrylics, continued to predominate. Among the artists was Eduardo Úrculo, who died this year (2003), a rare traveller between social criticism, Abstraction and even Pop. Also Luis Gordillo, who had started out on his automatic drawings the previous year. The most widely represented was Darío Villaba, who exhibited his figures encapsulated in *Plexiglas*, the point of departure for his international launching. There were artists who were new at the Biennale, others who were already habitual..., but again a pavilion that was "serious," which is why the atmosphere of diversion prevailing that year at Venice was not noticed. This was demonstrated by Hernández Pijuán's thoughtful dimension, Orcajo's technological landscapes, and Cruz de Castro's personal relationships.... After twelve years at the head of the Spanish pavilion at Venice, Luis González Robles handed over the baton, in 1972, to painter Ceferino Moreno. This was the first occasion for many years that the selection of works of art would be the responsibility of an artist, although Moreno had wide-ranging experience in the organisation of artistic events. Luis González had been a competent curator, but his latest exhibitions had not been as lively as the first. A change was necessary. And the orientation of the Spanish pavilion did indeed change radically with the new man in charge.

In the first place, Ceferino Moreno theoretically refuted what had constantly been repeated at Venice: that Spanish art was basically expressionist and expressive. Going back to Velázquez and Zurbarán and drawing support from Picasso and Juan Gris, Ceferino Moreno talked about rationalised art. For the first time, a curator concentrated on a single trend and expressed it. But he didn't do so through a large number of artists, but rather by focusing on a relatively small group, at least in comparison with what was usual at the Spanish pavilion. In all, the offerings included nine artists, with works by José María de Labra, Francisco Echauz, José María Iglesias, Jordi Pericot, Salvador Victoria, José Luis Gómez Perales, Luis Lugán, Joaquín Mouliaa and Amador Rodríguez. Some, such as Labra and Iglesias, had been at the Biennale before.

All of them, to a greater or lesser degree, had participated in the different experiences which since the fifties had been aimed at finding a space for geometric and analytical art. Some had a very direct relationship with the Computer Centre at Madrid's Complutense University. And it must not be forgotten that some (Pericot, among others) helped to introduce optic and kinetic trends into Spain.

In general the pavilion had look of unity; and above all it had recovered the Rationalist tradition that is also present in Spanish art and which until

Jose María Labra
"Espiral triangular" (Triangular Spiral)
Spanish Catalogue, 1972

then had not been seen very much at Venice. It covered an aspect that had been developed many years previously in our country. Already in the last third of the fifties, the Equipo 57 had, in its manifesto, called for the elimination of all emotional and individualistic facets in art objects. The experiences of the Russian Constructivists were revealed with the same passion that they wished to leave invisible in their works. Many artists looked at themselves through them. In 1960 the first exhibition on "Spanish Normative Art" was staged in Valencia, and in 1968 the first exhibition of the Antes del Arte (Before Art) group, which considered the art-science relationship and concerned itself with the relationships of Constructivism, kinetic art and optical art. These were the experiences that served as a prelude to the 1972 pavilion, which constituted a novelty in programming.

The Spanish pavilion at Venice did not open again until 1978. In 1974 there was no Biennale, as a result of the crisis concerning the statutes. In 1976 it remained closed, but that was nevertheless the year when the greatest exhibition of Spanish contemporary art that had ever taken place in the city was held. We shall talk about it next.

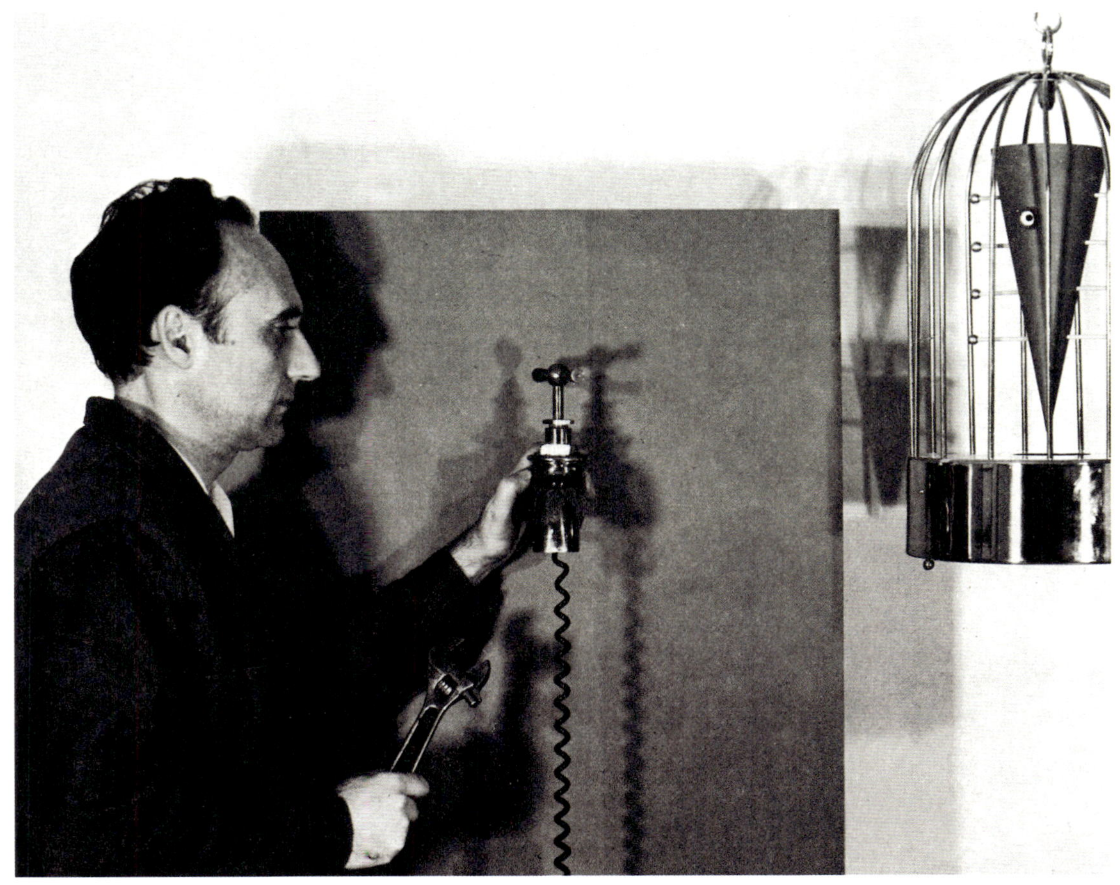

For the first time, a curator concentrated on a single trend and expressed it

Luis Lugán
"Cuatro grifos sonoros" (Four Noisy Taps)
Spanish Catalogue, 1972

The 1976 Biennale: Spain. The Artistic Avant-Garde and Social Reality, 1936-1976

Projects and Ins and Outs

The first Biennale without Franco continues, for Spain, to be the most significant of those that have taken place until now, although –or precisely because– the country was not officially invited and a committee that had nothing to do with the State undertook to put together a very special display. Of course, the exhibition was not held in the Spanish pavilion, but in the central building in the Gardens, and it is still remembered by those who had an opportunity to go to it. It's true that it was controversial, and also true that agreements and understandings were left by the wayside, but it undoubtedly contributed to systematizing part of the history of Spanish contemporary art.

The plan for an extra-State Spanish exhibition –that from the outset voluntarily mixed politics and art– had been conceived before Franco's death, but nevertheless it had to be resolved after the decease of the Head of State. This circumstance led to some problems: the first was the doubt as to whether or not it was appropriate. The Biennale had decided, some months after Carlo Ripa di Meana had become its director, that Spain was not going to be officially invited to Venice. At that time –this was in 1974– Franco had not yet died, and the aim was to deprive Franco's Spain of its voice. The dictator's demise in 1975 caught the organisers on the wrong foot and a theoretical reformulation had to be contrived: the exhibition would be a call to attention for the managers of the transition. If there was a moment of doubt relative to the invitation, it was dissipated by the very recent memory of the executions by firing squads during Franco's last days and of the police repression in the Basque Country. Franco's supporters still held positions of responsibility in Spanish political life and there was –as later shown– a danger of reaction.

In fact, the story of Spanish participation in this Biennale began on March 20, 1974, when a new Board of Directors was appointed and Carlo Ripa di Meana, an heir to '68, was anxious to make Venice a place of art and commitment. He wanted to denounce the situation in countries subject to a dictatorial system. Spain was practically the only Western European country that lived under a regime lacking the most elementary political rights. It was natural, and almost obvious, that his sights should be set on it. Carlo Ripa decided to prevent official Spanish representation and to make way for avant-garde critics and artists with a clear stand in the anti-Fascist struggle.

However, during the initial months of his management, the idea that Ripa would later present had not yet taken shape. As a matter of fact, it appears that there were contacts with the Ministry of Foreign Affairs with a view to programming the usual exhibition in the pavilion. To this end, Luis González Robles had sent a letter to Ripa on August 14, 1974 (in reply to a previous letter from another member of the Board of Directors) in which he proposed a selection for the Spanish pavilion consisting of Cuixart, Feito and Equipo Realidad. It was a significant proposal aimed at temporising.

But Ripa was ruminating over another idea, certainly as a result of his exchange of impressions with painter Eduardo Arroyo, a member of the Biennale Arti Visive Committee, as well as the opinions that he was able to exchange with the rest of the committee and with some Spanish intellectuals. In October 1974 a number of feelers were sent out in order to measure the support that a manifestly anti-Fascist exhibition could summon up in our country. The first noteworthy incident took place on the 18 of that month, when Arroyo was arrested at Valencia airport (he had returned to Spain clandestinely), where he had gone for the

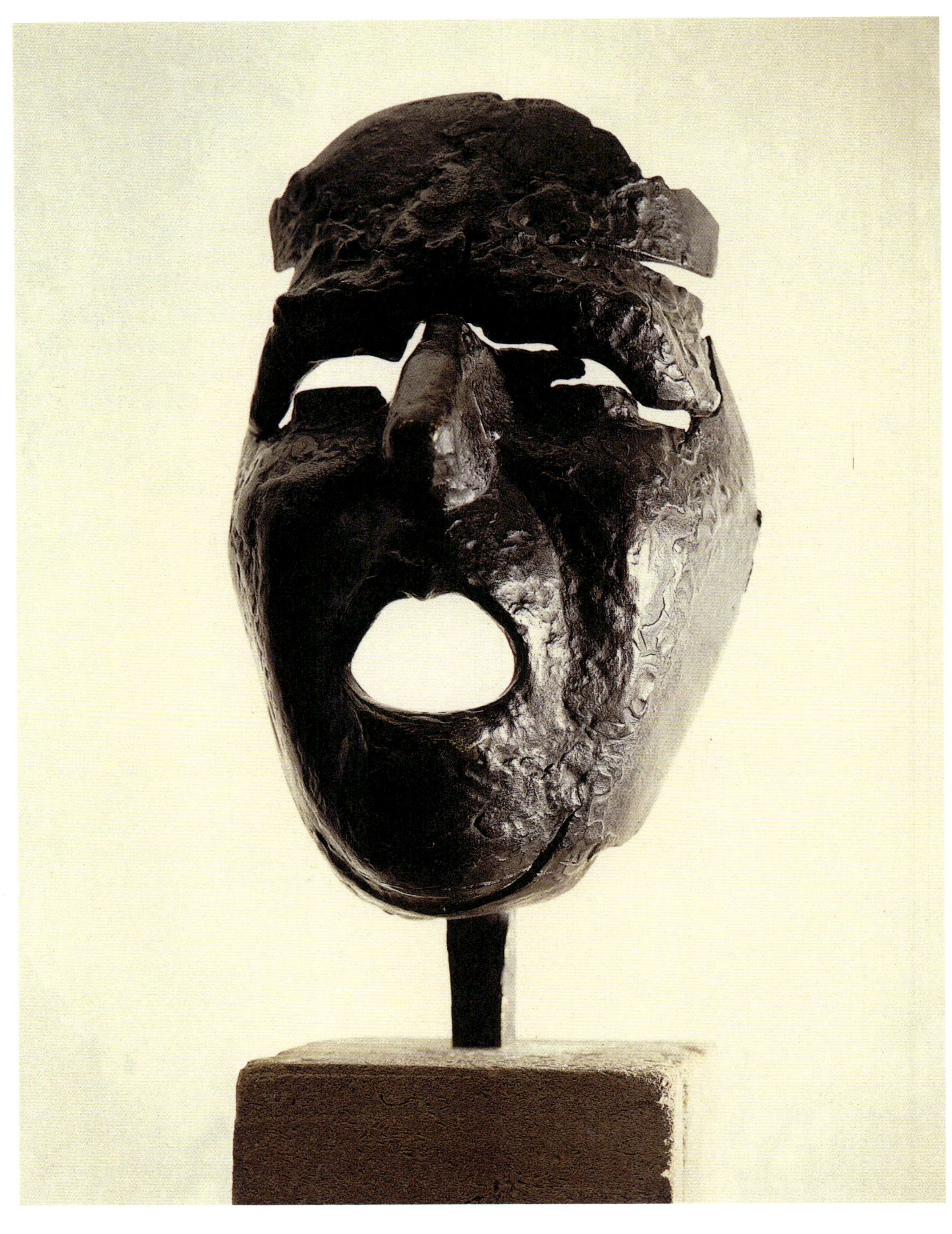

Julio González
"Máscara de Montserrat gritando"
(Mask of Montserrat Screaming)
Reina Sofía National Art Centre

The series of pictures by Julio González of the Montserrat became an emblem which the 1976 Biennale did not wish to omit

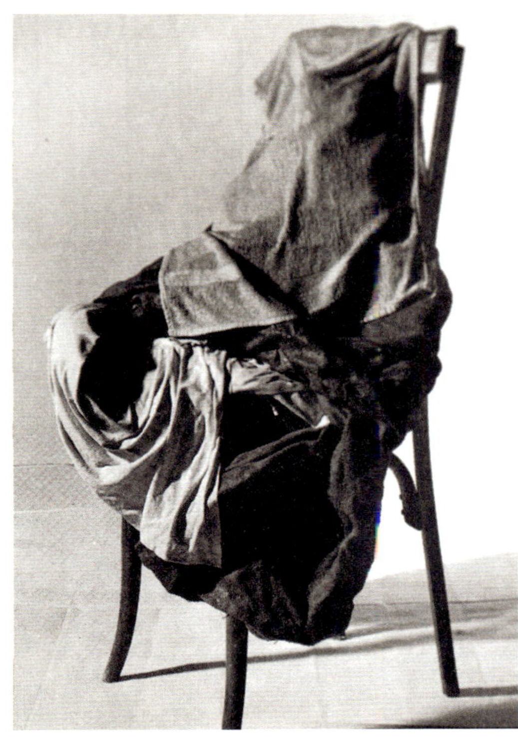

purpose of organising an exhibition of Spanish artists for the 1976 Venice Biennale.

The Biennale raised its voice of protest, and denounced the case, as it did when Alfonso Sastre, Genoveva Forest and six other Spanish intellectuals were arrested. The need for the proposed exhibition, said Ripa, had been demonstrated, since it responded "to the need to confront the serious restrictions that prevailed in many parts of the world of art, culture and freedom." Arroyo, married to an Italian national, obtained his release a few days later, and was expelled from Spain.

Until the holding of the Congresso Internazionale della Nuova Biennale, which took place from May 30 to 31, 1975, the first official proposal on the theme of "Spain" was not publicised. The congress was attended, on the part of Spain, by Eduardo Arroyo and the members of the Equipo Crónica, consisting of Rafael Solbes and Manuel Valdés, as well as Alberto Corazón. Raffaele de Grada, a member of the committee of the Arti Visive sector of the Biennale, then outlined the reasons why, in the opinion of the group, Spain should be the focal point for the 1976 Biennale. "I do not think that anything is more important at this time than showing the true face of a country that has itself shown a deformed face, a face of conservatism and at times of a false modernism recovered by the regime."

However, this Congress had taken place only to point the way. It was necessary to wait until July and the Convegno Internazionale Progettuale for more specific suggestions on the projects to be executed and the general activities for the coming years. Apart from the Spaniards who had attended the previous meeting, art critic Tomàs Llorens was invited to this colloquium. Although Llorens is now an indisputable figure on the international art scene, at that time he was unknown. He had been a professor at the schools of Architecture at Valencia and Portsmouth, and had taken up criticism for a journal directed by Aguilera Cerni. His presence, however, was very significant in so far as it showed the wish of the group involved in the project until then to obtain the collaboration of art theoreticians. Indeed, one of the severest criticisms levelled at the future committee was the large number of artists on it and, of course, their over-representation.

Llorens was entrusted with submitting a proposal on what the future exhibition dedicated to Spain would be. For the time being he was asked to produce "a proposal." But since no further consultations had taken place although only a year remained before the exhibition was due to be held, it can be assumed that the Biennale

In the opinion of the group, Spain should be the focal point for the 1976 Biennale

Antoni Tápies
"Silla con vestido" (Chair with Dress)
Italian Catalogue, 1976

management had complete confidence in Llorens. In his speech to the Convegno, the critic outlined a clear objective: he wanted to organise an exhibition in which the Spanish artistic avant-garde over the past forty years would be analysed, and to submit for debate "the implications of this project relative to a theoretical problem with a more general objective –that of the relationship between cultural (and specifically, in this case, of the artistic avant-garde) and political production." He would not be interested in the art of "official culture," but rather in the art generated despite it, both within and outside the country. This point of departure, which acknowledged the existence of two cultures, was one of the arguments used by the project's detractors, since other sectors of criticism and of history of art minimised the importance of the so-called official culture.

In any event, and in particular in so far as Spanish art at the Venice Biennale was concerned and the manner in which its proposals had been reflected at it, Tomàs Llorens was of the opinion, and wished to demonstrate, that for years the Biennale had been a showcase in which Spain had exhibited a distorted reality: "This image of a so-called Spanish avant-garde art similar to that of other European countries whose political organisation was different, apart from being used domestically as an instrument for interference in artistic production, had been converted into an instrument for political propaganda in favour of Franco's regime, for international as well as for national purposes."

The idea having been defined, the chairman decided to appoint a committee to implement it. Its members would be: Antoni Tàpies, Antonio Saura, Oriol Bohigas, Agustín Ibarrola, Valeriano Bozal and the members of the Crónica (Manuel Valdés, Rafael Solbes, Alberto Corazón and Tomàs Llorens). Manuel García would perform the duties of secretary. It would be the Committee of Ten. Moreover, Inmaculada Julián, Víctor Pérez Escolano, Josep Renau and José Miguel Gómez would help with consultation and specific organisational matters. In the Biennale's definitive catalogue, this list of collaborators was enlarged to include Antonio González Cordón, Vicente Lleó Cañal, Fernando Martín Martín, Ludolfo Paramio and Ignacio de Solá-Morales. Later on, when the exhibition was taken to the Miró Foundation, the name of Simón Marchán appeared. The task of preparing the spaces for displaying the exhibits was undertaken by Martorell, Bohigas and Mackay-Barcelona. Although Eduardo Arroyo participated in the committee's arrangements (some people even talked about "Arroyo's exhibition"), he did not form part of it. He was already doing other things for the organisation of the Biennale.

On September 8, 1975, the Board of Directors of the Biennale, on deciding the general theme for the 1976 exhibition, which was: "Cultural Environment, Participation and Structures," also defined the special project "Spain: The Artistic Avant-Garde and Social Reality, 1936-1976." At the International Congress of representatives of countries participating in the 1976 Biennale, held on January 9 and 10, 1976, it was provisionally approved, and on the 31st of the same month it was definitively accepted. As of then, the project –headed by Tomàs Llorens and Valeriano Bozal– gradually took shape. The stages gone through by this project can be seen from the paperwork collected by Manuel García, secretary to the committee.

Although at the beginning the possibility of an inter-disciplinary exhibition had not been envisaged, it was progressively decided to incorporate this aspect, undoubtedly in response to the criticisms being made. The programming and ideological grounds of the proposal (explicitly stated in an internal document) were soon defined. The aim was to analyse the relations between art and politics and between intellectuality and politics; to study Spanish art within the ambit of the class struggle; and to consider the relationship between art and the working classes. Moreover, it consisted of offering a view, which was neither ingenuous nor immediate, of the commitment of artist and intellectual; to address the problem of artistic idiom –given that a change of contents and subjects no longer appeared sufficient; and finally to ascertain whether the capitalist organisation of culture would constitute a system of appropriation, in which case there should be a move towards supplanting this traditional organisation of culture.

And all this was to be circumscribed within the past forty years, in which the periods corresponding to political and artistic events –from the Civil War to the latest commitment– would have to be mentioned. Finally, the issue was brought up of an alternative language and organisation of culture and artistic production.

However, the setting into motion of the project caused uneasiness in some Italian Communist circles, which channelled their protests through composer Luigi Nono, painter Emilio Vedova and art historian and critic Giulio Carlo Argan. Nono and Vedova enjoyed great esteem in Venice, where they had played an important role during the reform process of the Biennale. Carlo Ripa knew that their opposition could cost him the support of other people, precisely among the Communists who were allies in the "government" of the Biennale but were nevertheless very critical of his management. This was the situation and –pressured by the aforementioned Nono and

Vedova– he decided to broaden the consultations and approached José María Moreno Galván, a person of great standing, an art critic and Communist, whom his Italian companions had contributed so many times to releasing from Franco's gaols, also Vicente Aguilera Cerni, one of the most well-known critics in Spain at that time, with wide-ranging contacts in Italy –especially as a result of the international critique prize awarded to him by the Biennale in 1958, and finally, Rafael Alberti, the poet. This was a Communist option that at the same time, through Aguilera, would keep the most progressive Catholic sectors happy.

Especially Moreno and Alberti were people who, in respect of their political significance –according to Nono and Vedova– could not be left out. The last and brutal death throes of the Franco regime demanded, in their opinion, that those in charge of the exhibition should have a strong political commitment. In this connection it is possible to understand the letter sent by Vedova to Saura on December 22, 1975, in which he said that "an exhibition of such cultural and political importance" would need a new committee.

At the same time, both criticised the project under way, whose structure, in their opinion, would not differ from the traditional concept of the exhibition. At the same time they reproached its lack of an interdisciplinary aspect, which according to the dissidents was essential. Nono said about the latter, "Arroyo's exhibition is too limited. The Biennale initiative should not be confined to paintings and sculptures, but rather take into account all the voices and expressions of Iberian culture, thereby contributing to the spirit of unity of the Spanish democratic forces." But basically the question was not that. If only the foregoing problems had been at issue, they could have been solved without any difficulty. What really annoyed Nono was that the Biennale had delegated the organisation of the event to a committee that had not been agreed by consensus, and that the wide democratic political spectrum in Spain had not been consulted. At the same time he was vexed that names as charismatic and committed as those which he had proposed had not been taken into account.

This was the state of affairs –and pressured in this way– Carlo Ripa di Meana summoned the above –mentioned people to Venice so that they could in turn submit a proposal for the exhibition. There was an initial interview, which was summarised as follows by Vicente Aguilera: "Alberti, Moreno Galván and I coincided in everything. We did not merely want an `exhibition´; we also aspired to a set of interdisciplinary expressions in consonance with the category of Spanish artistic culture and with the requirements of our historic moment. We demanded that they should be combined, not divided up. We asked for the maximum qualitative and historic rigour, assuming that the reality of our wide-ranging democratic culture would impose itself. But above all, we demanded that culture should be the point of departure for attaining concord and freedom for all individuals, all peoples and all living cultures within our frontiers (which should be specifically and unequivocally delimited). Likewise we requested cultural recognition for the positive role of the immense democratic segments of Spanish Catholicism."

After this first meeting, Aguilera Cerni and Moreno Galván (Alberti had had to return to Rome) met again with the Biennale's Board of Directors, which asked them to draw up a draft proposal containing their points of view. So they made an emergency draft (it was done in record

The last and brutal death throes of the Franco regime demanded, in their opinion, that those in charge of the exhibition should have a strong political commitment

time), divided into eleven sections, covering from visual arts to cinema, music and theatre, and including as a counterpoint the analysis –in respect of architecture– of certain manifestations of Fascist art. They indicated that the purpose of the exhibition would be to demonstrate the vigour of Spanish culture, to contribute to the unitary underpinning of the democratic process, and to highlight the position of national reconciliation. At the same time, it was pointed out that the draft would have to be critically reviewed and then submitted in Spain for the consideration of artists and personalities in culture and politics in all the democratic segments of society.

It was the beginning of January 1976 and there were two exhibition proposals for Venice. This was an absurd situation: some people had been asked to draw up a new plan while the original plan was still in force. In the event that the latest plan were to be accepted, there was not enough time for making the proper arrangements to ensure its success. However, the first invitations were already being sent out for the plan headed by Tomàs Llorens and Valeriano Bozal.
One of the inevitable questions asked was the extent of knowledge of those involved in these groups regarding what was going on. It seems that, at least initially, Llorens, Bozal and the rest of the committee were unaware of the double–dealing being carried on by the Biennale. Aguilera, for his part, knew that Arroyo was working on the exhibition, and intimated that he knew of the presence in Venice of Manuel García. But he said he had no knowledge of the composition of the rest of the committee, nor of the progress of the plan. In any event, although he and Moreno knew nothing about the basic contents of the exhibition, they had heard some news through Luigi Nono and Emilio Vedova. At least it appears that the latter had been in contact by telephone with Moreno Galván in order to tell him that the Biennale, in principle, was not counting on him. We also know that Vedova had knowledge of the participation of Saura and Tàpies on the committee responsible for the project. Therefore, when Vicente Aguilera and José María Moreno Galván arrived in Venice, they were aware of some things that had been divulged by Nono and Vedova. However, it is not surprising that they did not know about the project in its entirety.

Perhaps Ripa was secretly hoping that both groups would get together and organise a joint exhibition. A vain hope. Vicente Aguilera, Moreno Galván and Alberti would not have wanted to join a venture that had already begun (nor would this have pleased the other group). Moreover there was the “Arroyo problem.” This painter was not much liked by the others –especially Moreno Galván. Ripa soon realised that it would be impossible to reach an agreement: ”... they stated some prejudices concerning Arroyo that immediately put an end to the conversation. They reproached him for having painted a controversial picture of Dolores Ibarruri, *La Pasionaria*. Conducting themselves in this way they created an embarassing situation for us, because Arroyo is an artist and we were unable to censure his work from a political point of view. Furthermore, Arroyo is a Biennale curator....” Moreno Galván, who was by no means conciliatory, was unable to contain himself when criticising the painter of the controversial picture, against whom he levelled some very harsh words.

In any event, after the Christmas holidays –specifically on January 11, 1976, Aguilera and Moreno Galván learned from the press that the project of the so-called Committee of Ten had already been accepted. After reading the news, their reaction was swift. Both, separately, wrote letters to the President of the Biennale: Vicente Aguilera’s letter was sent from Milan on January 12; that of Moreno Galván, from Madrid, was dated the 18 of that month. The two letters were revealing and coincided in expressing disappointment that nobody had talked to them clearly, and that the advanced state of the project –which was already under way– had been hidden from them. Both also said they had nothing against those responsible for the project, although Moreno Galván did stress his lack of agreement with Arroyo. Nevertheless, that was not the end of the story: a few days after the news had appeared in the press, Vicente Aguilera received a telegram from Carlo Ripa, telling him that the decision to accept the project, which had already begun, had not yet been formalised, although (and this should be made clear), those involved had been assured that it would be implemented.

Indeed, the Llorens and Bozal team, already informed about much that had occurred, began to show that they were upset about the situation, and on January 20, 1976 they sent a letter to Ripa expressing this malaise, which was caused as much by the problems raised concerning their project as by the doubts relative to the suitability of some of the members of the team. They provided information on the activities carried out until then, and requested written approval both of the project itself and of the committee. They urged that formal invitations be sent to artists and institutions, that the budget be defined, and that the funds be handed over.

Meanwhile, Ripa, taking his time, went to Paris on January 28 for the purpose of meeting Santiago Carrillo. He wanted to know what the consequences would be of sticking to the first project. Ripa was worried about the contentiousness that was beginning to divide Spanish artists and intellectuals –especially within the Communist Party– in respect of the Biennale

Ripa was worried about the contentiousness that was beginning to divide Spanish artists and intellectuals

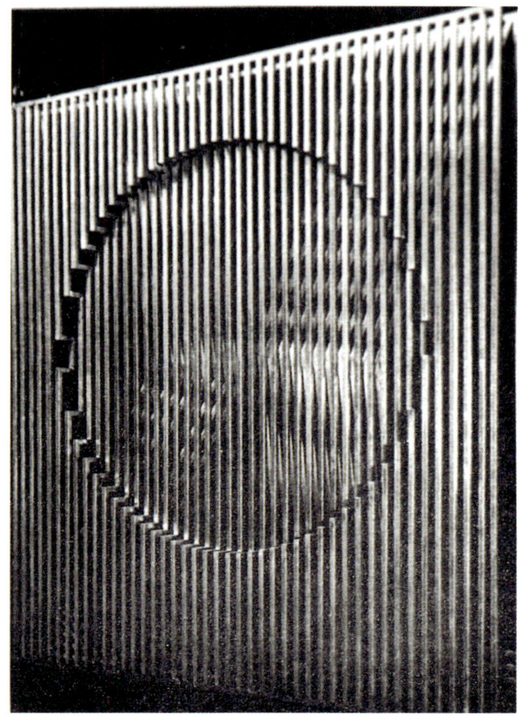

dedicated to Spain. It seems that Carrillo showed caution, saying that he shared the concern of the president regarding the possible breach to which this exhibition could lead. His recommendation to Ripa di Meana to beware of the artists because they were "bad tempered" came to the notice of the press.

Three days after this meeting, on January 31, at the annual meeting of the Biennale's General Council, it was decided to hold a vote on the two projects submitted. By 18 votes in favour and two abstentions (by two Christian Democrats) the project headed by Llorens and Bozal was adopted. It appears that the interview with Carrillo had served the interests of Carlo Ripa.

At the same time, the interdisciplinary nature that Nono and Vedova had wanted for the Spanish exhibits (fully accepted by the Aguilera-Moreno-Alberti trio), was something important that could not be disregarded, and so it was also taken into account. Not all the projects suggested at that time could be implemented, but they contributed to better knowledge of Spanish culture.

During the month of February, the Committee of Ten worked assiduously, accelerating the rate of contacts that would enable the exhibition to be installed on the dates planned; at the same time it was a month of negotiations between the Biennale and different spheres of Spanish political life, since the support of all the democratic forces was sought. A member of the Biennale's Executive Board went to Madrid towards the end of February for the explicit purpose of ensuring the presence of the Catholics. Anxious to obtain the consensus of the democratic forces, Ripa had planned the setting up of a "Guarantee Committee" concerning which he was seeking the opinion of specific Spanish political sectors. The committee was unable to modify the plan already under way and its only real aim was to bring about a rapprochement between different positions. Ripa di Meana proposed the following names: Vicente Aguilera Cerni, José María Moreno Galván and Rafael Alberti (in clear search of an agreement between the parties that in any case was impossible). He also proposed Camilo José Cela, José Bergamín, Vicente Aleixandre, Salvador Espriu, José María Castellet, Joan Fuster, Raimon, Josep Renau, María Teresa León, Juan Goytisolo, Alfonso Sastre, Genoveva Forest, Luis María Xirinacs, Juan Antonio Bardém, Lola Gaos, Agustín Ibarrola, Dolores Ibárruri, Nuria Espert, Ricardo Salvat, Luis de Pablo and Fernando Arrabal. Some of these people were still in exile, and one of them –Forest– was in prison.

With this list in his pocket, the representative of the Biennale had a number of meetings in

Eusebio Sempere
"Móvil" (Mobile)
Italian Catalogue, 1976

They unanimously agreed that they would not be displeased if the Spanish Government were not officially invited to the exhibition

Madrid, basically with Christian Democratic groups, with whom he wished to reach an agreement and sound out their opinions. The document drawn up after the contacts were established was of exceptional interest, in that it gives us information about the ideas held by Italy on Spain and its public figures, and at the same time it introduces us to the play of interests which guided some politicians in our country.

Among other well-known figures, the representative sent by the Biennale, mentioned Ruiz Giménez, who was not in favour of Dolores Ibarruri being on the committee, "as a politically qualified person"; he said the same thing about Genoveva Forest, who was in prison, as someone "whose presence would surely provoke irritation in Spain, specifically in moderate circles"; he would be in favour of talking to Santiago Carrillo, who was also missing from the list submitted to the Socialists, which would be "politically dangerous for today's Spain." Enrique Múgica, Organisational Secretary of the Socialist Party, obviously also thought the same; he suggested contacting other exponents of Socialism such as Alfonso Guerra and Luis Yáñez.

Contact was made in the office of Gil Robles with the members of the team made up of the five Christian Democratic parties. They unanimously agreed that they would not be displeased if the Spanish Government were not officially invited to the exhibition; moreover, they also said it would be useful to hold a political meeting shortly with the Communists and Socialists and organise a meeting with the three secretaries; at the same time they should prevent the presence of Dolores Ibarruri on the committee and promote that of Vicente Aguilera. There were a lot of doubts about Luis María Xirinacs.

There was also an interview with Pedro Altares, described in the document as a "Socialist, future director of *Cuadernos para el Diálogo*, when it becomes a weekly." In his opinion, the exhibition was not developing along clear lines and the list of guarantors was totally absurd, especially on account of the presence of Dolores Ibárruri, Forest and some others whom he said he didn't know who they were. As far as Altares was concerned, it would be necessary to ensure the active presence of Aguilera Cerni and –in the words of the document– of "Eduardo Chillida (Basque, Catholic, a Democrat, of the Basque Nationalist Party, an expert in contemporary art); Tàpies (it would seem useful to include him on the committee); Saura (the filmmaker); Saura (the painter); Juan Benet (novelist with a lot of authority) and Antonio Fernández Alba (architect, very well known in Italy, independent). He also proposed Antonio Buero Vallejo (playwright, condemned to death, leftist, not Communist); Miguel Delibes; José Luis López Aranguren (professor of ethics, expelled from the University)." Other meetings likewise took place with Óscar Alzaga, Xavier Tussell..., and a number of significant figures in Spanish culture and politics.

According to the report submitted by Massimo Andrioli to the president of the Biennale after his meeting in Madrid with the main leaders of Christian Democracy, "almost all Spanish contemporary culture is, in one way or another, opposed to the regime; [...] the Communists have a majority –although not exclusive– presence in this picture. Immediately after the Communists, it's the Social Democratic group that has the greatest presence in the intellectual field." The Christian Democrats wanted to eliminate from the list suggested by Ripa di Meana all names that were "excessively political" such as those of Ibarruri and Forest and add figures strictly from the cultural field. The popularity of Vicente Aguilera Cerni was clear; he enjoyed a consensus among the Catholics.

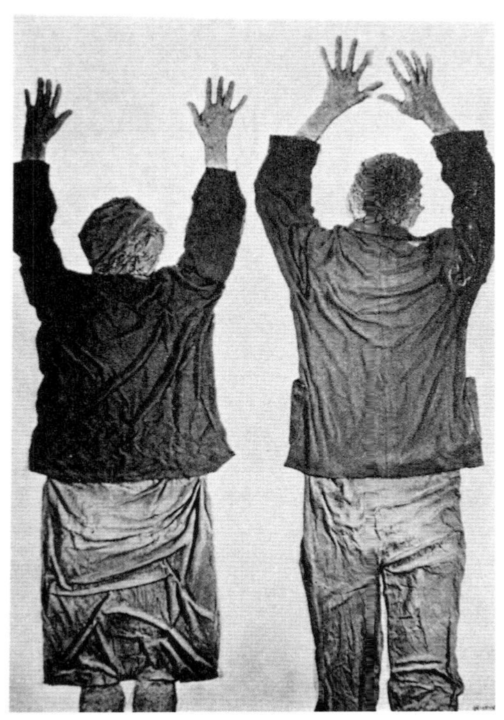

And precisely Aguilera, on knowing that the Biennale had included him in the Committee of Guarantee, agreed in principle to form part of it, as placed on record in a letter sent to Ripa di Meana. However, the letter states that Aguilera still expected that there could be a confrontation between the project that was already under way and that which he and Moreno Galván would draw up in order, following comparison between them, to consider the coinciding points as definitive and discuss the other aspects "on a scientific level." But this was not the intention of the president of the Biennale.

Echoes of the organisation of the Biennale had already started to reach Spain. On February 28, an article appeared in the daily newspaper *Informaciones* signed by José Luis Orosa which depicted the Spanish exhibition to be held in Venice as an axis around which the discord between Communists and Socialists was being catalysed. The malaise had already reached Spain and especially involved some artists from the Basque Country, although also some from Madrid.

The matter became more virulent in May of 1976 with a new intervention by Aguilera. According to him, it was absurd to organise an exhibition based on a dichotomy of official culture/non-official culture, since the former had not yielded anything worthwhile under the Franco regime. "If we make an exception for Dalí and Eugenio d'Ors" –he said– "there has been nothing valid in the anti-democratic sector during the war and post-war periods. Therefore, organising a Biennale of `anti-establishment culture´ in our country would be to admit that another culture had existed, and that is not true. Therefore, the exhibition would be based on false premises from the start." At the same time he considered that the physical space allocated by the Biennale to the Spanish exhibition was not sufficient, and also thought it unjustifiable that some of the artists on the project committee planned to exhibit their own work, wherefore they would be "self-invited inviters." Finally, Aguilera Cerni expressed his disagreement regarding the system of selection of the committee.

Until then the members of the Spanish Biennale Committee had not joined the fray that had been whipped up around them, prudently remaining silent. Only Inmaculada Julián, in an extremely polite article, had responded to another by José Garnería –who was from Vicente Aguilera's circle. The other statements by the members of the committee had been limited, when they made them, to commenting on matters of composition and organisation of the exhibition. But finally, one of those involved in the affair, Antonio Saura (perhaps the least expected) decided, in an interview granted to Ramón Chao, to reply to Aguilera Cerni. Saura declared, referring to the critic, "His conduct in Venice, getting himself invited after having placed the validity of our work in doubt, [...] constitutes one of the many actions that he has taken in order to disprove a project about which he had full knowledge [...] His task over the past few months has consisted of carrying out systematic obstruction."

Aguilera's reply to Saura was concise. In just a few lines he outlined his position in respect of the painter's words. He said that he did not want to enter into an argument, but at the same time he reserved the right to: "... institute any judicial action that might be appropriate in view of said declarations."

Argan and Arroyo also had opposing opinions. The former stated that the lack of political culture on the part of the Franco supporters meant that there had not been any censorship

Juan Genovés
"Contra la pared" (Against the Wall)
Italian Catalogue, 1976

problems at Venice, wherefore an exhibition programmed by the Biennale would necessarily be repetitive. On the other hand, he didn't foresee any problems with that exhibition having to co-exist with another held at the pavilion, which could be devoted to the country's most recent production. Eduardo Arroyo refuted this alleged lack of cultural policy under Franco. He asked, "Why can't it be understood that Franco had realised that modernism was the best mask for repression? [...] How can Mr. Argan say that General Franco didn't have a cultural policy if Franco himself would have agreed with him? Because, how is it possible to talk about repression in a country so full of advanced painters, in other words, "of opponents"? Fortunately, the Spanish painters do not all agree with Messrs. Argan and Franco."The juxtaposition would not have pleased Argan. The dispute was taking on rather unorthodox tones.

Independently of these issues, at the Biennale they were worried about whether the current Spanish Government would want to exercise its right over the pavilion, which to all intents and purposes enjoyed something very similar to diplomatic status. There was a possibility that Madrid would try to use the benefits of extra-territoriality in order to organise its own exhibition, parallel to that of the Biennale. In that case, the Biennale could have recourse to article 10 of its new Statutes in which it was specified that participation in the events of the autonomous body was subject to direct and personal invitation to the artists by the Board of Directors. This clause, however, had never been activated because the Biennale (receiving a lot of criticism for this reason) had never intervened in the actions of the individual pavilions. But the problem never arose. A proposal was made by Spain –without very much conviction– to open the Spanish pavilion and dedicate it to Cerdà, the Catalan town planner whose centenary was being commemorated at that time, but no battle was waged on that account, and so there was no chance of losing it.

The weeks prior to the opening of the Biennale were peppered with incidents that were immediately reported in the press. Some artists, such as José Caballero and Canogar, expressed their annoyance at having been excluded from the exhibition then under way. The former, in a letter dated April 14, 1976, wrote to Tàpies telling him that he himself, proposed for the Grand Prize at the First Mediterranean Biennale in Alexandria, had been vetoed by González Robles on account of his political leanings. So now there were complaints about the new discrimination.

Other artists, however, such as Chillida and Oteiza, refused to participate in the Biennale, given that in order to defend the identity of Euskadi (the Basque Country), they wanted it to have its own space.

Opinions were divided. On July 5, a large group of Spanish intellectuals and artists drew up a manifesto in which they accused the exhibition of being based on outmoded ideas, of indulging in opportunism, and of putting a brake on truly social art, while at the same time they placed the representativeness of the Spanish Committee in doubt. The Madrid Plastic Arts Association wrote a communiqué along the same lines.

As a counterpoint to these declarations, another was written, signed by about five hundred artists of the "Co-ordinator of Plastic Arts and Democratic Culture," in which Lola Gaos, Olea and Bardem, among others, backed both the organisers and the project, which for them represented with truth and clarity the avant-garde world of art of the past forty years. It was in this heated atmosphere that the days prior to the opening of the Biennale arrived. All those invited by the organisation were already in Venice; the Biennale President himself, accompanied by several of his advisers had gone to Madrid and Barcelona between June 5 and 10, in order to personally invite artists, intellectuals and political groups of the opposition associated under Coordinación Democrática (Democratic Co-ordination). In particular they approached Marcelino Camacho, the leader of the trade union Comisiones Obreras; Felipe González, Secretary General of the Socialist Party; and different exponents of Christian Democracy, among whom was Ruiz Giménez. But Coordinación Democrática did not unite all segments of the opposition in our country around it. Neither the anarchists nor other revolutionary leftist organizations who were not members of unitary bodies, were invited to Venice. The Biennale representatives themselves attributed this situation to their lack of knowledge about the reality in Spain, thereby casting doubt on their

At the Biennale they were worried about whether the current Spanish government would want to exercise its right over the pavilion qualifications for organising an exhibition of this kind. At the press conference on July 16, the above-mentioned declarations by artists and intellectuals were read out. During the questions and answers period the meeting heated up. Julián Pacheco asserted that the only legal democratic regime existing in Spain –in other words, the Republic– was not represented at the Biennale, and announced the immediate removal of his works from the exhibition. The dispute grew more intense when cinema director Miguel Herbeg directly accused the Biennale of following Carrillo's line of argument and showing the same works in the Spanish exhibition as during Franco's time. Finally, he concluded by requesting that groups such as the FRAP, the FAI and others be allowed to have their interlocutors at Venice. A representative of the Basque nationalist groups also had his say, although he did not give his name and asked not to be photographed for fear of reprisals.

The day after this press conference marked by discord, the members of Democratic Co-ordination were expected in Venice. On their first official trip abroad they were going to the Italian city in order, through their presence, to approve the Spanish exhibition. The absence of Santiago Carrillo and Felipe González, who excused their non-attendance at the last minute, was significant. Antonio García-Trevijano, to whom the Spanish Government had not granted a passport, was also absent. Tierno Galván, for his part, sent his excuses in writing.

But the most notable absence was that of the representatives of the Basque people. On the day after the aforementioned event, and on the occasion of a press conference given at the City Hall, a note was distributed explaining the reasons for their absence. As stated, of the three unitary bodies existing in the Basque Country –the Democratic Assembly of Euskadi, which represented the "pro-Spanish left"; the Basque Government in exile which represented the "nationalist right"; and KAS (Coordinación Abertzale Socialista - Radical Nationalist Basque Co-ordination), only the first two had been present at a meeting called on July 16 in Madrid by Democratic Co-ordination in order to finalise the attendance at Venice and the message to be read in the Doge's Palace. The Asamblea Democrática (Democratic Assembly) and the Government in exile were of the opinion that they could not be represented on the Co-ordinator because it did not take all the alternatives into account (in other words, KAS); for that reason they refused to go to Venice.

The Co-ordinator argued that the Basque Country had indeed been invited, but that as it lacked a single democratic organization, there could not be an elected delegate. But this reason was interpreted by the Basque journalists as an excuse. The three already-existing bodies could have been convened, in the same way that Catalonia was represented by two alternatives (Assemblea and Consell). The Biennale responded by saying that KAS did not form part of Democratic Co-ordination and that therefore it was excluded from the invitation extended by the Municipality of Venice. Notwithstanding the absences, an unusual assortment of people was milling around at that time in Venice, housed in the Doge's Palace, where, according to *El viejo topo* (The Old Mole), the polysemous "... presence of the people and works of the Spanish State caught up in a tangle of problems, interests, protagonisms, vanities, deceits, ingenuities, \`politics´ of the good, not bad and very bad" was seen. On July 17, most of the Spanish representatives were officially welcomed. The president of the Biennale, Carlo Ripa di Meana, emphasized the nature of the meeting of Italian parties and trade unions with the "authentic Spain"; the Mayor of Venice, Mario Rigo, quoting Ortega and Unamuno in a long speech, described the special political circumstances that surrounded the Spain of the time and its struggle to achieve democracy.

Everything took place in the usual orderly manner characterising these events until an incident was on the point of shattering it. After the meeting had begun, the representatives of the different regions of the Spanish State learned that only a representative of Democratic Co-ordination would be given the floor, on behalf of all the rest. There were whispered discussions, momentary alarm and threats to leave the room. Finally an agreement was reached; everyone would be entitled to speak. The person most applauded was Roca Junyent. In general emphasis was placed on the need to recover democratic legality and to re-establish the statutes of autonomy drawn up during the Republic. After these declarations, representatives of the co-ordinator of Basque Socialist and *abertzale* (radical Basque nationalists) groups tried to get a note read in which two members of the Venice City Council were invited to visit Euskadi, but failed to do so.

The voices of Camacho and Ruiz Jiménez were not heard; they were the ones most sought after by the Italian press. Nor was a colloquium held with those present; it was not possible to clarify what the Spanish opposition thought about the partial amnesty that the Spanish Government had just granted. This news, together with the presence of our country's delegation in Venice, captured the attention of the media. In general, a feeling of disappointment reigned as the meeting drew to a close.

To conclude with the "politics" concerning the 1976 Spanish Biennale, we shall refer once more to the Basque issue. Chillida, Oteiza and Ibarrola had been invited to participate in the exhibition. Tomàs Llorens and Manuel García had interviewed them personally in the Basque Country at the end of April. As Llorens tells it, in a letter dated May 21, 1976, addressed to Luis Peña, at first they expressed no objections, but after Chillida had consulted some "young Basque artists,"he changed his opinion a few hours later. Oteiza did the same thing. A committee was immediately formed around them which demanded that Euskadi should have its own pavilion. An attempt was made to approach those responsible for the Spanish pavilion in order to obtain a space, but this was an unforeseen contingency and was not approved. So they decided to ask the Biennale representatives to give them a pavilion which was rightly theirs as a people who, as fighters against Fascism, "aspired to their national liberation."

Vittorio Gregotti, representative of the Arti Visive (Visual Arts) Committee of the Biennale, told them that they would need a specific programme and explicit political support in order for their request to be viable. The reply was not long in coming, and another eight letters from as many Basque organisations reached the president of the Biennale. At the same time, the Basques issued a communiqué reinforcing their proposal. In it they described themselves as a subjugated people, crushed between two centralisms –the Spanish and the French. The note was signed by a broad spectrum of collectives, ranging from Basque political prisoners and exiles to different weekly newspapers and publishers, and including the Assembly of Basque Professionals. In view of the manifesto, the Italians, imbued with a spirit of solidarity, decided to leave a space in their own pavilion for the *ikurriña* (Basque flag). Symbolically they were given a space, but only symbolically. In fact, Ripa's promise that the Basque Country would have its own pavilion from that year on, was never kept.

Finally the idea of a Basque exhibition was dropped, but representative events took place later on, outside the Biennale Gardens. Basque culture made its appearance in the city through cinema and songs. Singers Mikel Laboa and the Arza brothers were given a magnificent welcome, and films and documentaries were projected under the title *Euskadi en lucha* (The Basque Country in Struggle), showing images of the main events that had taken place over recent years, with special emphasis on the incidents in Vitoria. Those were the Basque days at Venice.

Results

After its long political and problematical gestation, on the morning of July 18 –forty years to the day after the beginning of the Fascist uprising, the Biennale exhibition "Spain: The Artistic Avant-Garde and Social Reality, 1936-1976" opened to the public. The incidents which had punctuated its preparation were echoed continuously in the media that was reporting on the exhibition. In Italy in general there was a positive response. In Spain the reactions were varied and even conflicting. Whereas some of the critics pointed to its conceptual rigour, others again insisted it was impossible that an "official culture" could have confronted another "unofficial culture" during the Franco years.

In any event, in the reactions that were produced, there was constant looking back at the controversy surrounding its setting in motion. Tomàs Llorens regretted the fact that very few people had taken the time to appreciate the results obtained; and that the majority, paying no attention to the exhibition itself, had focused exclusively on the issues prior to its "legitimising."

Before analysing the different sections of the exhibition, it is necessary to observe what is fundamental to us these days but of which nobody at that time seemed to be aware: the absence of women in the exhibition. Not a single woman artist was represented. Forty years of anti-Fascist culture without a single female exhibit. Of course, it was not only the responsibility of the curators: they availed themselves of what society indicated to them was important. It was only later that the history of art and feminist critics rescued so many women from anonymity. But we had a Maruja Mallo, a Remedios Varo, a Juana Francés..., who deserved an invitation and a viewing of their work.

Bozal and Llorens had opted for a historical project. In it would be an explicit proposition: the analysis and "correction" of the image that the biennale had been offering of the Spanish avant-garde –"an image that was necessarily `ideological´ (in the worst sense) and `false,´ due to having been implicitly hidden from the political context in which art was then produced in Spain." A similar image had been deliberately used *abroad* by the dictatorship "to support the assertion that it was also, in its different way, a special kind of democracy." For its part, inside Spain, the selection for international exhibitions was being used "as an instrument of repression and `clipping´ aimed at channeling and domesticating the ideological outbreaks of artistic trends." The methodological guidelines of the project drawn up by the curators was based on "a) the highlighting of any aspect directed at a rational *reading* and interpretation, in historic and theoretical terms, of the diachronic current of artistic production; and b) the avoidance of simplistic moral judgments in the name of that species of abstract humanism that is usually the appendix of bourgeois ideology." It was a matter of avoiding at all costs "the temptation to present art either as the victim or the moral denunciation of the Spanish dictatorial regime." The project –continued Bozal and Llorens– was aimed at demonstrating that the Spanish avant-garde had been moulded from the inside, at its primary source, "by the process of an ideological struggle that was part of the class struggle, and that this had happened within the structure of a general movement by Spanish society in the pursuit of an abstract model of the `normal capitalist society.´"

It was on these premises that the exhibition was based and was structured into two major sections. The first was related to the artistic events that had taken place during the Civil War, and to the artists in exile. The second undertook a chronological and visual analysis of art in post-war Spain. Methodologically speaking, the

Methodologically speaking, the proposal was highly didactic. There was an awareness that the Civil War did not put a complete brake on artistic creation

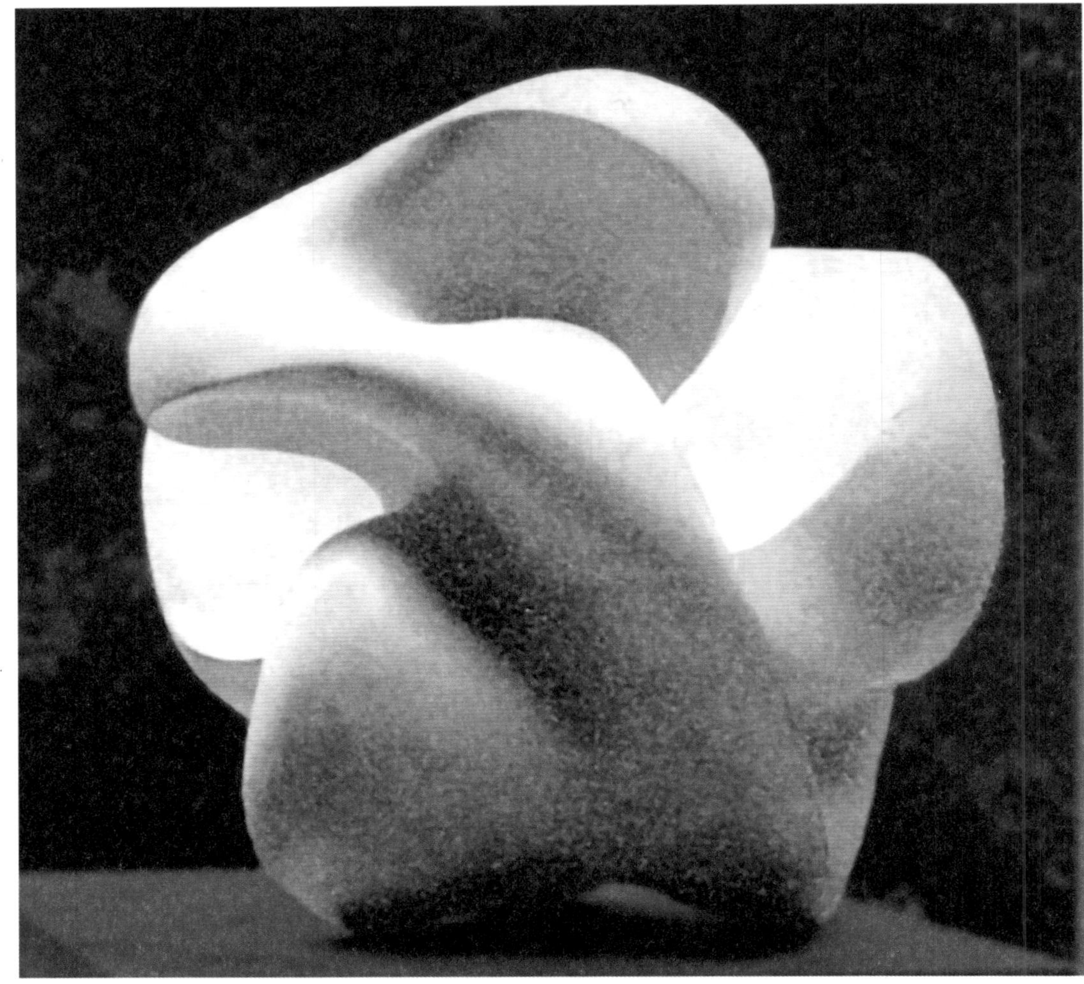

proposal was highly didactic. There was an awareness that the Civil War did not put a complete brake on artistic creation, but rather brought about a significant qualitative change. During it many artists were converted into propagandists, and it became clear that the so-called directed art could have outstanding formal characteristics. It also became clear that in wartime, events could be organised –although outside Spain– such as the Spanish pavilion at the 1937 Paris International Exhibition. There were two reasons (the posters and the pavilion) for reflecting about the relationship between art and contents, and about the creative possibilities in time of war. The offerings also included a reflection about the influence of exile on art. That was the end of the first part of the exhibition. In the second, those events and artists which, in the judgment of the organisers, were basic to art culture from the post-war period to the start of

Equipo 57
"Escultura II" (Sculpture II)
Italian Catalogue, 1976

the transition (in which Spain was immersed at that time), were dealt with chronologically. It was almost necessarily the most difficult and awkward section, since it was a matter of choosing between different names, and on some occasions it appears that objective criteria were not of primary importance.

As a point of departure, there was the Civil War itself, in which poster-painting acquired a crucial dimension. Already in the summer of 1975 Inmaculada Julián had been asked to collaborate in assembling an exhibit of posters at Venice that had been done by the Republican side. The Civil War poster-design revealed an emotional power that was on display here. Never until then had it been possible to bring together such an extraordinary collection of Republican posters because the plan was to show only the production of the anti-Fascists and ignore the posters of the Franco regime. The researcher, rather than highlight trends or artists, was determined above all to supply information about their mission in the war. Therefore, she grouped the posters according to subject matter, from the calls to battle to the advice proffered to the civilian population in the rear, including the posters bearing instructions to the people or offering aid to different territories or fronts, or to health or the artistic heritage.

The distribution according to subject matter proved to be very appropriate. However, some criticisms were made about the selection –the most important being about the extremely few anarchist posters shown. Nevertheless, some of the most significant works of the Spanish Civil War were at Venice: among the anonymous ones (well over a third of the total number) were *El Frente Popular* (The Popular Front), 1936 and *Los trece puntos de la victoria* (The Thirteen Points of Victory), 1938. Among the signed posters was the work of poster designers as well known as Arturo Ballester, with his *Loor a los héroes* (Praise to the Heroes), 1937; Goñi, with his very direct *I tu? què has fet per la victòria* (And you, what have you done towards victory?), and also Renau, Castelao and Souto....

In the midst of the war, the Republic, artistically speaking, was responsible for a fundamental landmark: the pavilion at the 1937 Paris International Exhibition. Attempting to take to Venice the works that had been exhibited there was a wonderful idea, although unfortunately and necessarily it only achieved partial results. However, the attempt constituted in itself a point of reference that causes us to meditate about the specific historic moment, about the impact of the war, and about the cultural policy of the legitimate Republican Government.

Choosing that pavilion as one of the points of departure for this exhibition was not, as far as Antonio González Cordón, Vicente Lleó and Víctor Escolano (those responsible for this project) were concerned, a gratuitous act, but rather the result of critical meditation. The meaning was not only symbolic, "but rather that of a real will to understand the processes of cultural production." If, indeed, the pavilion was the paradoxically spontaneous and meditated cry of the artists faithful to the Republic, it also was an exhibition of art decidedly at one with the most brilliant approaches of creative production of its time. The building that housed the exhibits, designed by Josep Lluis Sert and Luis Lacasa (with the points of view of the former predominating) was in harmony, in that exhibition, with other European structures also forming part of the Modernist movement.

In Paris, the sculpture by Alberto Sánchez, *El pueblo español tiene un camino que conduce a una estrella* (The Spanish People have a Path that Leads to a Star) had been erected at the entrance to the Sert building. Inside, among other magnificent sculptures, was *Pagès català i la revolució* (Catalan Peasant and the Revolution) by Juan Miró, photomontages by Renau, the Montserrat by Julio González, ceramic works by the then very young Llorens Artigas and above all the *Guernica* by Picasso. The only non-Spanish participation in the pavilion was that of Alexander Calder with his *Mercury Fountain*, in which an iron spade inscribed with the word Almadén was accompanied by another inscription, *"Por esto luchan las fuerzas invasoras"* (This is what the invading troops are fighting for). The Almadén mercury mines, had been besieged by Franco's troops, as a priority objective. They were our equivalent of the modern Iraqi oil wells.

It was not possible to exhibit the *Guernica* in Venice although some steps had been taken in that direction. However, Picasso's bronze bust *Cabeza de Mujer* (Woman's Head) and a pair of etchings *Sueño y mentira de Franco* (Dream and Lie of Franco), by him, were there. Miró was represented by one of the works that was a symbol of Spain at war: the lithograph *Aidez l'Espagne* (Help Spain). His *Pagès* was not there. Drawings and sculptures by Julio González (not the same, but on the same subject as those at Paris) were also exhibited. And there were photographs and the original plans of the Republican pavilion together with the model; but Alberto Sánchez's *Star* had been lost. Calder took his *Fountain*, which was the subject of one of the most curious episodes at the Biennale. The fumes from the seven hundred pounds of mercury necessary to make it work threatened to intoxicate anyone who came near. The mercury had to be removed and replaced by coloured water.

The war ended in the defeat of the Republicans. And with defeat came exile. Valeriano Bozal and Tomàs Llorens organised a number of artists who had declared in favour of the Republic around the image of a "lost future." They continued to work –some for a very short time, until they died. They were all artists in exile– either the radical exile that prevented their return home, or the other, no less radical, domestic exile which prevented them from fulfilling themselves. They were artists whom war and alienation had conditioned in such a way that, in the words of the organisers, "their only common denominator was that they had been deprived of the possibility to develop within a `normal´ social context." Some of these artists were the eight who exhibited their work in this section: Julio González, Alberto Sánchez, Josep Renau, Picasso, Miró, Óscar Domínguez, Luis Fernández and Enrique Castelo. Very different degrees of relationship with exile could be observed in them. Some, like Picasso, had already chosen a more spacious homeland before the war, but the world –that is, his new mother country– was not complete without the part of it that first of all was off limits to him and then he himself vetoed: the land of his birth. Others among the artists selected had also settled outside Spain even before the war, but they were exceedingly affected by the events that occurred here, as happened with Miró who lived as a recluse in Majorca, and those who died without being able to return... as well as some who many years later came back to walk about on the streets of Valencia in their unmistakable way. They were all artists marked by exile.

The option of presenting the artists who had been in exile could not be rejected in this exhibition, but some other names could have been included. Again we recall Maruja Mallo, exiled in Buenos Aires, and Remedios Varo, who died in exile in Mexico –once more, forgotten women.
Julio González, an artist who died only three years after the end of the war, was indeed remembered. His works took a long time to reach Spain and to become known and valued here. His daughter Roberta made a donation to the Spanish Museum of Contemporary Art in Madrid, which amounted to the first step towards his recovery in Spain. Later, Tomàs Llorens himself, on organising the Valencia Institute of Modern Art, would succeed in bringing most of the work of this sculptor to this institution. Julio González had lived in Paris since 1900 (he had been born in 1876). Although far from his own country, the events of the Civil War had affected him tremendously. The theory proposed by the organisers was that the Montserrat series on which Julio González had worked until his death was inspired by events of the Civil War. Given that these sculptures were related to the rebuilding of the 1937 pavilion, we shall review the different works done after 1950, among them *Hombres cactus I y II* (Cactus Men I and II).

Alberto Sánchez left Spain for Moscow in 1938, accompanying a group of children as their drawing teacher. He never returned; he died in the Soviet Union in 1962. The country that took him in was not a paradise for art at that time: the Constructivist opening–up had been obliterated by the Stalinist iron–handed imposition of conformity. Alberto provisionally gave up sculpture –to which he would return in the fifties– in order to design theatrical costumes (which he had already done in Spain) and stage sets. The war constituted a hiatus in his life and career. His work was only partially shown at the Biennale. Nevertheless, we were able to perceive the difficult relationship that he was able to establish between avant–garde approaches, which were plain to see in his work, and his wish to make contact with popular art. It was in the pursuit of this difficult synthesis that his efforts were directed.

Josep Renau went into exile after the Civil War. His role during the conflict, consisting of contributing to safeguarding the national artistic heritage, has been recognised by widely-differing circles. He came to the realisation when the Second World War ended that his new country would be that of exile. Therefore, he tells us, he worked and lived as intensely as possible, producing markedly critical work. He took a series of photomontages to Venice, dating from 1936 to 1975 –all of them with a political slant.

The inclusion of Óscar Domínguez in this list of artists who had been "marked" could be questioned. This painter moved to Paris when he was just over twenty years old, and lived in that city until his death in 1951. Interested in Surrealism, his accentuation of certain features of his work during the course of the thirties and forties was interpreted by Llorens and Bozal in relation with the events in Spain –a hypothesis which, to say the least, appears to be a risky point of departure for analysing the work of the artist from the Canary Islands.

Luis Fernández also left early for Paris, specifically in 1924. The Biennale served to recover the work of this painter which was as interesting as it was little known to Spaniards. The interpretation of the organisers was that the change which took place in his painting at the end of the thirties ("... a formal and self-repressive regression through the history of art") corresponded to the parallel process of some Spanish poets and intellectuals in exile.

Enrique Castelo continues today to be the least known of all the artists selected –at least in Spain. For the organisers, this painter illustrated the type of artist who, having moved to Paris in 1939 on account of his disagreement with the political context, was obliged to make his living from marginal work although he was able –perhaps for that very reason– to retain his creative freedom.

To conclude, Miró –who returned to Spain in 1940– and Picasso, who never returned, were included in this group. There was only a small number of works exhibited for each of them, which was justified by the organisers by the fact that they were both so well known.

After this first major section, the plan of the exhibition offers us, in chronological order, the artistic events linked to avant-garde art from the Civil War to the present time. One of the objections made to the organising committee was that some of its members were represented in not just one but in several different sections of the exhibition. Perhaps the selection could have been more careful in this respect, and perhaps artists could also have been left out of the organisation, or only have acted in a consultative capacity. At the same time, this method of proceeding meant that there had necessarily to be a choice between the artists linked to each of the trends, and here there were always differing opinions. In general a clear process was perceived, limited by significant absences (on inevitable occasions). On the other hand, the unbalance that occurred between some of the periods could have been due to easy access to specific works.

The first thing on which the organisers focused was the attempt to recover the avant-garde art that had been produced in our country in the forties. These experiences were included in the exhibition through the work of Ángel Ferrant and the Dau al Set group. The presence of Ferrant was undisputable; overcoming the negative post-war atmosphere, he had continued the research that he had begun before the conflict. His feeling for organic structure and sense of play in composition remained among the best

> The plan of the exhibition offers us, in chronological order, the artistic events linked to avant–garde art

contributions to 20th-century Spanish sculpture. He took drawing, engravings and sculptures to the Biennale that were dated from 1950.

However, fault was found with the Dau al Set group, not on account of its undeniable value on the post-war art scene, of which it was the first great reference, but because only one of its members –Tàpies– was present. A group cannot be understood through only one of its components, and it was told so at the time. The organisers answered the critics by emphasizing the lesser interest that the works of Cuixart and Tharrats, whom they had not invited, held for them. They had tried to get Ponç to come, and requested him to bring paintings and drawings of that period, but it appears that he made his participation conditional on the parallel exhibition of three pictures of his current production. Even if that was so, an effort could have been made. Ponç should not, under any circumstances, have been absent from Venice, and the presence of Tharrats or Cuixart, although minimal, would have been necessary in order to make the offer coherent. Tàpies remained as the only guide to introduce us to the Catalan Surrealism promoted by his group. The criticism was justified.

The second section of the historic review provided by the exhibition was called, “Between Testimony and Freedom: 1954-1964.” This space in time was in turn divided into five sub-sections. In that of “First Approximations” we find a work by Millares, four by Saura and two by Lucio Muñoz. The three appear to be directed at what we would call “informalist orthodoxy.” El Paso (The Step) accounted for the second section, represented by Millares and Saura. Once again the organisers ran into controversy as to why only two of the group’s components were present. Their reply was not very convincing: “We haven’t invited Feito or Rivera because the El Paso group

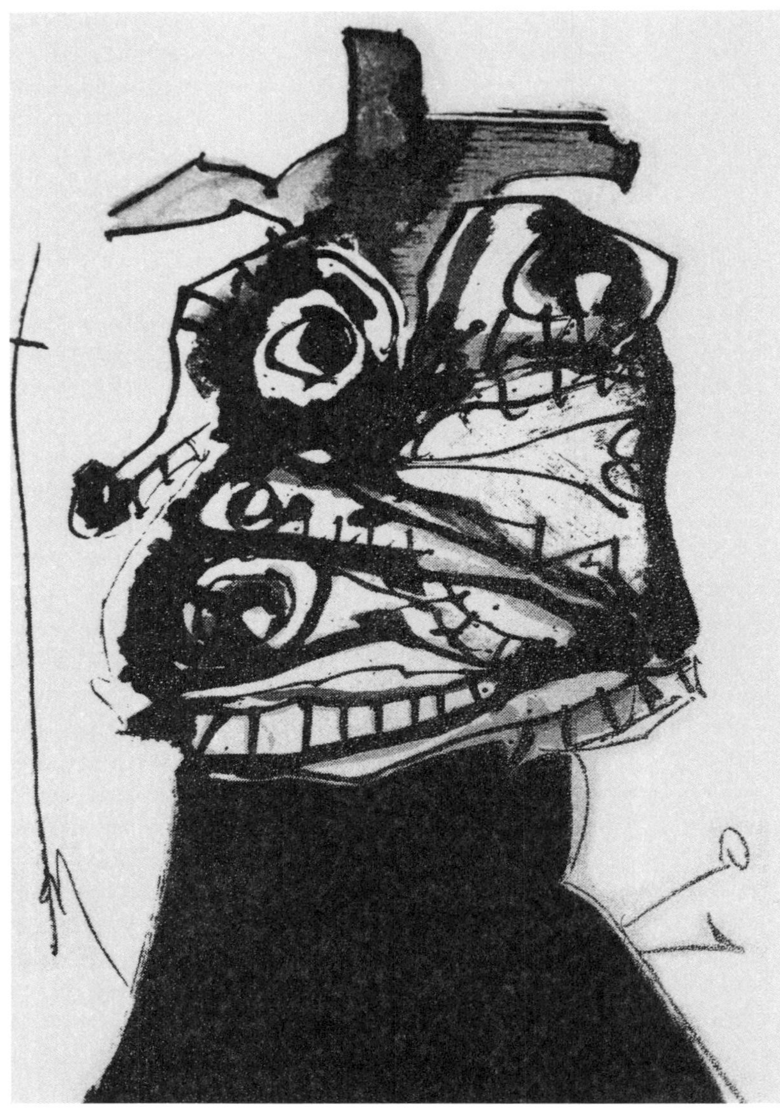

[...] seemed to us sufficiently complete with Saura and Millares. As for Canogar, his type of painting is already on display in the contribution by Genovés."

The case of Canogar was particularly significant. He was not included either as a member of El Paso (covered by the aforementioned Saura and Millares), or within the currents of "social reporting," since Juan Genovés was to occupy the space provided. However, these do not seem to have been the only reasons. We know about many artists drifting apart following the differences that arose between them on account of the important role that some played in the different international exhibitions programmed by the State. We are sure that this issue, which we have mentioned before, would not nowadays lead to the maximalist positions adopted at the time. But in those days of political emergency, the decisions were experienced intensely and were often sustained by strongly-felt ideological arguments.

Returning to our exhibition, in the next section, "Testimony of Violence," Millares, Lucio Muñoz and Guinovart submitted works of explicit commitment, with titles such as *Homúnculo*, *Tríptico a Miguel Hernández* and *Personaje caído* by Millares, *Facistol* by Lucio Muñoz and *Ávila 63* by Guinovart. El Paso was becoming "academicised" and some of its members, together with other artists, set forth their points of view in the new historic dimensions, which necessarily required another "step" towards greater explicitness in denunciation.

Next, a fourth section, "Utopian Spaces," constituted an emphatic counterpoint to the previous one. An attempt was made to mark the gap between the irrationality and romanticism of Spanish Informalism and the rationality and

Antonio Saura
"Retrato imaginario de Felipe II" (Imaginary Portrait of Philip II)
Italian Catalogue, 1976

scientific analysis that artists such as the members of Equipo 57 (Team 57) made of visual perception. Apart from the differences between their formal resources and their contents, both were guided by a deep sense of ethics (this was the thesis of the organisers). It was these ethics that caused different Informalist artists to produce their "testimonies of violence," and the members of Equipo 57 their research on form and space aimed at achieving art that could be translated into useful products by entering the sphere of design. There was a will to undertake social service that inevitably reminds us of the evolution of Russian Constructivism.

Eusebio Sempere and the Equipo 57 contributed a large number of works, while there were two by Oteiza not considered in consonance with programming ideas. Although Oteiza had withdrawn from the exhibition, these two sculptures were kept in it because they belonged to private collections. These, together with a work by Alfaro made up the "Utopian Spaces," which brought the review of the first post-war Spanish avant-gardes to a close. Both Sempere (who entered several gouaches, dated from 1953 to 1960, in the Biennale) and the Equipo 57 constituted clear exponents of the regulatory trends in Spain, of which they were the precursors. The Equipo 57, with the personality of its members consciously diluted within the team as a whole, wished to respond through its plastic art to the needs of its time: but the field of design in which they would necessarily have been destined to implement their ideas had no place in the Spain of that time. Alfaro's conceptual and compositional clarity was shown in *El cercle i la línia* (The Circle and Line), dated 1959.

A last, slightly cryptic, section entitled "Archeology of Practical Reason," only contained works by Tàpies. Later, when the exhibition was taken to the Joan Miró Foundation, it was placed next to the "Testimonies of Violence." After all it was more closely related to this sphere, because of what it represented as a link with the special circumstances of Catalonia, than with the alleged flight from Informalism.

Following the proposed chronological and thematic order, we now come to what the organisers called "Areas of Realism: 1959-1964." Towards the end of the fifties, both Informalisms and regulatory trends entered into crisis. The trends such as Pop, and later Op, did not have much of a chance in our country. However, social or critical realism would be decisive.

In the "Areas of Realism" at Venice the story did not start with the Hondo group, as might perhaps have been foreseen, but rather with a magnificent but strangely placed Saura. Behind him, the significance of the "Popular Images" was stressed, with their common interest as a conduit, through art, for a fully-fledged system of political propaganda. Engraving was their main vehicle of expression, both with a view to reducing the price of production and also because it was considered the most appropriate procedure for their social interests. For illustrating the proposals of "Images", Francisco Álvarez, José Luis Delgado, Agustín Ibarrola, Arturo Martínez, Monjalés, José Ortega, Manuel Ortiz Valiente and Ricardo Zamorano were chosen.

Under the title of "Phantoms, Nightmares (and other) Anecdotes" this section on realisms was concluded. Eduardo Arroyo, Jorge Castillo, Juan Genovés, José Hernández and Modesto Roldán were responsible for showing us the world of the incubus and the succubus. Arroyo was here; his painting responded more to the anecdotal part suggested by the title than to that of the potency of nightmares. Genovés only exhibited one picture. Jorge Castillo, the creator of a tortured world, as well as Jorge Hernández of the *Caballeros del eterno retorno* (Knights of the Eternal Return) which represented him at Venice, were good choices. The inclusion of Modesto Roldán was more questionable. One of his pictures was entitled *Recuerdo insistente de la Guerra Civil en el lado fascista* (Persistent Memory of the Civil War on the Fascist side).

One of the most successful things about this exhibition was the appropriate naming of its different sections. From the title, "The political objective (the limits of meaning) is narrowed: 1964-1972," we understand how the artists of the time became increasingly interested in the political situation. By narrowing their objectives, many artists went through a clear process of protest and denunciation.

The political changes of 1962 had promoted economic development and a timid feeling of freedom. In view of the apparent opening-up, it was a matter of clearly stating some political objectives. This process, which had already begun, now acquired a new quantitative and qualitative dimension. Many artists, previously concerned with formal matters, changed their goals and undertook realistic projects that were belligerent in nature. However, there was not just one way of expressing commitment. Indeed, the organisers of this exhibition displayed two ways, expressed by two different groups of artists. In the first place, they showed those who had chosen the use of symbolism, or emblems, for political denunciation. Secondly, they exhibited another group that had chosen to adhere to iconographic meaning. So we find the duality of artists who, through the choice of a topic, transcribed a value and represented an attitude, as opposed to others who were interested in a particular event or a specific object through which to channel their denunciation.

Based on this dual way of publicising political commitment, the organisers presented two sub-sections: "Emblematic Games" and "Iconographic Systems (limits of reference)." In the first there was work by Alfaro, Guinovart, Tàpies, Genovés, Ràfols Casamada and Joan Brossa; while the second, "Popular Images," was illustrated by Valencia, Eduardo Arroyo, Jorge Castillo, the Equipo Crónica and Manuel Millares.

The theoretical discussions in Spain about Realism involved theoreticians and artists during the start of the sixties. As against the "avant-garde in the European manner" of previous years, many thought that the time had come to return to their own context in order to practise the criticism that the situation demanded. Bozal and Llorens themselves recognised that, even though they had supported the analytical avant-gardes on different occasions, they would have to revert, at this juncture, to assuming the commitment required by the current circumstances. However, not all the artists who were meeting to discuss this possibility, were in agreement with the so-called conversion. This was the case of Alfaro, who continued to believe in the social function of a "true" avant-garde. Basically, the issue was the old question that had rocked the foundations of the avant-gardes since the beginning of the century: the possibility of revolutionary formalism.

But the requirement of a real contact –and of its external transposition– with the socio-political situation of the time caught on with the artists. In the case of Alfaro, his commitment was resolved through symbolism or emblems. Thus, without foregoing his experiences with form (he was in the midst of a very interesting process of evolution), he conferred a specific denotative meaning on his works, thereby being able to consider himself almost a paradigm of the "emblematic games" proposed.

Genovés contributed to this section pictures such as *Contra la pared* (Against the Wall), *Hombre colgado* (Hanging Man) and *Detrás del azul* (Behind the Blue), which were obvious symbolic images. Other artists also evolved their own particular emblems. Some of them –such as Ràfols Casamada– had opted for commitment following more formalistic language to which they would subsequently return. He himself exhibited *Morir en Vietnam* (To Die in Vietnam). Joan Brossa, among other subjects chose Ché Guevara as a point of reference; Tàpies was becoming increasingly becoming aware of his Catalan identity; Guinovart, with his powerful *Homenaje a Picasso* (Tribute to Picasso), offered testimony –through the image of wheat, the food of the people, and continuous references to the *Guernica*– of their daily effort to survive.

"Iconographic systems (limits of reference)" was the second sub-section of this section. Here stress was laid on realism assigned to specific iconographic systems. The presence of "Popular Images" was logical, although it was possible to object that only the Valencia group had been chosen, and that moreover their works appeared in two different sub-sections –the one on which we have been commenting, and another entitled "Areas of Realism," which failed to contribute to contextualising their role with precision. Nor was the Valencian group the most significant one in the country. Probably the close relationship of the organisers with the Valencians, with the consequent facility of access to their works, was the reason for their active presence at Venice. Apart from "Images" the sub-section comprised: Millares, some of whose works had a direct bearing on political issues; Arroyo, who was included here on account of his explicit and very direct way of making fun of reality; Jorge Castillo, with his suggestive titles of *Palomares*, *Homenaje a Franco* (Tribute to Franco), *Franco Clown* and *Francisco Franco, doble retrato* (Double Portrait). Finally, the Equipo Crónica completed the exhibits.

The last section of the exhibition was called "Painting, Critique, Significance: 1967-1976." It consisted of situating the contributions of Spanish art over these past ten years. Of all the undertakings of the Venetian exhibition, this was surely the most obscure. Perhaps the proximity of the events prevented a convincing systematisation. At the same time, emphasis was placed on some artists to the detriment of others. First of all, Llorens and Bozal considered one of the oldest claims of the avant-garde: the relationship between art and daily life. This link, which had never been established, was proposed as a return trip between painting and daily life, and was exemplified by Luis Gordillo, Guinovart and Tàpies.

Among the following sub-sections ("Dialectics Code-Process," "Reductions" and "Role Games") the first focused on the New Abstraction that, as opposed to Constructivist Rationalism, had emerged shortly before this Biennale and was "officially introduced" in 1975. Illustrating it were Ràfols Casamada, Teixidor, Broto, Xavier Grau, Carlos León, José Rubio and Gil Tena. This new generation of lyrical abstraction had a counterpoint in Spain in a new "rationalist" abstraction on which emphasis could have been laid. Moreover, Minimal, Body and Land Art were not properly represented, although they did have an ephemeral presence, thus demonstrating an effective contact with the European avant-garde. On the other hand conceptual art was shown in "Reductions," through the installations by Antoni Muntadas and Francesc Torres, two of its best exponents.

The meaning of "Role Games," with works by Eduardo Arroyo and the Equipo Crónica was not so clear, thus failing to provide a convincing conclusion to the exhibition. This time the dialectics between the painters were not understandable and the finale was nothing if not confusing.

However, it was not strictly the end. In a last section, under a meaningful title, "Hors texte" a number of works were displayed by artists mostly included in previous sections. This was not the case of Julián Pacheco, but he removed his works, nor of Alberto Corazón. Some works were very eloquent, such as the *Paredones* (walls used by firing squads) by the Equipo Crónica in reference to the last great outbreak of violence on the part of Franco's Government –the barbaric shootings of September 27, 1975. As a hopeful counterpoint there was *El abrazo* (The Embrace) by Genovés.

Alberto Corazón was given the job at this Biennale of making a kind of "historic tape." It was displayed on a board on which the historic context of the forty years under review was documented by means of photographs, diagrams and articles. It was their theoretical justification. Moreover, he was the author of an article about iconicity as a basic problem, broken down into three units: iconographic-anthropological analysis of images of women that had appeared during a one-week period in the Madrid press; a study of the covers of *ABC* on every July 18 from 1939 to 1976; and a proposal regarding the process of construction and reproduction of images. It was the first time that women had appeared in the exhibition (as objects of study, not as active subjects). But what aroused misgivings about this "tape" was the fact that some historic events had been left out. Furthermore, the Italian translation led to some confusion. So there were accusations of Manichaeism and partiality in the reconstruction of history. But we are all aware of the difficulties involved in this type of endeavour.

Another note of historic recovery (this time directly appealing to people's feelings) was an installation consisting of a recently-laid table: on it, were some cards waiting for dinner guests who would never arrive: Antonio Machado, Pau Casals, Luis La Casa, García Lorca, Manuel Azaña, Aurelio Arteta, Miguel Hernández, Josep Torres Clavé, Carles Rahola and Juan Bautista Peret. This installation portrayed victimisation to some; to others it was romantic and restored a sense of immediacy and participation to the exhibition. Perhaps, on account of the lack of a "revolutionary spirit" in the exhibition, viewers were seeking out this type of exhibit. That is why some of them remembered the wall provided for visitors, where they could write, and which was covered with petitions for amnesty and freedom.

The general distribution of the space was entrusted to architects Oriol Bohigas, Josep Martorell and David Mackay. They found a central pavilion that had undergone excessive alterations over the course of its history. The choice was made for simple spaces –perhaps too simple at times, as when the sculptures were mounted on tables covered with white cloths. That could have been attributable to a lack of funds. The two parts of the exhibition: war and exile as opposed to historic review, were effectively delimited and the itinerary was marked by a symbolic red carpet on a black floor. Alberto Corazón's wooden panel also helped to separate the spaces.

After the closing of the exhibition, its echoes were heard for a long time: furthermore, old controversies were rekindled. Comments and criticisms focused on the system of choice of participants, on the significant absences, on the excessive presence of the organising artists. The staging itself was also questioned. From a strictly political standpoint, objections were made about the disproportionate protagonism of

The general distribution of the space was entrusted to architects Oriol Bohigas, Josep Martorell and David Mackay

the Communists and the neglect of the different regions of the Spanish State. The organisers replied to all this by asserting that they had acted in accordance with criteria of "representativity," not of "totality"; that they had granted the organising artists their right dimension, and had left the staging in the hands of experts. As to political considerations, they acknowledged substantial participation by the Communists, but denied that there had been manipulation by the Party. They also recalled that the most virulent attacks on their project had precisely been made by the latter. With regard to the issue of the regions, the organising committee expressed its clear belief that art is a symptom of a particular social system, but not its voice, and that it cannot represent regionalism.

However that may be, with its failures and its successes, its arguments and its agreements, the exhibition "Spain: The Artistic Avant-Garde and Social Reality, 1936-1976" was a timely review of Spanish culture during the forty years of Franco's dictatorship.

The organising committee expressed its clear belief that art is a symptom of a particular social system, but not its voice, and that it cannot represent regionalism

The Biennales of Democracy

During the two years between the 1976 Biennale and the following one in 1978, the political situation in Spain had been changing rapidly. In the final months of 1976, Franco's Cortes voted for a new bill and Spaniards gave the go-ahead to political reform. The first elections were held on June 15, 1977, and Suárez's centre party won.

Therefore the 1978 Biennale took place within the co-ordinates of a democratic Spain. The Ministry of Foreign Affairs retook possession of the pavilion that had been temporarily vacated and called upon José María Ballester to direct it, in association with Vicente Aguilera Cerni, Antonio Bonet Correa and Francesc Vicens; the first was most closely connected to cultural management and the other three were directly linked to the fields of history, art criticism and the management of major museums. It was a curatorship of consensus –in a way, "redress" for Aguilera Cerni and recognition for consolidated figures in contemporary art.

The art situation in Spain during the final years of the seventies underwent a point of inflection at all levels. The period of transition included a modernising process that would be apparent throughout the following decade. Suddenly –artistically speaking– the imperious need for critical realism was no longer there and trends linked to those of Europe and North America were established. The experiments in *Povera*, Minimal, Conceptual and Behavioural art, which had timidly appeared in previous years, confirmed this link with countries abroad, although we had already reached a time of "return to painting," of reconciliation with the easel.

But for the time being, in 1978 an art could still be observed that was seeking a relationship with natural and ecological processes. This was the general theme chosen for the 28th Biennale, the last directed by Ripa di Meana in an Italy that was convalescing after the assassination of Aldo Moro. Specifically, the title of the exhibition was "From Nature to Art, from Art to Nature." It was more suited to action in a broad sense than to pictorial and sculptural practice. In this connection, the sheep with blue patches "exhibited" by Menashe Kadishman, in a clear reference to human intervention in nature, and the controversial inflatable cow with its corresponding stud bull, attracted great attention. It was the culmination of a period during which "happenings" and different types of action had predominated in Venice.

The Spanish pavilion focused on the subject proposed, since not for nothing had it been the foreign curators themselves that year who had decided on the topic, in agreement with the Biennale. In this "natural" context, the reflections of José María Ballester warned against the romantic illusion of giving up technology, since science and technology "are the engines that require the transformation of cultural tradition in order to adapt it to the new conditions, which change continually." In this sense, it was possible to understand a pavilion that displayed as much work by civil engineers as by "technological" or "romantic" artists. There was no wish to forgo intervention in nature by new creators –engineers, architects– who contributed to changing it. So, in the pavilion, "could be seen in different areas the response of technology and the reflection of artists about the same problem: the transformation of the natural setting under the influence of human action."

The result of this approach was a pavilion in which a rational compositional plan was followed, which nevertheless harboured romantic references to nature, and at the same time

There was no wish to forgo intervention in nature by new creators –engineers, architects– who contributed to changing it

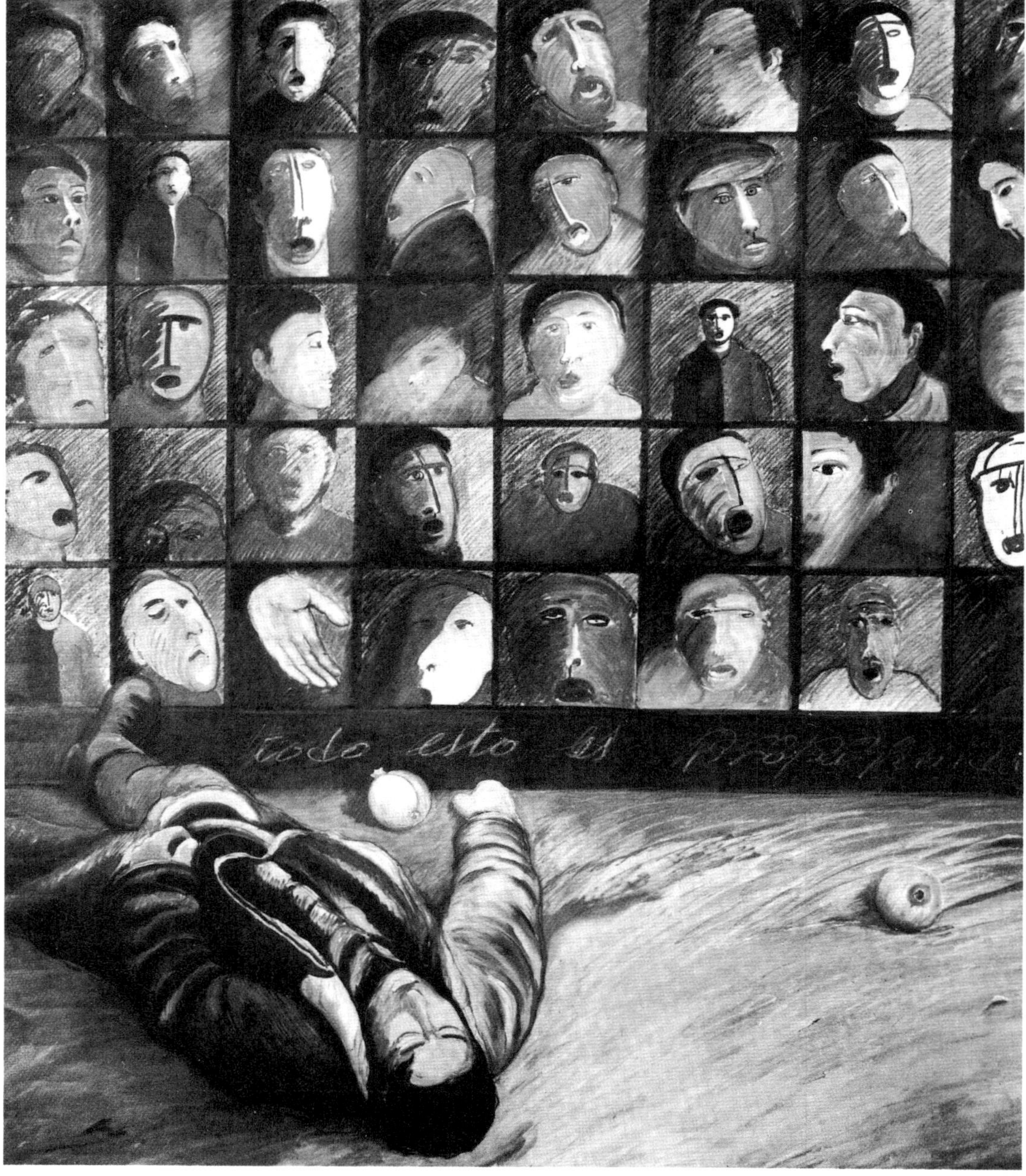

Juan Martínez
"Sólo propaganda" (Only Propaganda)
Spanish Catalogue, 1980

constructions linked to engineering. In comparison with what could be seen in other pavilions at the Biennale, something was borne in mind that the others had practically omitted: the transformation of the landscape by means of town planning, architecture and engineering, which were illustrated through the joint work of José Antonio Fernández Ordóñez and Julio Martínez Calzón. For their part, Juan Navarro Baldeweg and Nacho Criado, who both introduced conceptual art to our country, participated with assemblages such as those of the evocative sculptures of protest by Pilar Palomer and Josefina Miralles, which were considered assemblages. José María Yturralde contributed some poetic technological notes to Venice, through his cubic flying structures.

Spain had finally gone to Venice with ideas for "environmental art." But these schemes lost intensity against the international background, although in no case did they disappear.

Neo-figuration was the tie linking the artists selected by Ceferino Moreno for the 39th Biennale in 1980. As we will recall, this curator had managed the last Spanish pavilion before the crisis, in 1972. At that time he had drawn up a very clear and systematic proposal and the Ministry of Foreign Affairs entrusted him again with the organisation of the exhibition.
In his proposal, Ceferino Moreno bore in mind the guidelines of the Biennale, to the effect that artists who had emerged over the past ten years should be chosen to exhibit at Venice. He decided, as opposed to his policy on the previous occasion, to invite a group of artists forming part of the neo-figurative trends, among whom there was a single sculptor –Javier Aleixandre– and six painters: Eduardo Arranz Bravo, Rafael Bartolozzi, Luis Delacámara, Juan Gomila, Juan Martínez and José Luis Pascual. All of them (except perhaps the sculptor) were united in their commitment to painting directed at social criticism. We do not find in them such concrete references or specific resources as those used by the painters of Crónica de la Realidad, but there was the expression of a degree of disillusionment. As Ceferino Moreno wrote, it was no longer a case of political rebellion, but rather of a "nonconformist attitude in respect of social structures that influenced the most recent Spanish art."

We previously added a "perhaps" on introducing the work of Javier Aleixandre in social criticism. It was certainly not as explicit in him as in his colleagues. It is possible that his beautiful sculpture *Homenaje a Goya* (Tribute to Goya), recreating a nude *maja*, had more to do with kinetic interests and aesthetic propositions than with the message, but in any case it brought back recollections of Bacon's enigmatic beings and their inevitable feeling of defencelessness –in the ultimate analysis a complaint, a judicial appeal against society.

As well as through neo-figuration and criticism, the painters were connected by a great mastery of drawing. This was demonstrated by the Arranz Bravo-Bartolozzi tandem; they shared a workshop and projects and painted the human figure; the first in a more dramatic way and the second in more of a Pop style. José Luis Pascual, with an exceptional sense of humour, flirted with the techniques used in comics. Juan Martínez and Delacámara were painters of the anxiety of grandiose figures who devoured the space; Gomila was the most given to gesture, destroying images with rapid and vigorous touches.
Again, Moreno's eagerness to systematise provided a good point of reference for the Spanish pavilion in Venice. During the next two exhibitions, in 1982 and 1984, Luis González

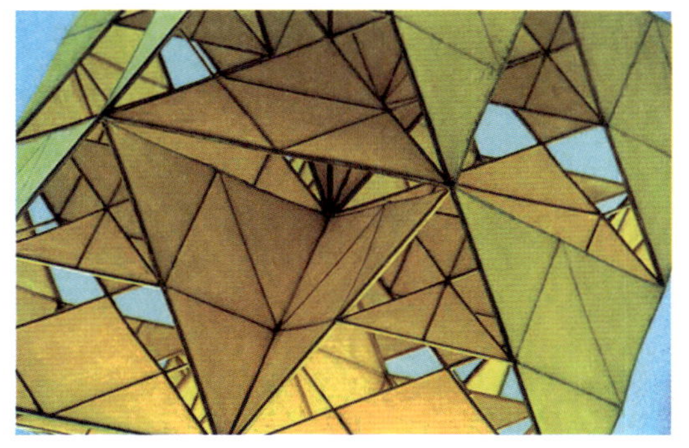

José María Yturralde
"Estructura volante. Octaedro"
(Flying Structure: Octahedron) / 1978 Biennale

The most that could be talked about were the recent neo-figurative signs, although there were new forms of abstraction as well

Robles would once more be in charge. Since then the curator's name has not once again been mentioned.

González Robles had not left any particular resentments behind him. Despite having belonged to Franco's civil service, he knew that the boycott to which he had been subjected in previous years was not directed against him personally, but rather against the regime that he represented. When the Ministry of Foreign Affairs called on Luis González again, it was resorting to an option that it considered safe. It trusted a curator who in the past had so successfully prepared the ground at the Spanish pavilion. Words such as "trans-avant-garde" and "post-modernism" would soon become familiar on the international art scene. But for the moment in Spain the most that could be talked about were the recent neo-figurative signs, although there were new forms of abstraction as well. González Robles attempted to reflect the current diversity by programming an eclectic exhibition. He remarked, "... our time must not be characterised by this ideology or that, or by this or that style; we have chosen figures, artists who represent themselves and therefore not a particular group but rather a social moment."

Of the five artists selected, two had already exhibited at the Biennale –also as protégés of González Robles: Cruz de Castro and Josep Guinovart. Guinovart had evolved from figurative work to abstract formulation and matter painting. He exhibited a single work, *Entorno* (Environment), measuring 2 by 33 metres, which was placed along the length of the pavilion's central gallery. Cruz de Castro was then going through a very gestural period, akin to Abstract Expressionism. Their options were thus very different from each other, and also from the figurative works that accompanied them, such as, for example, *Homenaje al barroco* (Tribute to the Baroque) by José Abad, in which he imparted Dadaist resonances to sculptures highlighted by the power of the "object found" and also by poetic composition. Nor did they have anything to do with the works of Eugenio Chicano, who took his own particular tribute to cinema to the Biennale, in the form of pictures with photographic and Pop significance. Finally, Rosa Torres, contributed her landscapes characterised by schematic formality and chromatic gesture.

The next exhibition programmed by González Robles, in 1984, was a surprise, since the whole pavilion was given over to a single artist –Antoni Clavé, born in 1913. The entire space was occupied by 105 works by him, among which there were paintings, sculptures, posters and set

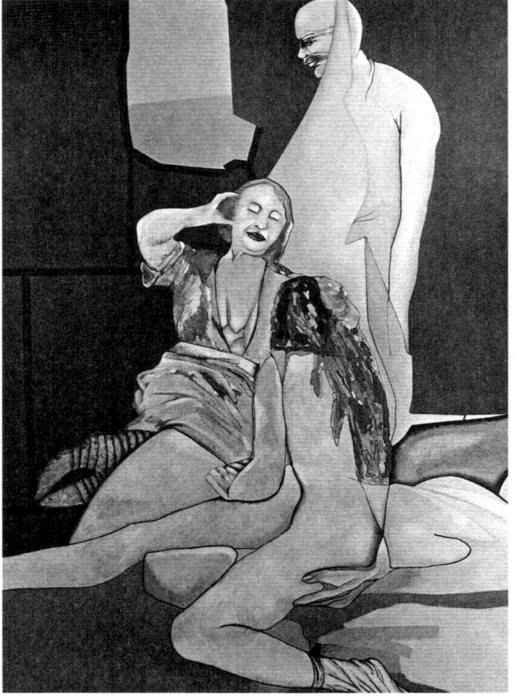

Rafael Bartolozzi
"Figures penúltimes" (Penultimate Figures)
Spanish Catalogue, 1980

designs. In consonance with the general orientation of the exhibition, "Art and Arts –the Present Time and History," Spain was not the only country that chose this formula of historic review. Clavé, an artist who had been forced into exile by the war, was seen as a figure who needed to be recovered.

However, in the light of González Robles's career, his choice of Clavé was totally unexpected, given that until then he had attempted to emphasize the latest generations of artists in the exhibitions that he had directed. This choice, to the contrary, fell within the context of "recoveries due." Antoni Clavé had nearly always worked outside Spain, compelled by circumstances, and he was only slightly known here notwithstanding the great value of his production. The then director of Cultural Relations, Miguel Ángel Carriedo, probably aware of the controversy to which a selection of this kind for the Venice pavilion could give rise, signed a memorandum –together with the director-general of Fine Arts, Manuel Fernández Miranda– recommending that the cultural institutions should support artists who had reached the maturity and projection achieved by Clavé. Given that it was a case of emphasizing a single artist, the catalogue contained several articles, among which was the magnificent review of the artist written by Corredor-Matheos.

Antoni Clavé had started out in illustration and publicity posters, of which some, dated 1934, were on display. He continued working in France, along these lines and in scenography, until the fifties, when he decided to devote himself to painting and sculpture. He had met Picasso –an artist of the greatest importance for him– during his exile in France. Clavé developed some very singular genres, always within the category of abstraction and matter, in which he revealed himself to be a virtuoso. His tricks with paper (wallpaper and crumpled paper...), the use of *collage*, the contrasts of areas of light, his beautiful *trompe-l'oeils*... comprised a very special and unpredictable body of work. The first series by which he became known was the *Guerriers* (Warriors), of which some examples could be seen at Venice, and to which he returned in 1982. His latest work, finished that same year, could also be seen at Venice: it was a large triptych six metres long. At the same time there was a good selection of sculptures or manipulated objects, among which were his cupboards, rescued and painted, in a lesson of daily life and poetry.

In 1986 the curatorship of the Venice Biennale was for the first time in the hands of a woman, Ana Vázquez de Parga. She had worked in different galleries, such as the Biosca y Ponce, and at the beginning of the eighties was practising as an independent curator. Her organisation of an exhibition on Frida Kahlo, at a time when this artist was practically unknown in Spain, was worthy of note. The choice of Ana Vázquez meant a qualitative step forward in the policy of the Ministry of Foreign Affairs. The profession of an independent curator untrammeled by institutional ties, a concept that in one way or another had been seen before, was now "officially" recognized.

Ana Vázquez gained theoretical support for her exhibition offerings from the work of the well-known critic Francisco Calvo Serraller. This author brought up for discussion some significant issues concerning Spanish art over the past ten years. He took the 1976 Biennale as the point of departure and indicated that at that time art was still marked by strong political commitment. But now, ten years later, that commitment had evaporated. The new artists hardly knew anything about the Franco regime which they had only

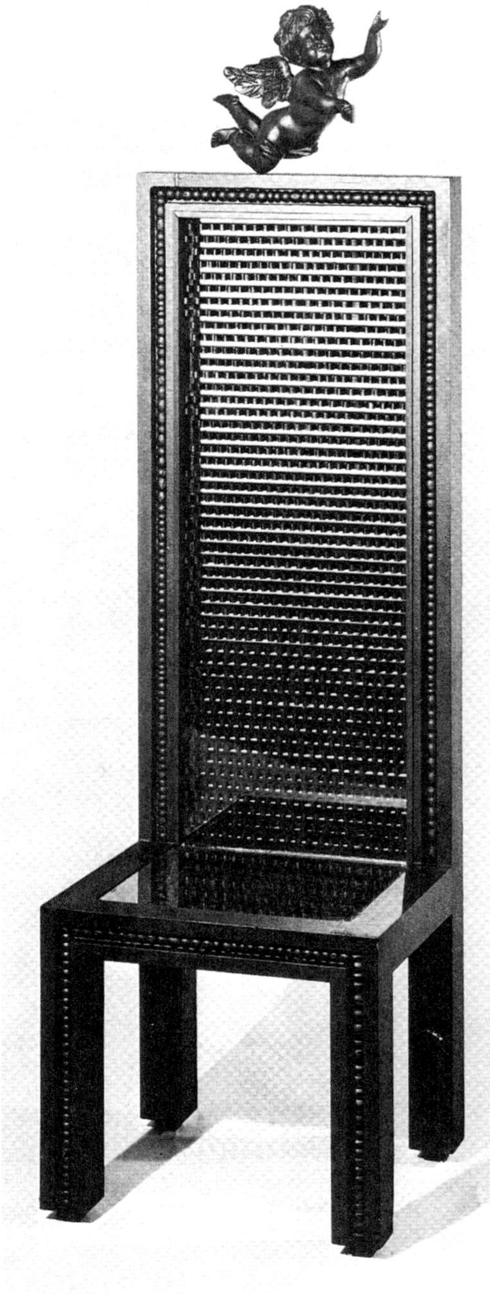

José Abad
"Homenaje al Barroco II" (Tribute to the Baroque II)
Spanish Catalogue, 1982

experienced in their childhood; the world in which they lived was full of outside influences. Calvo Serraller pointed out that over the past few years there had been a burgeoning in art, affected precisely by these relations with the outside world, but warned that, "the new Spanish art has been marked by haste and the most uncontrolled wish for international standardisation, with all that an attitude of this kind *also* entails of a negative nature." The avidity to grasp all that was foreign only accentuated the contradictions of many artists who were not yet in a position to exhibit their personal work.

At this stage, there were not many artists who could represent Spain without resorting to imitation. Among them, were those selected for this exhibition, whom the critic said carried out "a type of coherent and well-consolidated work, which gives the impression of being far removed from the ingenuous anxiety and opportunism that have characterised many young artists in this country."

The artists concerned were Miquel Navarro, Ferrán García Sevilla, José María Sicilia and Cristina Iglesias. Miquel Navarro took his emblematic *ciudades* (cities). He himself acknowledged the influence of Constructivism on his volumes, but I would especially like to mention the Suprematism of Malevich in this connection, and the recollection of his *planites* and *arquitectones*. Visually, the ceramic matter contrasted with the use of zinc and lead, which performed not only a material function of counterpoint, but also a formal one. Ferrán García Sevilla showed us his idiom of complex symbolic ingenuity; Sicilia, his very personal dramatics; and finally Cristina Iglesias, who had not taken long to return to Venice, took her sculptures of iron, reinforced concrete and pigment. These were vertical structures that needed the support of a wall. She was beginning to look like one of the most solid sculptors in the Spain of the period.

Precisely as far as María Corral (curator at the next Biennale in 1988) was concerned, sculpture was the artistic discipline that benefited from the greatest number of interesting artists. She programmed another of the emerging sculptors, who was, however, already fairly well recognised. This was Susana Solano, who shared the space with Oteiza, in the following formula: established-older-male-artist/young-female-artist-with projection, which was repeated at future exhibitions.

During the period under review, María Corral was the director of Exhibitions at the Madrid Pensions Fund Foundation. Shortly afterwards she would be

The new artists hardly knew anything about the Franco regime which they had only experienced in their childhood; the world in which they lived was full of outside influences

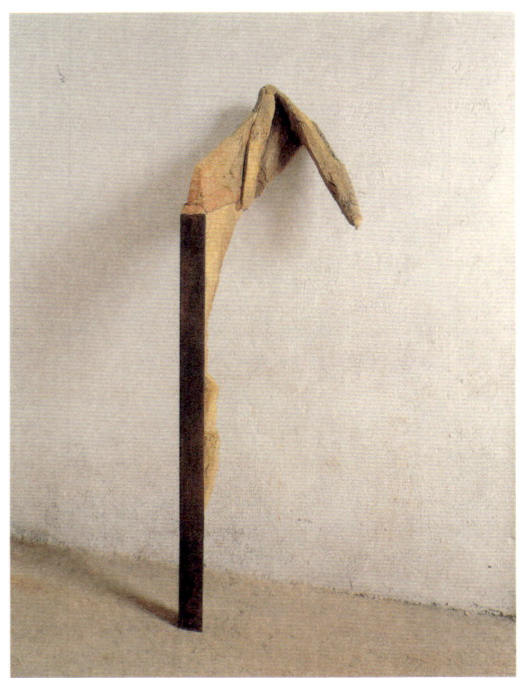

Cristina Iglesias
"Sin título. N 6/4" (Untitled. N 6/4)
Spanish Catalogue, 1986

the director of the Reina Sofía National Art Centre. She was a woman of prestige, like many of those who would have important responsibilities in the field of art during those years.

There was no doubt about the seriousness of her proposal. Oteiza, an outstanding and controversial figure, had refused to participate in the 1976 Biennale on account, as we recall, of his wish for independent representation of the Basque Country. He was the great unknown sculptor, to be rescued for international viewing of his work since it had remained hidden following his decision to abandon sculpture and devote himself to political and cultural activities. On display at Venice, above all, was his fruitful decade of the fifties, during which he had produced his paradoxical *cajas vacías* (empty boxes) or *cajas metafísicas* (metaphysical boxes). These were peculiar forms which, although possibly related to the geometrism of the Cubists and Constructivists, were also recognised to have sources in primitive cultures. But visual experience of Oteiza's work transcended these recollections, given the magnitude of his sensitivity relative to his paradigmatic concern with hollow spaces.

Susana Solano belonged to the generation born in the forties; among the representatives of the Spanish sculptural scene, she was probably the best to accompany Oteiza's pieces. Her own sculptures gave off the same air of sobriety, and also generated a number of questions in respect of the "inside" and "outside." Solano's large pieces, her *Siete estaciones* (Seven Stations), contrasted with the relatively small ones by Oteiza, but they shared many theoretical and formal implications.

The 1990 pavilion took an entirely different direction. Its contrast with that of the previous

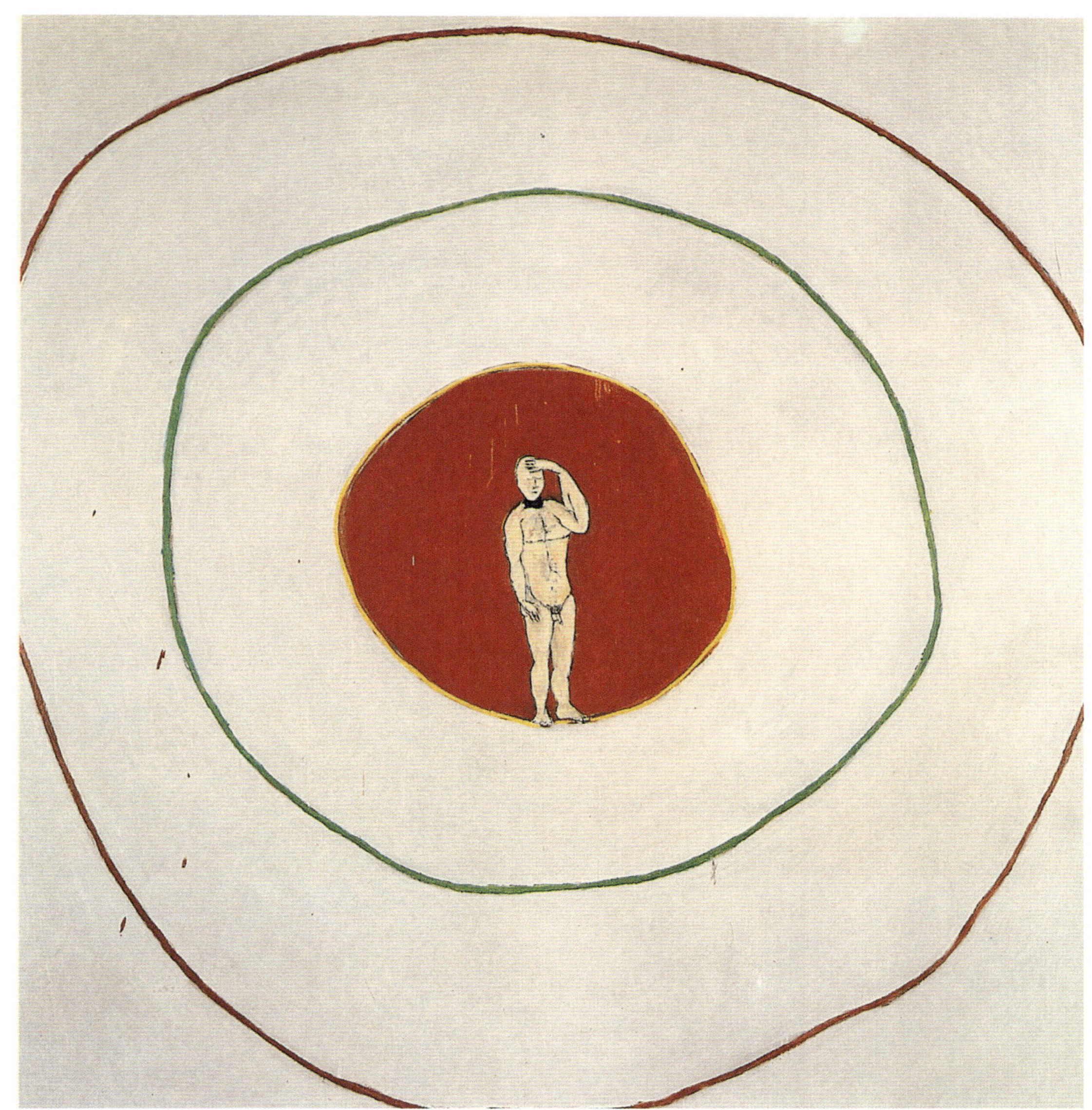

Ferrán García Sevilla
"Pariso 8"
Spanish Catalogue, 1986

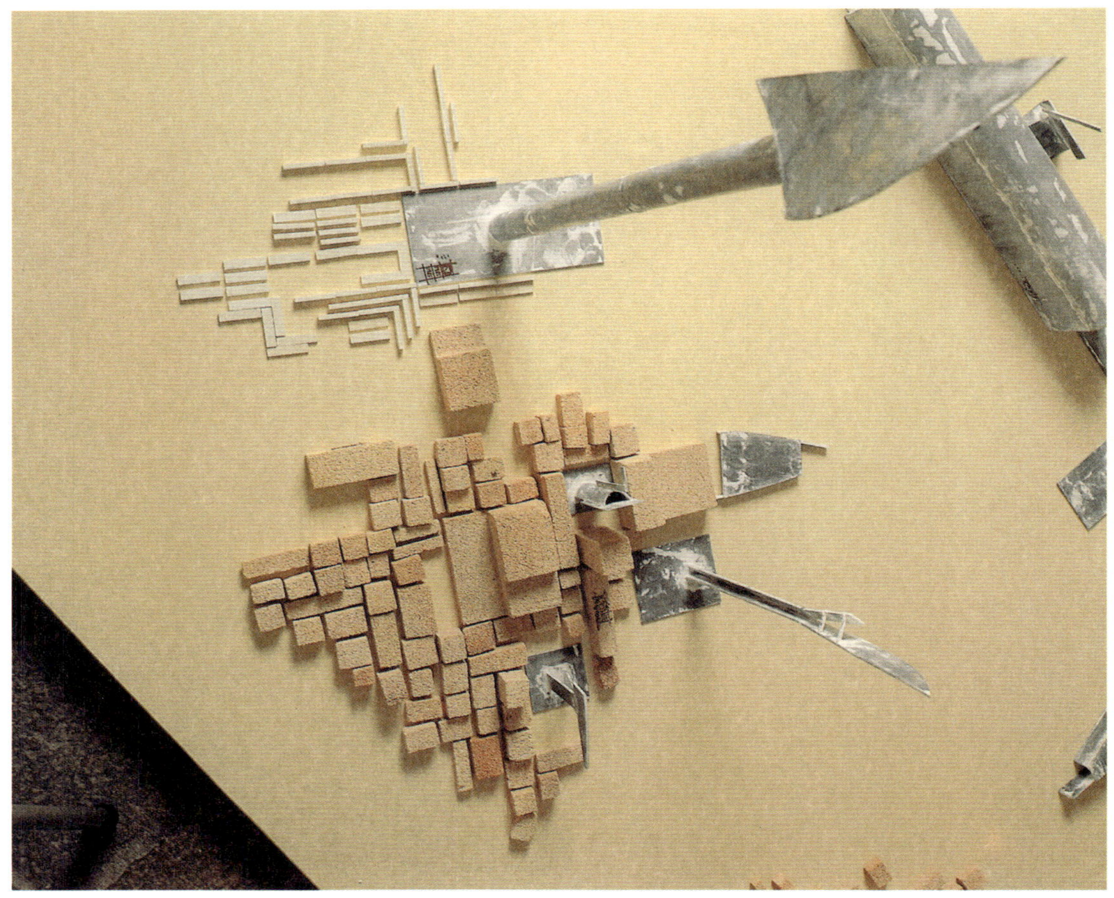

exhibition was the best example of the multiplicity of idioms existing in contemporary art –also in Spain. Not since 1978, when the re-opening of the installations at Venice led to our country's renewal of its links with the exhibition, had anything similar happened. But this time it was completely different. In 1978 the exhibition had concentrated on art's relationship with nature, and the pavilion was sober and thoughtful. Now, on the contrary, a party was being prepared for the wedding of two giants –the New York Statue of Liberty and the Barcelona statue of Columbus. This was a work of art in the purest procedural style, proposed by one of the most significant artists within this concept of art, Antoni Miralda.

Miralda, interested in the ritual of ceremonies and also in an entertaining "edible art," as well as having pacifist leanings that were seen in his first *Soldats-soldats*, presented part of a project in Venice that he had been preparing since 1986 and which would be completed in 1992. The purpose of the project was to marry these statues. The "wedding" would take place in 1992 to commemorate the Quincentenary of Columbus's landing in America. Prior to this, however, all the procedures of a traditional ceremony would have to be followed. The engagement ring had previously been exhibited in different towns and cities; its central "stone" was a television set projecting images of the engaged couple –the bride's lingerie, the trousseau and the bridal bouquet.... The banns were published in Venice, to enable those present to give their approval or voice their objections, as proposed by the artist with tongue-in-cheek and corroborated by Maria Lluïsa Borràs, curator of the exhibition who, as a matter of fact, was not too happy about an experience in which she had to wrestle with unexpected financial problems.

Honeymoon –which is what the project was called– took some of the objects to Venice that had already been circulated in other cities. Of course everything was very kitschy; there were hundreds of yards of pink and blue tulle, the bride's shoe, and a gigantic bouquet of flowers. If in all social ceremonies of this kind there is an element of kitsch, imagine what it was like –magnified and also falsified by the fact that the bride and bridegroom were non-existent. There was certainly good reason for the resulting outcry, but Maria Lluïsa Borràs left a living record of procedural art. In the final analysis, this specialist in architecture of Modernism had always been

Míquel Navarro
"Des del terrat" (From the Roof)
Spanish Catalogue, 1986

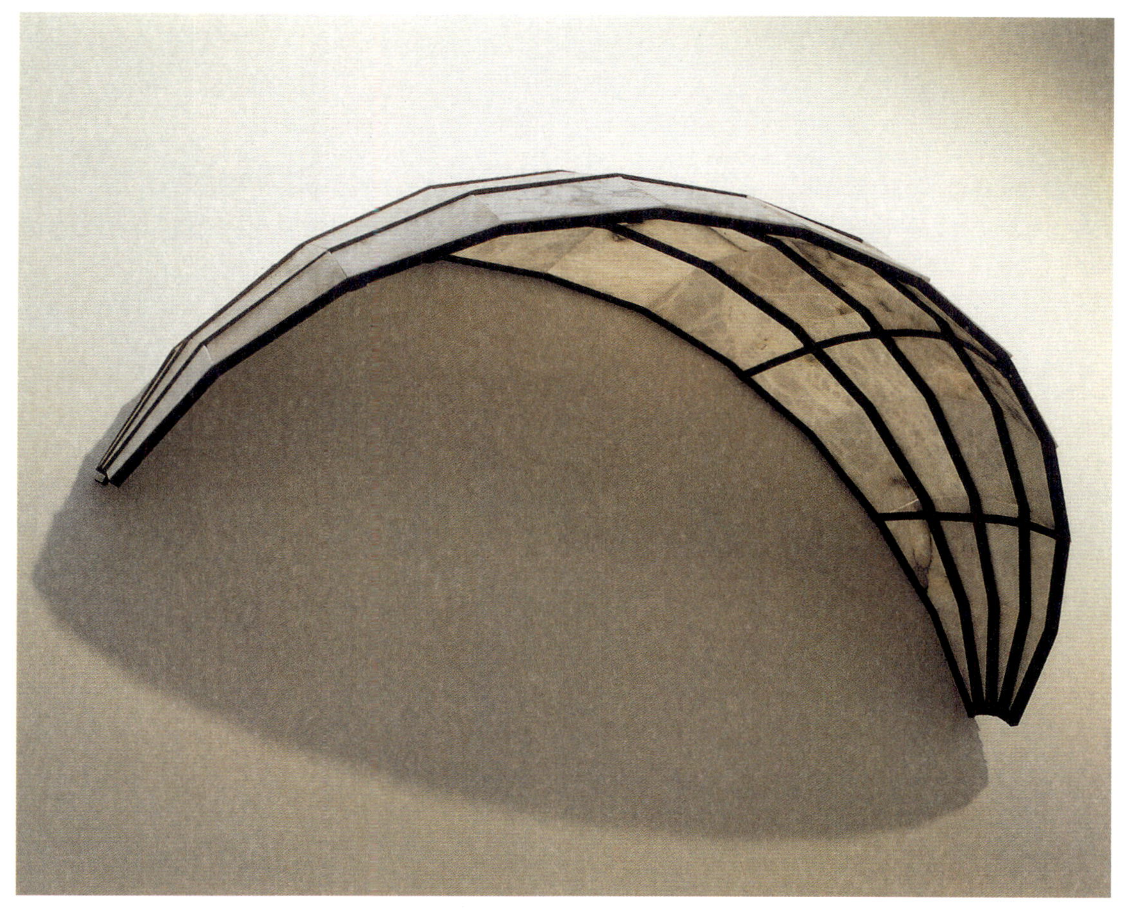

The 1990 pavilion took an entirely different direction. Its contrast with that of the previous exhibition was the best example of the multiplicity of idioms existing in contemporary art

caught by the Dadaist game, and here was something of that Dadaist "lack of respect."

At this Biennale the institution also paid tribute to Chillida, with an exhibition at Ca'Pesaro. Thirty of his sculptures, dated between 1951 and 1990, were chosen, apart from a large number of drawings and collages. It was necessary to forgo some large pieces because their weight would have been too much for the building, but it was nevertheless an impressive exhibition by the Basque maestro, who claimed to base his work on the dialectics between the full and the empty, matter and space; and who acknowledged as the best definition of his production one made by someone with nothing to do with the field of art who said, after viewing his sculptures, "I've understood, it's like music, but in iron."

The next Biennale was postponed until 1993, in theory so that the exhibition's centenary could be held two years later. But perhaps the real reason was so that it wouldn't coincide with Kassel; or, what is even more likely, that there were multiple management problems. The cultural agitator, Achille Bonito Oliva, was its new director, and he was programming a Biennale entitled, "Cardinal Points of Art," in which the idea of the

Cristina Iglesias
"Sin título" (Untitled)
Spanish Catalogue, 1993

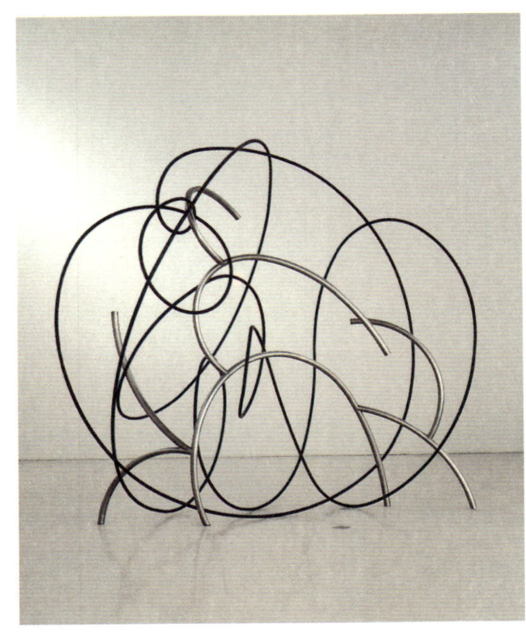

cohabitation of idioms would be illustrated. In this connection, a recommendation was made to the pavilions that they welcome artists from other countries. But this did not happen at the Spanish pavilion; another option was offered similar to that presented by María Corral. The project on this occasion was by Aurora García, art critic and historian, who from the start of the eighties had worked as an independent curator.

The curator staged the work of two artists, a man and a woman, of different generations. One of them, Tàpies, represented the strength of a consolidated career. The other, Cristina Iglesias, showed the coherent evolution of someone still young. The two had already participated in the Biennale –Tàpies several times in the fifties, and also in the 1976 exhibition; Cristina Iglesias in that of 1986.

Both worked on a project especially conceived for the Biennale. Tàpies went to stay in Venice some weeks before the opening of the exhibition, in order to put together *Rinzen* (in Japanese, "Sudden Awakening"). The assemblage was made up of different elements: in the centre there was an iron bed frame with a metal-spring-mattress hanging from the ceiling, with other spring-mattresses attached to it or lying at its foot, together with some coarse woollen blankets, and a folded pillow.... At one side, folding chairs painted white, in rows of two, some of them with a cross; at the other side a single chair facing the wall with a sign drawn on it. Three numbers on the wall, and a cross, constituted the sign. Without considering the interpretations that could be derived from the title, the graphics and the upturned bed, the space itself gave off a clear sensation of loneliness. Indeed, *Rinzen* had the semantic connotation of zen. I do not know whether this was its purpose, but the area seemed to be a place for meditation, a kind of atemporal temple. It was awarded the Biennale *Leone d'Oro* (Golden Lion) for painting.

If in former years perfect harmony had prevailed between Oteiza and Solano, the same thing occurred between Tàpies and Cristina Iglesias. Both partook of the poetry of silence. Iglesias, forceful in her work, exhibited bipolar spaces, with dual qualities of matter in which smooth surfaces alternated with the rough textures of dried leaves; the opaqueness of metal contrasted with the translucence of alabaster. The construction of her spaces was an invitation to move about, to stop, and to be surprised.

Two years later, in 1995, the Biennale celebrated its centenary with what many considered was a "return to order" in comparison with the results of the previous exhibition. For the first time there was a director who was not Italian: this was Jean Clair, who proposed a review of the human body over the course of the century. In one way or

The next Biennale was postponed until 1993, in theory so that the exhibition's centenary could be held two years later

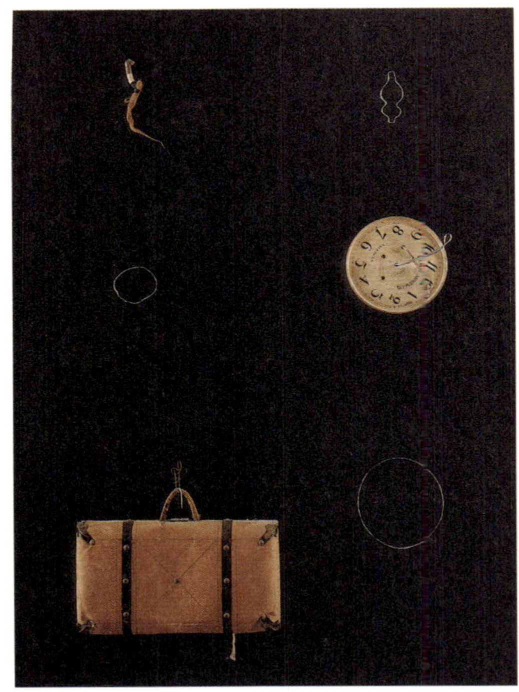

Andreu Alfaro
"Laocoonte"
Spanish Catalogue, 1995

Carmen Calvo
"Los parásitos viajan" (Parasites Travel)
Spanish Catalogue, 1997

another this was also the point of departure for the Spanish artists who went to the Biennale –sculptor Andreu Alfaro and painter Eduardo Arroyo. Both had already been to Venice on previous occasions: both were at the 1976 exhibition; and Alfaro, moreover, was invited by González Robles during the sixties. The exhibition was curated by Fernando Huici, art critic and habitual collaborator in many of the media. One of the first contributions was to the actual building of the Spanish pavilion, to which some outside changes were made in the form of the steel doors designed by Andreu Alfaro.

On previous occasions when an exhibition had been programmed with two participants, the intention had been that they should speak idioms with complementary features. Now the situation was entirely different. Arroyo, heir to the neo–figurative approaches of the sixties, with important links to Pop, had an outlook diametrically opposed to that of Alfaro, whose heritage came from the geometrisation of space aimed at approaching minimalist positions. Eduardo Arroyo took sixteen large-format canvases to the Biennale, practically all of which were from 1994 and 1995: children's stories, religious figures, Spanish myths, in most of which the human figure was the main referent. In them there were allusions to death, to violence, to nausea. A rather simple artistic formula, with flat colours, camouflaged axes and very clear and delimited explicit elements nevertheless conveyed a disturbing message.

Andreu Alfaro welcomed us at the Spanish pavilion door with the jambs that he himself had built out of steel bars. They traced a sequence which reminded us of some of his earlier pieces, as well as of the six colossal white marble sculptures that he named *Ramses*, consisting of polished blocks –modern columns of new spaces. The categorical expressiveness of this outside area contrasted with the *Ángeles* (Angels) inside, but not with the growing complexity of the *Laocoontes*. Even the material (tin for the first, iron, steel, marble and limestone for the second) spoke to us about the difference between the light, the ethereal, the volatile, as opposed to struggle, bravado and strength.

While this was going on in the Spanish pavilion, in the international exhibition other Spanish artists were presenting their works: Antonio López, who exhibited his nude figures of a man and woman, and also Miró and Picasso. Victoria Combalía, curator of the Spanish pavilion at Venice in 1997, had a critical view of current art. In the introduction to the catalogue, she said, "We are living at a time during which the world of

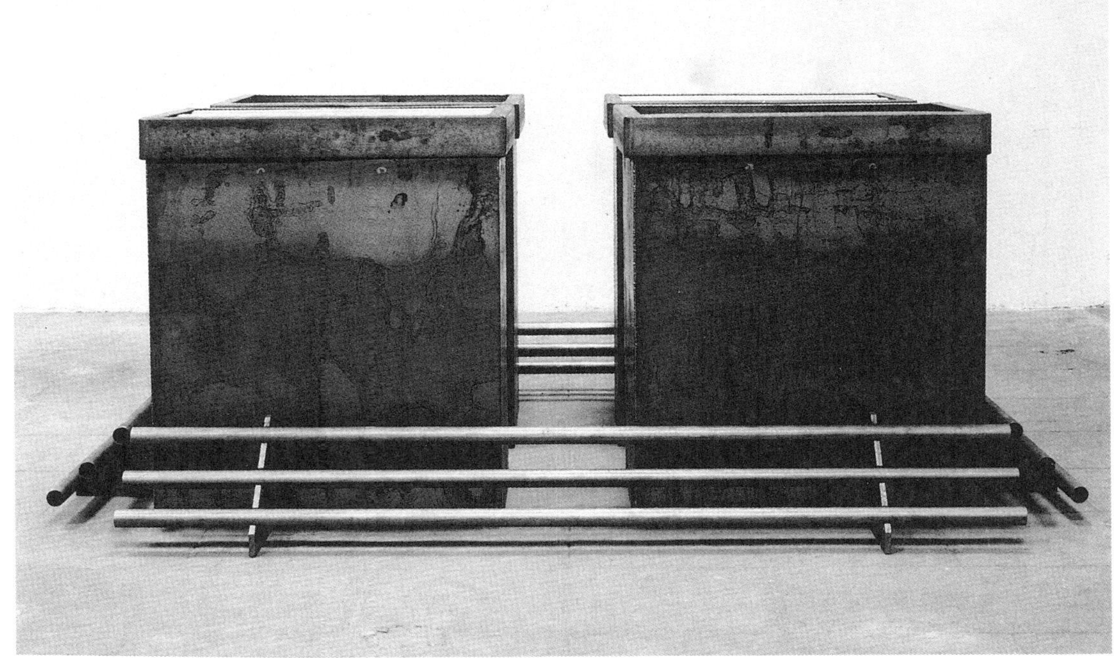

Susana Solano
"Estació termal N°2" (Thermal Baths No. 2)
Spanish Catalogue, 1988

His sculptures also took part in this movement, but nevertheless conveyed a very personal identity, with few but convincing planes and/or volumes

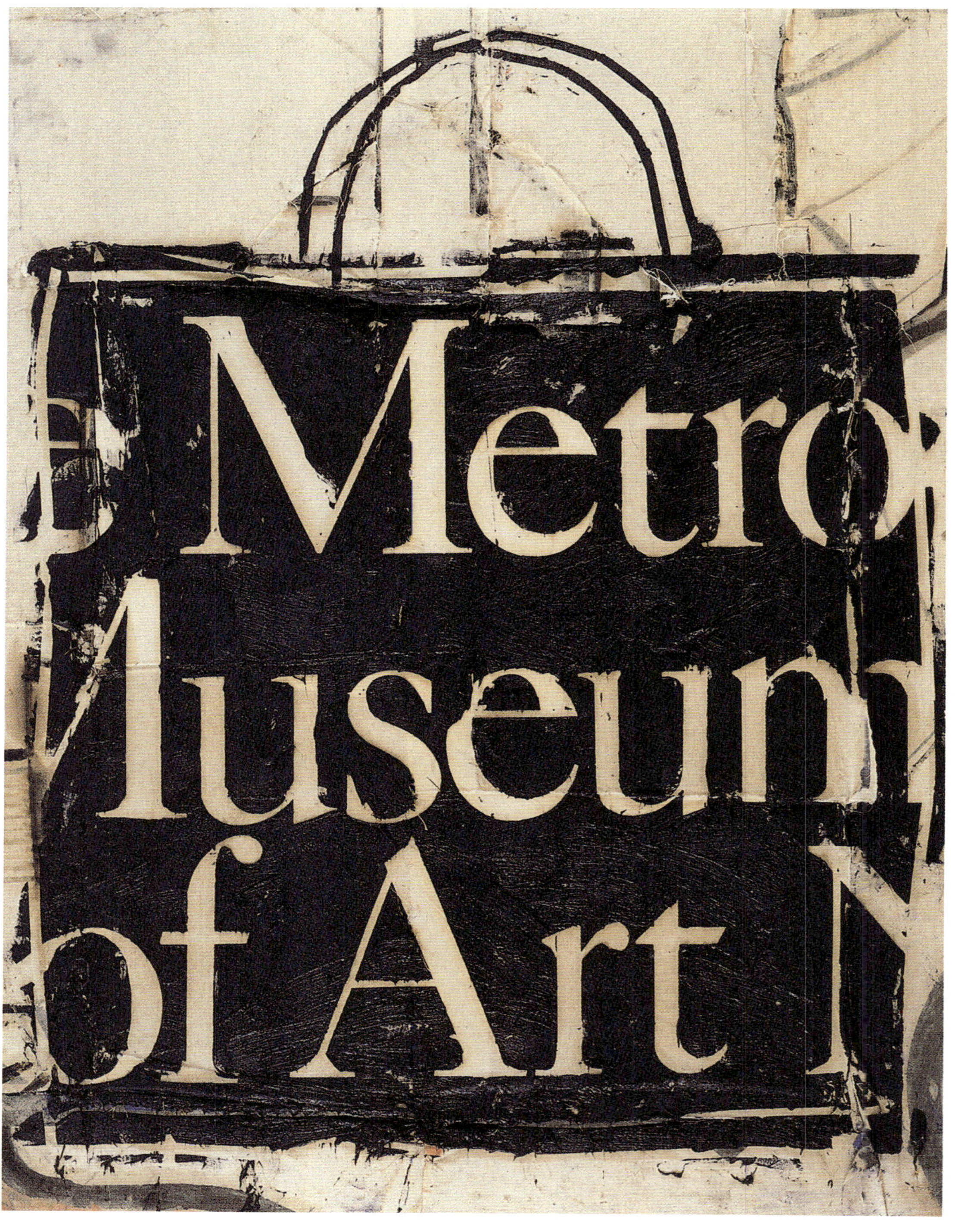

Manolo Valdés
"The bag"
Spanish Catalogue, 1999

contemporary art, in its eagerness to startle, is taking giant steps towards becoming a spectacle aimed at surpassing the media icons." Her option, ruling out these "vices," was to programme two artists: Joan Brossa and Carmen Calvo, whose works "are based on strongly personal worlds, each (in his or her generation) ignoring the reigning fashions; both are driven by the will to say something about the world and man's basic problems."

It was with the intention of counteracting the art–spectacle of commercial interests that the curator had chosen the aforementioned artists, in whom she had sensed their multiple nature. Joan Brossa, in effect, had been an artist who had included object poems in his experiments, but also "written poetry," film scripts, actions and other artistic expressions. Carmen Calvo, for her part, had trodden a path on which the boundaries between painting and sculpture had been eliminated. Both again made up a pair in which the much younger Carmen Calvo joined the veteran Brossa.

Joan Brossa took a selection of his object poems to Venice as well as some of his installations, works that he had produced between 1951 and 1994. Among the poems were depicted anxiety in *El regal* (The Present), in which an open penknife is seen in a box for luxury table knives, and irony in *Nupcial* (Wedding), which showed a wife tied to a diamond bracelet. There was also sarcasm –this time dark and tragic– in *Instal.lació*, conceived in 1986 and completed in 1990, in which a *garrote vil* (contraption for execution by strangling) was seen in front of a table prepared for an elegant meal: the last wish of a condemned man. In Brossa's work Dadaist and Surrealist links could of course be seen, but always bearing in mind the most committed and critical facet –something which always appears and remains behind the smile of the person who views his works.

Another poet in her own way was Carmen Calvo; this was corroborated by the *cuadros negros* (black pictures), the *pizarras* (slates) and the *Instalación/caja* (Installation/box) that she exhibited at the Biennale. There were backgrounds of rubber, backgrounds of slate, and on them objects, small constructions, apparent enigmas that little by little were elucidated. This artist, who made daily objects and fragments of pottery the basis of her compositions, had gone from an initial enthusiasm for "archeology" to another that was more descriptive –but both with great power of communication. Combalía, amongst other items, proposed a reading of her latest works (those that she took to the Biennale) in a code of female identity. In this way symbols could be understood such as hair, gloves, shoes and gynecological instruments.

This exhibition was very well received at Venice; its impeccable installation and its magic converted the Spanish pavilion into one of the most attractive national pavilions. Victoria Combalía's clear ideas had borne fruit.

Two years later, the last Biennale of the century, that of 1999, was held. David Pérez, professor and essay writer, was called upon to direct it. He decided again on two artists, Manolo Valdés and Esther Ferrer –again a man and a woman, although this time there was no generation gap. Both had appeared in art circles during the sixties– Manolo Valdés as a member of the Equipo Crónica and Esther Ferrer as a member of Zaj." But only at the time of their appearance in the art world did they find a point in common. Valdés was then immersed in painting of social criticism, and Ferrer in musical activity (which, apart from sonorous, was also tactile and visual) in a type of experiment that has been considered to precede conceptual art in Spain.

Both exhibited their latest production in Venice. Manolo Valdés, above all, with some beautiful heads -oils on sackcloth in which the influence of other artists was observed, and which no effort was made to hide. Passionate about different periods of history, he moved easily between them, giving himself up to the 18th century or the beginning of the 20th. His sculptures also took part in this movement, but nevertheless conveyed a very personal identity, with few but convincing planes and/or volumes.

Nearly everything about Esther Ferrer was surprising, from her autographed and manipulated face –so often the subject of her work– to her slender body, the support for her visual poems or performances. Likewise surprising were her questions, as current as, "Would you prefer NATO's next operation to be exclusively retransmitted by CNN or by the Art Channel? Why?"; or shocking photographs from *The Book of Sex*, some curious bits and pieces and, finally, her different projects, which at times only needed to be stated. One of them was *Within the Framework of Art*, a specific installation for the Venice Biennale of that year, consisting of a play of volumes, mirrors and frames in a constant questioning about the consideration of art and everything artistic.

The final proposal by the curator of the Spanish pavilion for that Biennale was the inclusion of multi-faceted musician Carles Santos, who gave one of his unique concerts. To a certain extent he became the connection between the different arts. Both he and Esther Ferrer fully demonstrated, by moving between the different disciplines, all the possibilities offered by creation in recent decades.

The first Spanish pavilion of the 21st century, that

of 2001, opened in Venice with a reflection about the idea of the city itself that was hosting the exhibition. The artists selected by Estrella de Diego with a view to establishing a “Venetian dialogue” were Ana Laura Aláez and Javier Pérez. For the first time, the whole weight of the exhibition was on the shoulders of two young people, whose work, however, was already fairly well-recognised.

Venice, in the imagination of the curator, was the city of light, of splendour, of surfaces, of water, of glass, and also of travel. That was why she chose these artists: “Javier Pérez, as a result of his professional career, represented glass and splendour, whereas Laura Aláez synthesised light and surfaces.” Face to face with the city and the space of the pavilion, each one re-interpreted them in their own way. Javier Pérez installed an enormous inverted dome in the central area, made up of gigantic drops of glass that murmured as they were reflected on the bluish surface of the floor. The Venetian elements succeeded one another –glass, drops, surfaces, reflection– with an intensity of contemporary euphuism.

The great volume of the piece necessarily moved viewers towards the lateral areas, where Ana Laura Aláez had changed the structure of the pavilion to the point of converting its bare walls into small sanctuaries marked by colour, as well as by sound, light and water. The artist, who confessed that her work had been directed more towards the idea of space than that of the city, nevertheless imparted some signs of Venetian identity, especially that of its sophistication. This was because, when night falls in Venice, and the tourists disappear into the neighbouring nightspots, it once more becomes the city that hides and protects itself, which shows off its most chic side, somewhat like the entire Spanish pavilion of that year.
For the fiftieth Biennale, Spain has made a risky choice which foreseeably will prove contentious. Rosa Martínez, with wide experience in the field of international exhibitions, has called upon a single artist, Santiago Sierra, currently living in México, who has divided the critics and the public. His latest actions basically consist of paying groups of people to do or let themselves be made to do a number of things, such as holding up a wall, staying in the hold of a ship, or getting inside a box. But not just any person will do. The artist “chooses” a physique, an age, a look. He finds profiles of immigrants, of the marginalised..., for the purpose of making the viewer feel uncomfortable and highlighting exploitation.

With a well-guarded secret, which will not be disclosed until the opening of the Biennale, the exhibition will contribute with its project to the mystery of the city, to the enigma that is always Venice.

For more than a hundred years, Spain has shown its multiform artistic face at the Venice Biennale, at times masking it, on other occasions revealing it to be significantly bare. Dozens of artists and hundreds of works have paraded through the *Giardini*. Many of them have not stood the test of time and nowadays are scarcely remembered in the art history books; they failed to reflect the dual quality of modernity required of a work of art according to Baudelaire: the contingency of the strictly contemporary and the immutability of the classic feeling. On reflecting only one of these facets, the artists denied themselves that of possible posterity. They belong to the legion of those only concerned with their own times, or only living for the past, who represented Spain for years. The works were also often those that pleased the Academy, which notwithstanding its liking for nudes, was suspicious of unembellished art.
But the time came for the mask to crack, and Venice as well saw those works that history today has shown are unforgettable. They are current and eternal, complete and without subterfuges, a part of their time and of all times. It was the close of the fifties and the artists refused to live under veils. Others followed them in the sixties. It was the great moment of Spanish art in Venice, systematised in the unforgettable exhibition of 1976.
Over the past three decades, Spain has always taken the correct choices to Venice, for an artistically-speaking correct country. Contemporary eclecticism has enabled the Spanish pavilion to carry out different experiments, which are a part of the reality of our art. The perspective of time will make it possible to discern whether or not the mask itself has been authentic.

Spain has shown its multiform artistic face at the Venice Biennale, at times masking it, on other occasions revealing it to be significantly bare

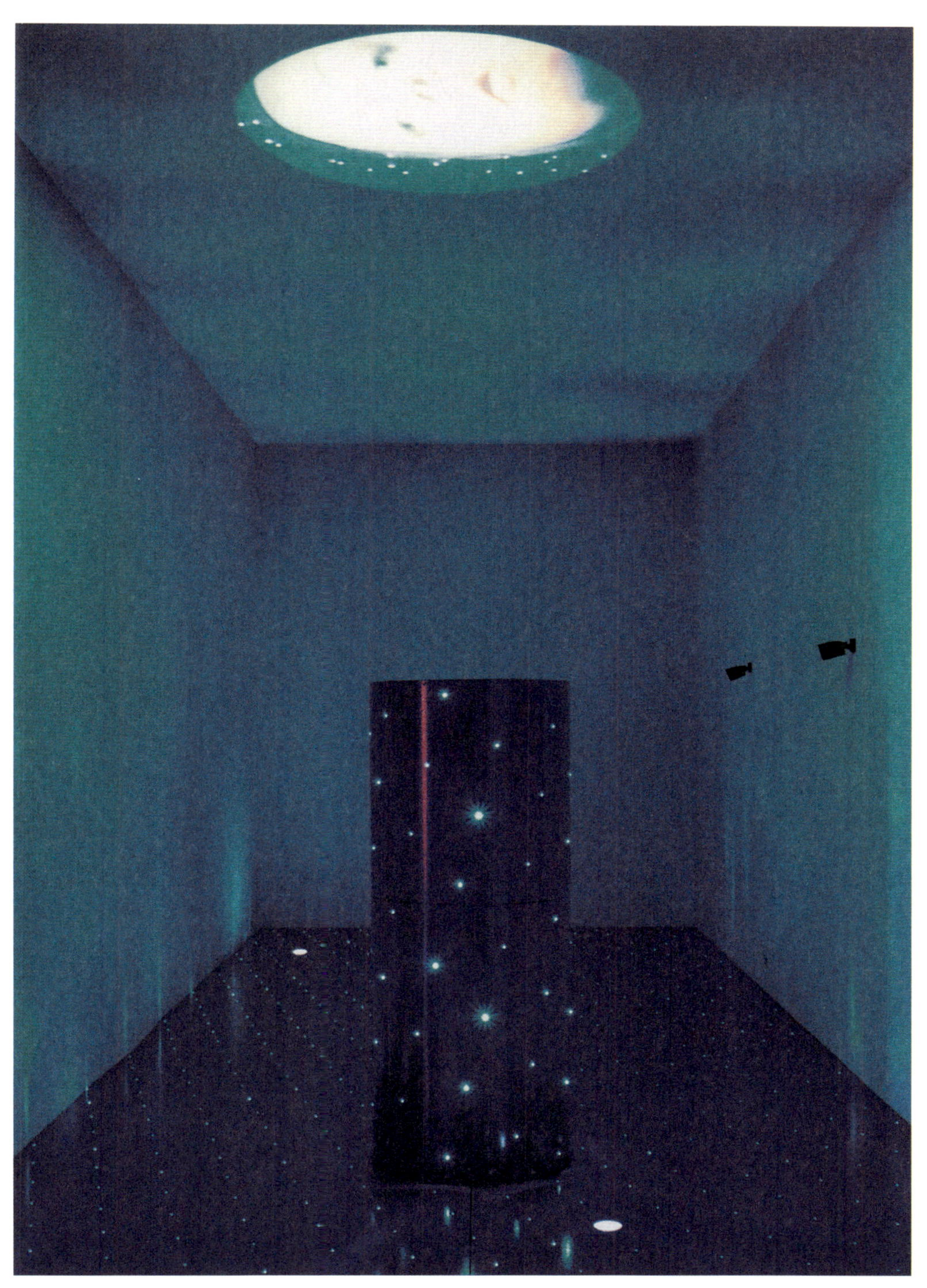

Ana Laura Aláez
"Liquid Sky"
Spanish Catalogue, 2001

The Other Spanish Artists at the Biennale

The Venice Biennale is a mosaic of exhibitions as varied as the countries that take part in it. But –today more than ever– it is also *the* major international show which, year after year, "chooses" its manner of understanding contemporary art and designs its programme on the basis of this concept. In this connection the curator is a determining factor. In recent years, depending on the various options presented by the curators, we have witnessed approaches ranging from historical to strictly contemporary, from transgressive to media-oriented. Whatever the approach, the programme adopted at Venice is indicative of the different current concepts of contemporary art.

The pavilions of the various nations that take part in the Biennale house the "official" proposals of the respective countries, which at times spring from specific, even political interests. However, the exhibitions programmed by Venice are more in line with the specific preferences of the curators. A heterogeneous group of Spanish artists have taken part in these exhibitions, some in retrospective or thematic exhibitions, and others in the emergent proposals of the Aperto.

The first years they took part in the Biennale, the Spanish artists who arrived in Venice did so in response to the invitation of Spanish curators, and in other instances were chosen by Italian juries. Nonetheless, during these years, Spain's and Italy's artistic policies shared the same goals and interests, so much so that their proposals were perfectly interchangeable.

A significant change took place at the 1948 Biennale when Picasso was directly invited by the organisers; Spain did not attend the event that year. Italy thus took on a leading role in the comeback of an avant-garde that had so far not interested the academics responsible for artistic affairs in Spain. Following the Second World War, Venice played a prominent role in this connection. It held various exhibitions that helped rediscover classical modernity and showed an interest in planning shows *by themes*. Later, in 1980, a new space, the Aperto, was opened to promote up-and-coming artists.

The various Spanish artists who were invited to the Biennale by the organisers of the events have been mentioned in the previous pages. Of these, Picasso (1948), Tàpies (1982) and Chillida (1990) were undoubtedly the most significant in that they represented a revival of quality. But other artists have also taken part in the various sections of the Biennale. We could cite, for example, Susana Solano, who in 1993 –five years after having her work shown officially in the Spanish pavilion– took part in the "Cardinal points of art" show with her work *Meditaciones n. 12* (Meditations no. 12). That same year the *Slittamenti* section featured Pedro Almodóvar as a creator who breaks genres, who is capable of "slipping" between them. Dalí was also remembered through Orson Welles, whose *Salvador Dalí: A Soft Self-Portrait* was shown.

Two years later, Antonio López, Miró and Picasso were represented at the Centenary Biennale. Works by Zuloaga, Anglada Camarasa and Sorolla were also shown that year in an exhibition that recalled past Biennales. The paintings in question were exhibited in Ca'Pesaro in Venice and therefore had strong emotional ties with the city. Nonetheless, the most significant exhibitions –as regards their implications for the future– were those designed to cater to younger artists or inventors of more novel languages. Such was the purpose of the so-called Aperto, which was established in 1980, though this was not the first time that artists of this kind had been invited to take part in the Biennale as up-and-coming names. Aguilera Cerni tells of how in 1958, Spaniards Jesús M. González, Rafael Ruiz Balerdi and Joaquín Pacheco took part in the section reserved for young artists whose work had never been shown at the Biennale.

The Aperto, which was installed permanently in the Corderie dell'Arsenale, beside the *Giardini di Castello*, was the brainchild of Achille Bonito Oliva and Harald Szeemann. Szeemann states that the aim was not simply to promote artists under thirty-five –as it was later interpreted– but also to provide exhibition space to artists who explored the "ramifications of art." The possibility was also considered of staging comebacks for artists with a long career but insufficiently acknowledged. Bonito Oliva, for his part, also regarded the Aperto as a place for young artists from countries without a pavilion of their own.

This section of the Biennale, the most dynamic according to some and a veritable "horror chamber" for others, was cancelled in 1995 when Jean Clair became curator. The 1993 Aperto, a project designed by Bonito Oliva, had been particularly controversial, full of dramatic effects –indeed, like the whole of that year's Biennale. Clair justified his decision as a question of priorities and by the need to reorganise the section. While some breathed sighs of relief at the prospect of a "return to order," many others expressed their disapproval of this measure. The protest, led by many curators of exhibitions all over the world, gave rise to the staging of various international shows under the name of the one that had been closed in Venice.

In a sense, the Aperto made a comeback in 1999, when Szeemann returned with the *APERTutto*, which aimed to establish a link with the 1980 Aperto but drew no distinctions between older and younger artists, and questioned the selection committees.

As for Spain's presence in this section of the Biennale, 1984 saw the significant participation of Miquel Barceló, undoubtedly one of the names that would thereafter be missed in the pavilion. Although still very young, he was already producing works as outstanding as his *Biblioteca* (Library), of 1984.

In the following Biennale held in 1986, María Corral –who was the curator of the Spanish pavilion the following year– was one of the members of the Aperto's Selection Committee. Sevillian painters Patricio Cabrera Rodríguez, Gerardo Delgado, Guillermo Paneque and the sculptor Juan Muñoz of Madrid were chosen. The first three belonged to a generation of Andalusian artists who worked intensely in the eighties, many of them immersed in a gestural art inspired by Abstract Expressionism. Muñoz, for his part, enjoyed a brilliant career the following years and, like Barceló, became a possibility –now lost for good– for representing our country in the pavilion. He showed his sculpture *El norte de la tormenta* (North of the Storm), an unsettling circular work in iron accompanied by a 45 rpm recording with the same title by composer Alberto Iglesias.

The Spanish artists who took part in the 1988 Aperto were: neo-conceptualist Federico Guzmán; Juan Carlos Savater, at the time a sort of modern post-Romantic landscape artist; and sculptor Ricardo Cotanda, whose work was reminiscent of *povera* with an industrial vein –three very different choices that reflected the eclecticism of the post-modern era that was soon to disappear. Pepe Espaliu, Pello Irazu and Perejaume took part in the following *Aperto* in 1990. These multifaceted artists had in common

The artists were not chosen on the basis of theme; on the contrary, we might say that it was the sum total of their exhibits that conveyed a vision of the contemporary art world

a high degree of conceptuality despite their very different poetic language. In this Aperto, the star of which was Jeff Koons, who staged a visual spectacle with Ilona, the Spanish artists, who introduced sculpture together with drawings and (in the case of Perejaume) photo assemblages, provided a thought-provoking counterpoint.

Pep Agut and Marcelo Expósito took part in the 1993 Aperto, the last before the section disappeared in the following Biennale. Expósito, an experimental artist with a critical intent, presented –at a time when video had not yet inundated international exhibitions– a work in this medium, *Tierra prometida* (Promised Land), from 1992. Pep Agut, who had shifted from painting to other fields, combined photography and composition using various materials. Another participant in this Biennale was an "outsider" with a Spanish passport: the Colombian-born architect and sculptor Carlos Blanco whose works, like marquees that contained a surprise, were erected in various parts of Venice, as they had been at Documenta in Kassel the previous year. Although the Aperto did not return as such, from 1997 onwards the *Corderie* played a somewhat similar role, though without the age barriers. That year only one Spanish sculptor took part in this section: once again the sculptor Juan Muñoz, whose work, which had embarked on a course of unstoppable development, was linked to the sculptures he had shown at the Palacio Velázquez some months previously. He participated in the exhibition organised by Germano Celant, with three significant sculpture groups.

In 1999 Antoni Abad and Ana Laura Aláez were chosen for the APERTuttto, which has been rescued by Szeemann –albeit with the aforementioned differences– and physically occupied a larger area, taking over adjoining buildings which preserved the flavour of the early years and provided over ten thousand square metres of breathing space. Aláez, who took part the following year in the Spanish pavilion, presented her *proyecto para estudio móvil para una artista del nuevo milenio* (project for mobile studio for an artist of the new millennium), a construction in which, once again, the artist was the protagonist. The works of Antoni Abad, three video projections, went down very well. The unsettling tightrope walker of *Últimos deseos* (Last Wishes) and the contradictory rat of *Love Story*, eating a romantic dessert, were a spectacular sight with the city of Venice as a backdrop.

After APERTutto Szeemann –who was appointed curator of the Biennale again in 2001– programmed *Plateau of Humankind*. The artists were not chosen on the basis of theme; on the contrary, we might say that it was the sum total of their exhibits that conveyed a vision of the contemporary art world. The Spanish artists selected on this occasion were Cristina García Rodero and Eulalia Valldosera and also Santiago Sierra, who went on to be the sole representative of the Spanish pavilion in 2003. On two successive occasions (first with Ana Laura Aláez and now with Sierra), being invited directly by the Biennale was a stepping stone for becoming "official" Spanish representatives. This artist staged one of his well known "remunerations," paying various people to have their hair dyed blonde. The photographer Cristina García Rodero contributed her enriching viewpoint with her photos of bodies, mud and water. Valldosera, for her part, adapted one of her ghoulishly everyday installations to Venice.

And this brings us back to 2003, the year of the fiftieth Biennale. In addition to the work of Santiago Sierra, which will be shown in the pavilion, Spain has staged the “Bac Boys” exhibition in which seven artists, using video as their medium, will erect installations in seven different areas, outside the *Giardini* Two are to be earlier works and one will be designed especially for Venice.

As we have seen, for Spanish art the Biennale is not confined to the walls of its pavilion; on occasions the artists included in the exhibitions organised by the Biennale (both those that pay tribute to highly prestigious artists and those that support new artists) have attracted the attention of both public and critics outside these walls. And so it should be, as it is a means of showing a complementary view of our country's art.

FINAL NOTES

These notes refer only to literal quotations expressly included in the book, although references to some significant publications which are mentioned and which contribute to an understanding of the history of the Biennale also appear. They are introduced in order. Use has been made above all of the documentation on the Biennale in the Archivio Storico delle Arte Contemporanee (ASAC) in Venice, especially the catalogues of all the exhibitions –both the general catalogues of the Biennale and the specific ones on the Spanish participation. We have also used as a basis our own book: *España en la Bienal de Venecia, 1895-1976.* We thank Manuel García for the documentation that he provided on the 1976 Biennale.

The Venice Biennale: Data for a Story

Alessandro Stella: *Cronistoria della Esposizione Internazionale d'Arte della città di Venezia.* 1895-1912. Venice, Fabris [1914].

F.T. Marinetti: *Discorso futurista di Marinetti ai veneziani,* July 8, 1910.

P. Orsi, A. Maraini, R. Bazzoni: "Programma," *XVII^a^ Esposizione Biennale Internazionale d'Arte-1930.* Venice.

Nino Barbantini: "Il laberinto e la strada," in *Biennali.* Venice, 1945.

E. Zorzi, R. Bazzoni, A. Maraini. "Regolamento per i premi," *XVII^a^ Esposizione Biennale Internazionale d'Arte-1930.* Venice.

G. Ponti: "Prefazione," *XXIV^a^ Esposizione Biennale Internazionale d'Arte-1948.*

Alan R. Solomon: "Stati Uniti d'America," *XXXII^a^ Esposizione Biennale Internazionale d'Arte-1964.* Venice.

Alberto Moravia: "Nata della contestazione. Dialogo tra Alberto Moravia e Carlo Ripa di Meana," in *Biennali 1974-1978. Cronache della Nuova Biennale.* Milan, Electa, 1978.

The Mask and the Reality: Spanish Art at the Venice Biennale

The First Biennales: 1895-1914

Valeriano Bozal: *Historia del arte en España.* T. II. Madrid, Istmo, 1977.

Juan Antonio Gaya Nuño: *Ars Hispaniae*, vol. XIX. Madrid, Plus Ultra, 1966.

Jean François Rodríguez: *Picasso alla Biennale di Venezia (1905-1948).* Padua, Cleup, 1993.

Arturo Lancellotti: *Le Biennali veneziane dell'ante guerra.* Milan, Alfieri & Lacoris.

From the Post-War Period to Wartime: 1920-1936

Nino Barbantini: *Biennali.* Venice, 1945.

Arturo Lancellotti: *Le Biennali veneziane de dopo guerra.* Rome, Prof. P. Maglione Succ. di E. Loescher.

Marco Mulazzani:*I Padiglioni della Biennale Venezia 1887-1993.* Milan, Electa, 1993.

José Francés: *XIX ^a^Esposizione Biennale Internazionale d'Arte-1934. Padiglione della Spagna, 1934.* Venice.

José López Rey: *XX^a^ Esposizione Biennale Internazionale d'Arte-1936. Padiglione della Spagna,* 1936. Venice.

The Wartime Biennales: 1938-1942

Antonio Maraini: "Introduzione," *XXI^a^ Esposizione Biennale Internazionale d'Arte-1938,* Venice.

Alexandre Cirici: *La estética del franquismo,* Barcelona, Gustavo Gili, 1977.

Eugenio d'Ors: *XXI^a^ Esposizione Biennale Internazionale d'Arte-1938, Padiglione della Spagna,* 1938. Venice.

Luis Felipe Vivanco: "Humillación a la pintura," in *Vértice*, no. 12, VII, 1938.

Marqués de Lozoya: *XXII^a^ Esposizione Biennale Internazionale d'Arte-1940 Padiglione della Spagna.* Venice.

Years in the Wilderness: 1948-1956

Renato Guttuso: "Pablo Picasso," *XXIV^a^ Esposizione Biennale Internazionale d'Arte,* 1948, Venice.

Alexandre Cirici: *La estética del franquismo,* Barcelona, Gustavo Gili, 1977.

Carlos Areán: *30 años de arte español*, Madrid, Guadarrama, 1972.

Carlos Cañal: *XXV Exposición Bienal de Arte en Venecia. Pabellón español.* Madrid, Directorate General for Cultural Relations, 1950.

Delfín Colomé: "La Bienal de Venecia en tiempos de Franco," in *Ars Mediterranea*, VIII, 1995.

Ángel Llorente: *Arte e ideología en el franquismo (1936-1951),* Madrid, Visor, 1995.

Enrique Lafuente Ferrari: *Catálogo del pabellón español en la Exposición Bienal de Venecia*, Madrid, Directorate General for Cultural Relations, 1952.

José Camón Aznar: *Artistas españoles en la XXVII Exposición Internacional Bienal de Arte de Venecia, Pabellón de España.* Madrid, Directorate General for Cultural Relations, 1954.

Marqués de Lozoya: in *Artistas españoles en la XXVIII Exposición Bienal Internacional de Arte de Venecia.* Pabellón de España, Madrid, Directorate General for Cultural Relations, 1956.

Luis Felipe Vivanco: in *Artistas españoles en la XXVIII Exposición Bienal Internacional de Arte de Venecia.* Pabellón de España, Madrid, Directorate General for Cultural Relations, 1956.

The "González Robles Era" and Ceferino Moreno's Participation: 1958-1972

Virgilio Guzzi: *Arte d'oggi. Storia di 8 Biennali.* Rome, Canesi, 1964.

Tomàs Llorens: "Vanguardia artística y política en la dictadura franquista: los años sesenta," in *España. Vanguardia artística y realidad social: 1936-1976.* Barcelona, Gustavo Gili, 1976.

Luis González Robles: *España en la XXIX Bienal de Venecia*, Madrid, Directorate General for Cultural Relations, 1958.

Vicente Aguilera Cerni: "España en la XXIX Bienal de Venecia," in *Punta Europa*, no. 33, September 1958.

Vicente Aguilera Cerni: "La Bienal entre dos fuegos," in *Revista*, no. 337, September 27 / 3 October, 1958.

Manuel Rivera, in an interview with J. Hierro: "Noticia de la Bienal de Venecia," in *La estafeta literaria*, no. 136, July 5, 1958.

Luis González Robles: *España en la XXX Bienal de Venecia.* Madrid, Directorate General for Cultural Relations, 1960.

Alfonso Sastre: "Arte como construcción," in *Acento cultural*, no. 2, 1957.

Luis González Robles: *España en la XXXI Bienal de Venecia,* Madrid, Directorate General for Cultural Relations, 1962.

Luis González Robles: *España en la XXXII Bienal de Venecia,* Madrid, Directorate General for Cultural Relations, 1964.

Vicente Aguilera Cerni: *Tras la XXXII Bienal de Venecia*, in *Suma y Sigue del Arte Contemporáneo*, no 7 / 8, 1965.

Genovés: *España en la XXXIII Bienal de Venecia*, Madrid, Directorate General for Cultural Relations, 1966.

Luis González Robles: *España en la XXXIII Bienal de Venecia*, Madrid, Directorate General for Cultural Relations, 1966.

Delfín Colomé: "Las bienales en tiempos de Franco," in *Ars Mediterranea*, VIII, 1995.

Luis González Robles: *España en la XXXIV Bienal de Venecia*, Madrid, Directorate General for Cultural Relations, 1968.

The 1976 Biennale: Spain. The Artistic Avant-Garde and Social Reality, 1936-1976

Letter from Luis González Robles to Carlo Ripa di Meana, reproduced in *Comunicación*, no. 31-32.

Carlo Ripa di Meana: "Il caso Arroyo e la risposta della Biennale antifascista," in *La Biennale*, Venice, October 26, 1974.

Raffaele de Grada: Speech at the International Congress of the New Biennale, May 30-31, 1975, *Minutes of the Congress*. ASAC, Venice.

Tomàs Llorens: Speech at the "Convegno Internazionale Progettuale," July 24-27, 1975, *Minutes of the Congress*, ASAC, Venice.

Luigi Nono, in an interview with Sandro Meccoli: "Alla Biennale c'è la febbre spagnola," in *Corriere della Sera*, February 25, 1976.

Vicente Aguilera Cerni: "La Bienal 76: ¿un ultraje a la cultura democrática española?" in *Guadalimar*, no. 13, May 10, 1976.

Carlo Ripa di Meana, in an interview with Rossend Domenech: "La Bienal recorda els 40 anys de la guerra d'Espanya," in *Avui*, August 13, 1976.

List submitted by Massimo Andrioli to the president of the Biennale. Files of M. García. José Luis Orosa: "Socialistas y comunistas desean que España no participe oficialmente en la Bienal de Venecia," in *Informaciones*, February 28, 1976.

Antonio Saura, in an interview with Ramón Chao: "Una exposición desmitificadora," in *Triunfo*, no. 700, June 26, 1976.

Vicente Aguilera Cerni: "Bienal. Aguilera Cerni responde a Saura," in *Triunfo*, no. 703, July 17, 1976.

Biel Mesquida, in *El viejo topo*, no. 2, November 1976.

Valeriano Bozal, Tomàs Llorens et al, "Vanguardia artística y política en la dictadura franquista: los años sesenta," in *España, Vanguardia artística y realidad social: 1936-1976*. Barcelona, Gustavo Gili, 1976. (Base text for the second part of this chapter).

The Biennales of Democracy

José María Ballester: *La Biennale di Venezia*. Milan, Electa, 1978, p. 197.

Ceferino Moreno: *Biennale di Venezia '80*, Ministry of Foreign Affairs, 1980.

Luis González Robles: *España en la Bienal de Venecia '82*. Ministry of Foreign Affairs, 1982.

Francisco Calvo Serraller: "Una nueva generación para una nueva época", in *España en la XLII Bienal de Venecia*, 1986, Ministry of Foreign Affairs-Ministry of Culture, 1986.

Victoria Combalía. "El porqué de nuestra selección," in *España en la XLVII Bienal de Venecia*, Ministry of Foreign Affairs, 1997.

Estrella de Diego: "Viaje a Venecia" in *España en la XLIX Bienal de Venecia*, Ministry of Foreign Affairs, 2001.

Chronology 1895 — 2003

Curatorship and Participants in the Spanish Pavilion at the Venice Biennale

During the initial Biennales there was no such thing as a curator. There were two procedures for exhibiting: direct invitation from the Biennale, or following selection by a panel from among the works submitted. However, this panel performed its task mainly in connection with the works of Italians not directly invited, although on occasions it also discriminated against those by artists of other countries. But usually the selection of foreigners was made by a committee, in the beginning called a "sponsorship committee." Later the position of person in charge of an international salon was introduced, while the position of curator was finally established –on the part of Spain– in 1920. At times the curator's duties were diluted within a larger committee.

In the Spanish case, there was no record during some of the first Biennales of what the procedure for the choice of artists was, although probably it would have been done by Italy with the collaboration of some Spanish artists with links to that country.

The list of participating artists was drawn up from those who appeared in the catalogues of the Biennale itself. Initially we gave the names both of those in the Spanish gallery and in the international ones. At the first exhibitions, Spain did not publish catalogues, and therefore we resorted to the Biennale's general catalogues. Some of the artists included as representing Spain had practically no links to our country, although they did represent it at one time or another.

1895

Spanish members of the Biennale Sponsorship Committee:

José Benlliure
José Jiménez Aranda
Joaquín Sorolla
José Villegas

Participating artists:

José Benlliure
Mariano Benlliure
Gonzalo Bilbao
José García y Ramos
José Garnelo Alca
José Jiménez Aranda
Emilio Sala
Salvador Sánchez Barbudo
Joaquín Sorolla
José Villegas

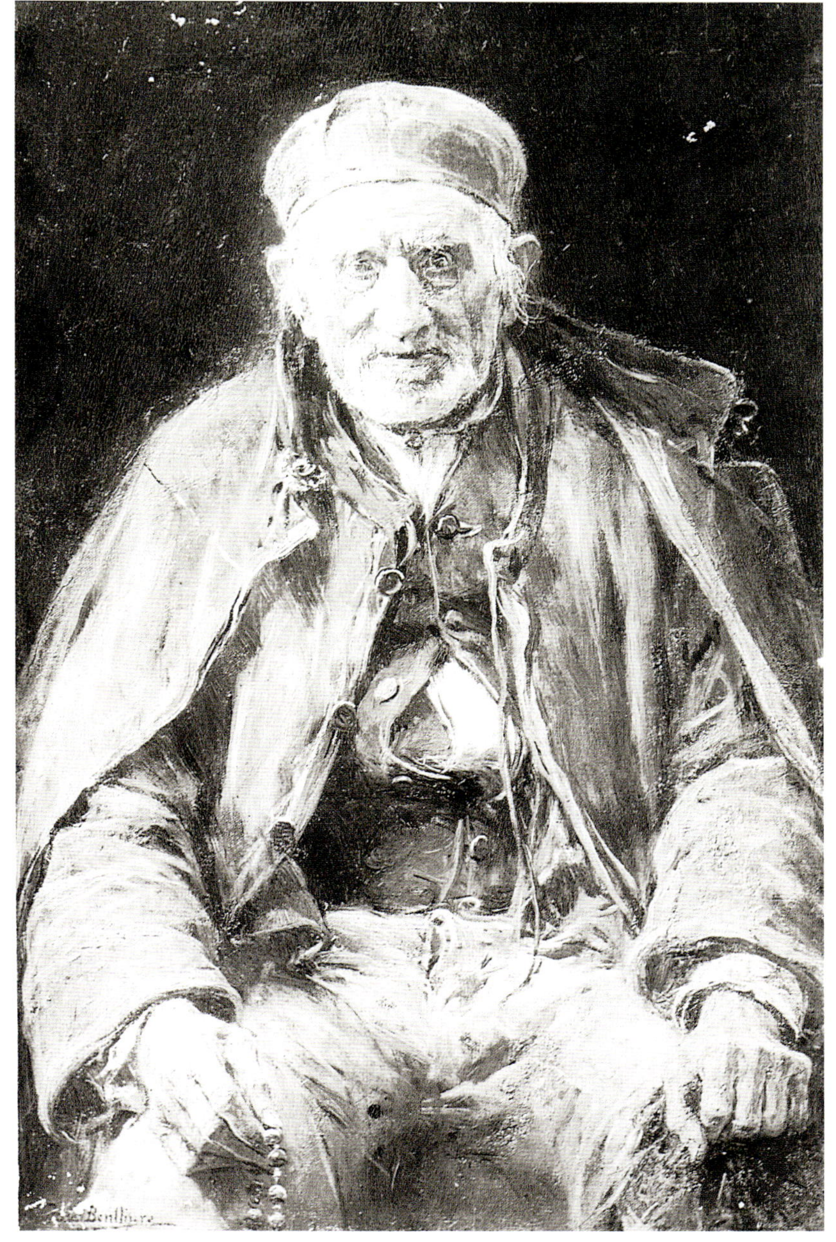

José Benlliure
"Viejo en oración" (Old Man in Prayer)
Photograph made available by the Casa Museo Benlliure

1897

Spanish members of the Biennale Sponsorship Committee:
José Benlliure
José Jiménez Aranda
Francisco Pradilla
Joaquín Sorolla
José Villegas

Participating artists:
José Benlliure
Antonio Fabrès
José Garnelo Alda
José Jiménez Aranda
Luis Jiménez
Ricardo de los Ríos
Salvador Sánchez Barbudo
Joaquín Sorolla
Ramón Tusquets
José Villegas

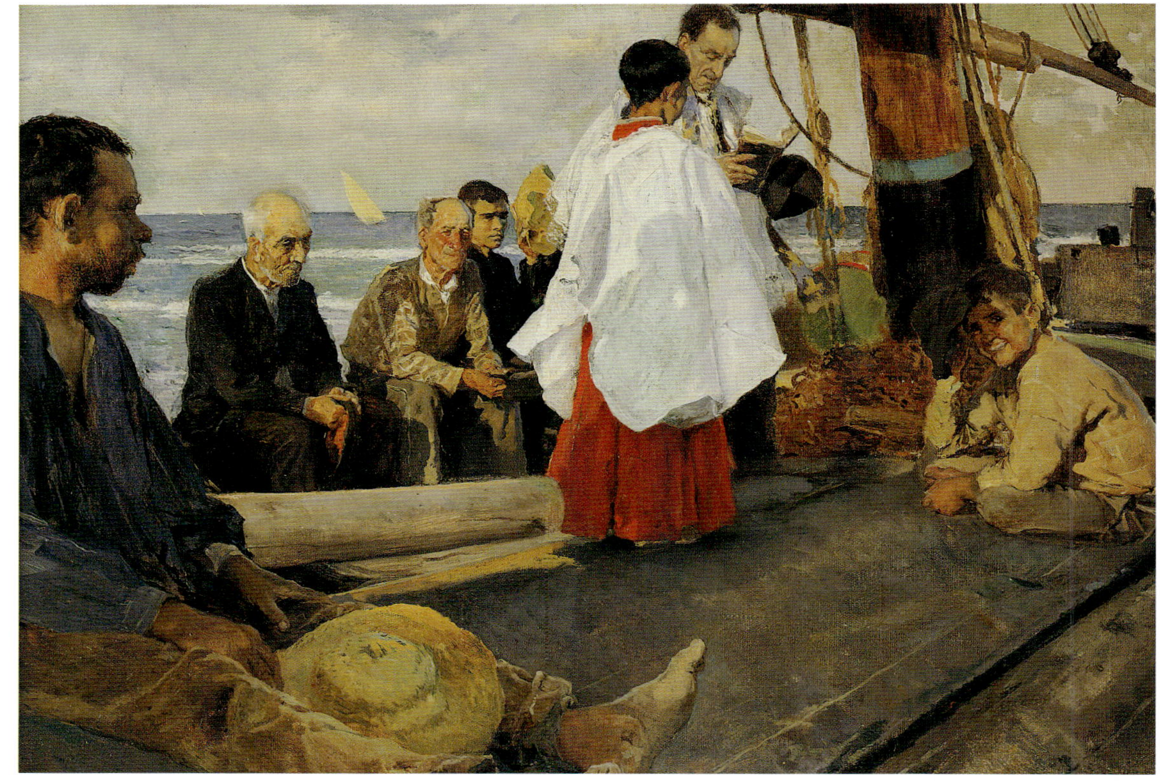

Joaquín Sorolla
"La bendición de la barca" (The Blessing of the Boat)
Asturias Fine Arts Museum

III Biennale

1899

Spanish members of the Biennale Sponsorship Committee:

José Benlliure
José Jiménez Aranda
Francisco Pradilla
Joaquín Sorolla
José Villegas

Participating artists:

Gustavo Bacarisas
José Benlliure
Mariano Fortuny y Madrazo
Joaquín Sorolla

IV Biennale

1901

Participating artists:

Mariano Benlliure
Joaquín Sorolla

1903

Participating artists:
Hermenegildo Anglada Camarasa
José Benlliure
Antonio de la Gándara
Joaquín Sorolla
Ignacio Zuloaga

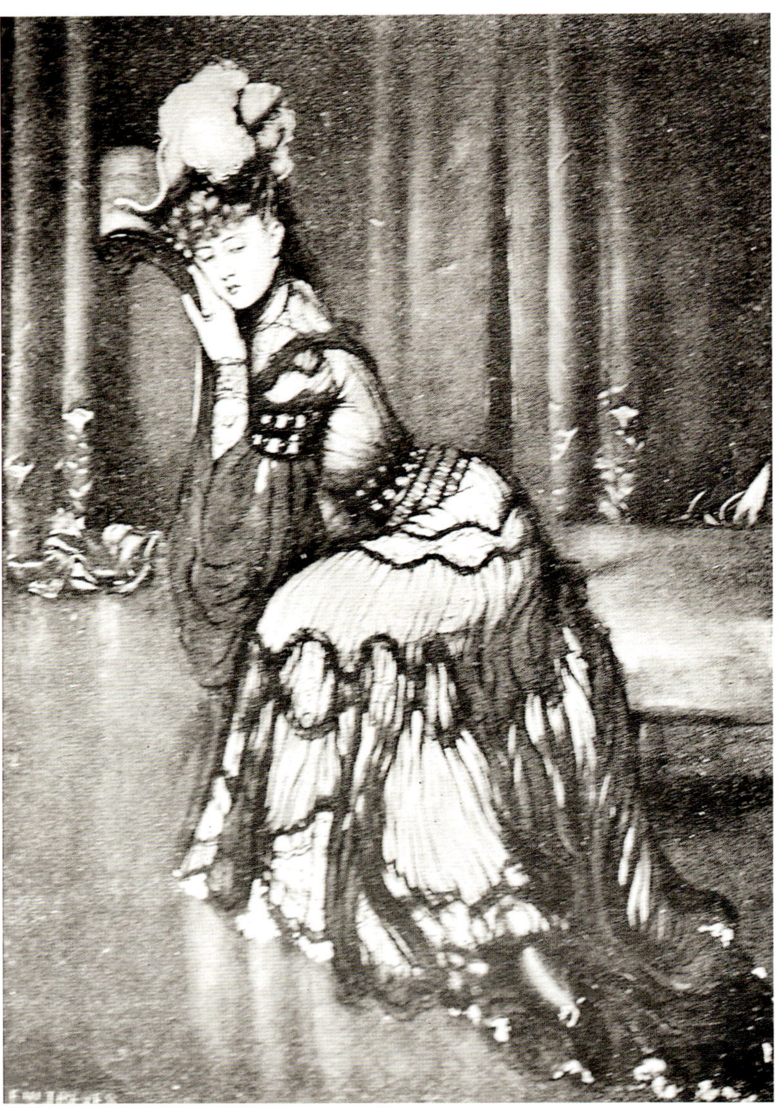

Antonio de la Gándara
"Retrato de la Señora Salvador" (Portrait of Lady Salvador)
Italian Catalogue

1905

Participated in the selection:
Ignacio Zuloaga, who formed part of the International Salons' Organising Committee and was in charge of proposing Spanish artists

Participating artists:
Fernando Álvarez de Sotomayor
Hermenegildo Anglada Camarasa
Gustavo Bacarisas
Manuel Benedito
Gonzalo Bilbao
Miguel Blay y Fábregas
Ricardo Canals
Ramón Casas
Eduardo Chicharro
Pío Collivadino (Argentina)
Francisco Durrio
Antonio de la Gándara
Francisco Iturrino
Luis Jiménez
Ángel Larroque y Echeverría
Manuel Losada
Enrique Marín e Higuero
Joaquín Mir Frinxet
Nemesio de Mogrobejo
Enrique Paternina García
Darío de Regoycs
Santiago Rusiñol
Joaquín Sorolla
Pablo Uranga
Ignacio Zuloaga

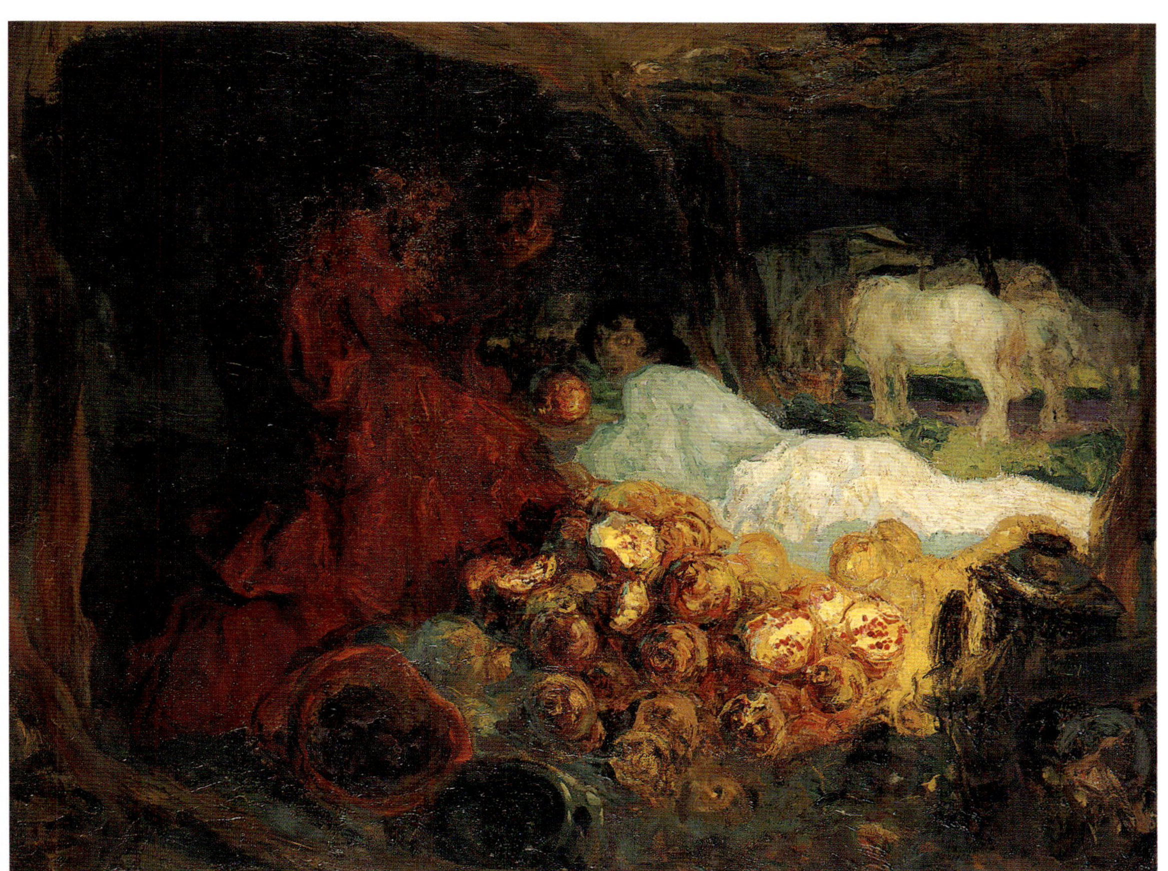

Hermenegildo Anglada Camarasa
"La gitana de las granadas" (The Gypsy of the Pomegranates)
Reina Sofía National Art Centre Museum, Madrid

VII Biennale

1907

Participating artists:
Hermenegildo Anglada Camarasa
Gustavo Bacarisas
Antonio de la Gándara
William Laparra
Santiago Rusiñol

IX Biennale

1910

Participating artists:
José Benlliure
Eduardo Chicharro y Aguera
Antonio Fabrès
José María López Mezquita
Enrique Martínez-Cubells
Antonio Ortíz Echagüe
José María Rodríguez-Acosta
José Ramón Zaragoza
Ángel Zárraga
Valentín de Zubiaurre
Ramón de Zubiaurre
Ignacio Zuloaga

1912

Participating artists:
Ángel Zárraga

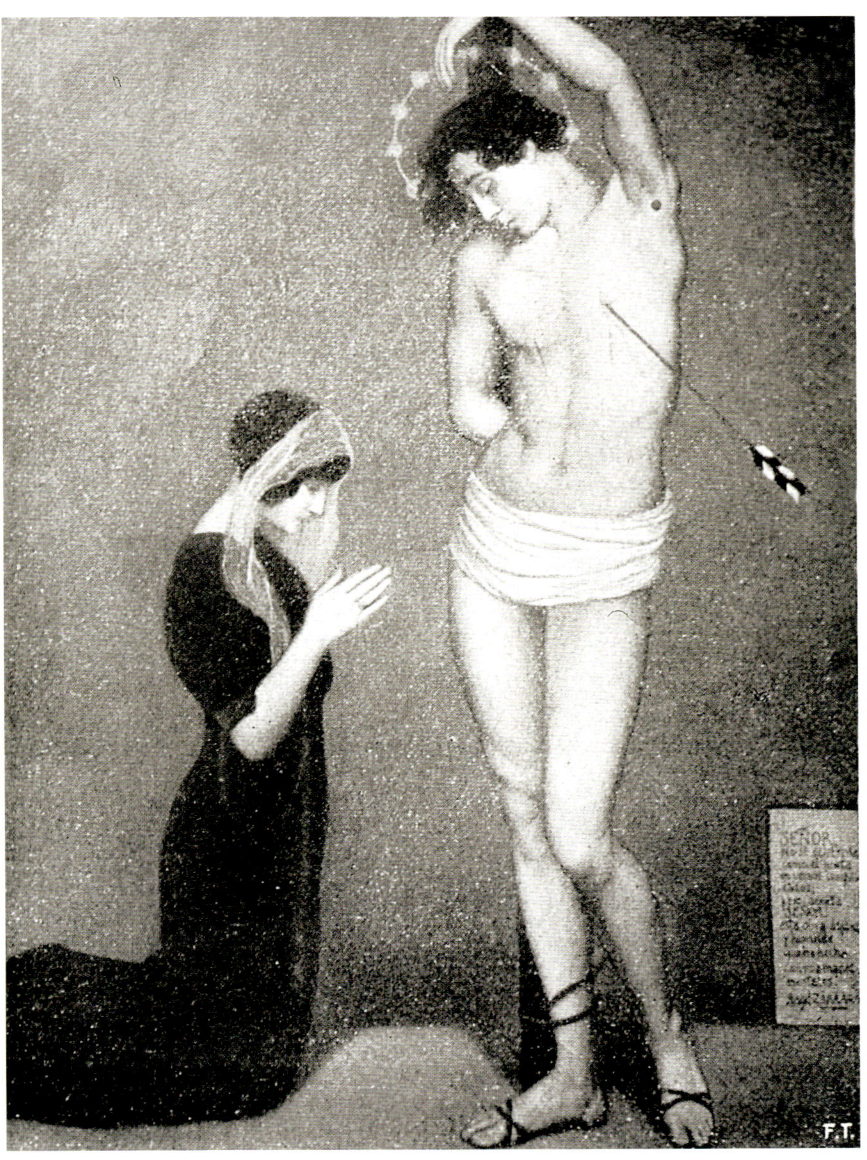

Ángel Zárraga
"Exvoto"
Italian Catalogue

1914

Participating artists:
Hermenegildo Anglada Camarasa (solo exhibition)
Mariano Benlliure
Manuel Benedito Vives
José Benlliure
Ramón Casas
Eduardo Chicharro
Eugenio Hermoso
José María López Mezquita
José María Rodríguez-Acosta
Santiago Rusiñol
Joaquín Sorolla
Ángel Zárraga
Ramón de Zubiaurre
Valentín de Zubiaurre

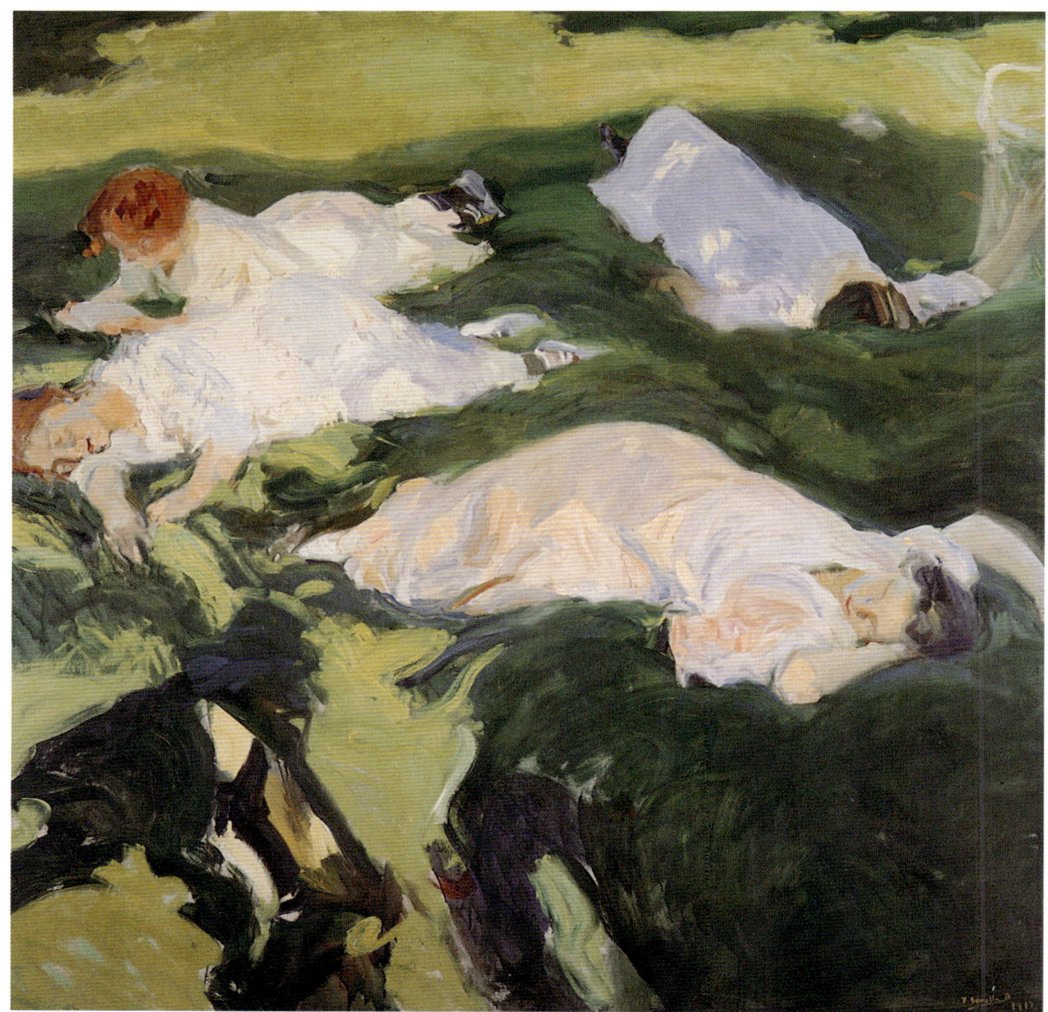

Joaquín Sorolla
"La siesta" (The Nap)
Sorolla Museum

1920

According to different sources, the following participated in the selection:
Mariano Fortuny y Madrazo
Vittorio Pica

Participating artist:
Federico Beltrán Masses

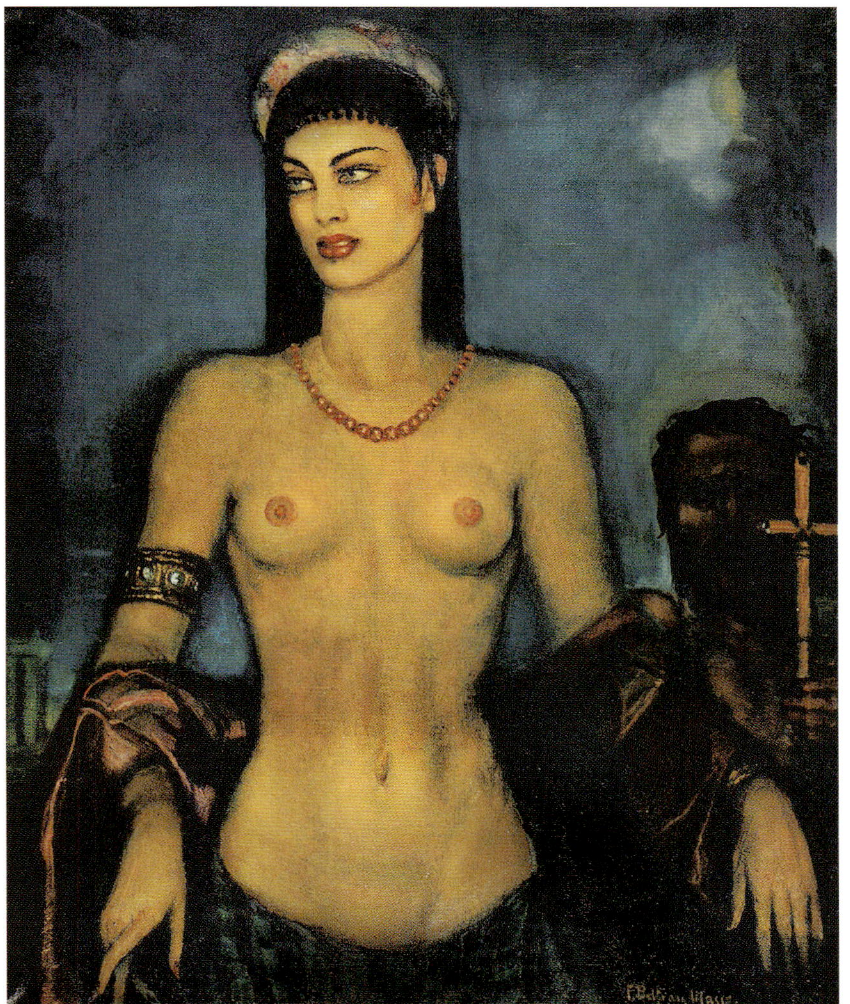

Federico Beltrán Mases
"Salomé"
Art Nouveau and Art Decó Museum, Casa Lis, Manuel Ramos Andrade Foundation

XIII Biennale

1922

According to different sources, the following participated in the selection:

Mariano Benlliure
Mariano Fortuny y Madrazo

Participating artists:

José Aguiar
José Benlliure
Gonzalo Bilbao
Joaquín Claret
Eduardo Chicharro
Mariano Fortuny
Mariano Fortuny y Madrazo
José Garnelo Alda
Eugenio Hermoso
José María López Mezquita
Eliseo Meifrén
Joaquín Mir Frinxet
Julio Moisés
José Moreno Carbonero
Antonio Ortiz Echagüe
José Pinazo
Nicolás Raurich
Santiago Rusiñol
Marceliano Santamaría
José G. Solana
Fernando de Sotomayor
Daniel Vázquez Díaz
José Ramón Zaragoza
Ramón de Zubiaurre
Valentín de Zubiaurre

XIV Biennale

1924

Curator:

Mariano Fortuny y Madrazo

Participating artists:

Fernando Álvarez de Sotomayor
Emiliano Barral
Manuel Benedito Vives
José Benlliure
Mariano Benlliure
José Bermejo Sobera
Gonzalo Bilbao
Ramón Casas
José Capuz
Manuel Castro Gil
José Clará
Eduardo Chicharro
José Chicharro
Augusto Colom Juan
Juan Cristóbal
Roberto Domingo
Rafael Forns
Mariano Fortuny y Madrazo
Enrique Galwey García
Aurelio García Lesmes
Emilio García Martínez
Luis Gil de Vicario
Eugenio Hermoso
Miguel Hernández Nájera
Moisés de Huerta
Luis Huidobro
Mateo Inurria Sainosa
Fernando Labrada
Francisco Llorens Díaz
José María López Mezquita
Victorio Macho
Gustavo de Maeztu

->

Enrique Martínez Cubells
Eduardo Martínez Vázquez
Eliseo Meifrén
Luis Menéndez Pidal
Joaquín Mir Frinxet
Julio Moisés
José Mongrell y Torrent
Antonio Muñoz Degrain
Eduardo Navarro
Néstor
Leandro Oroz Lacalle
José Pedraza Ostos
Enrique Pérez Comendador
José Pinazo
Nicanor Piñole
Buenaventura Puig y Perucho
Nicolás Raurich
Ricardo de los Ríos
Ramón Roca
José María Rodríguez Acosta
Santiago Rusiñol
José G. Solana
Rigoberto Soler
Joaquín Sorolla
Quintín de Torre
Ricardo Urgell y Carreras
Ricardo Verdugo Landi
Julio Vicent Mengual
José Ramón Zaragoza
Valentín de Zubiaurre

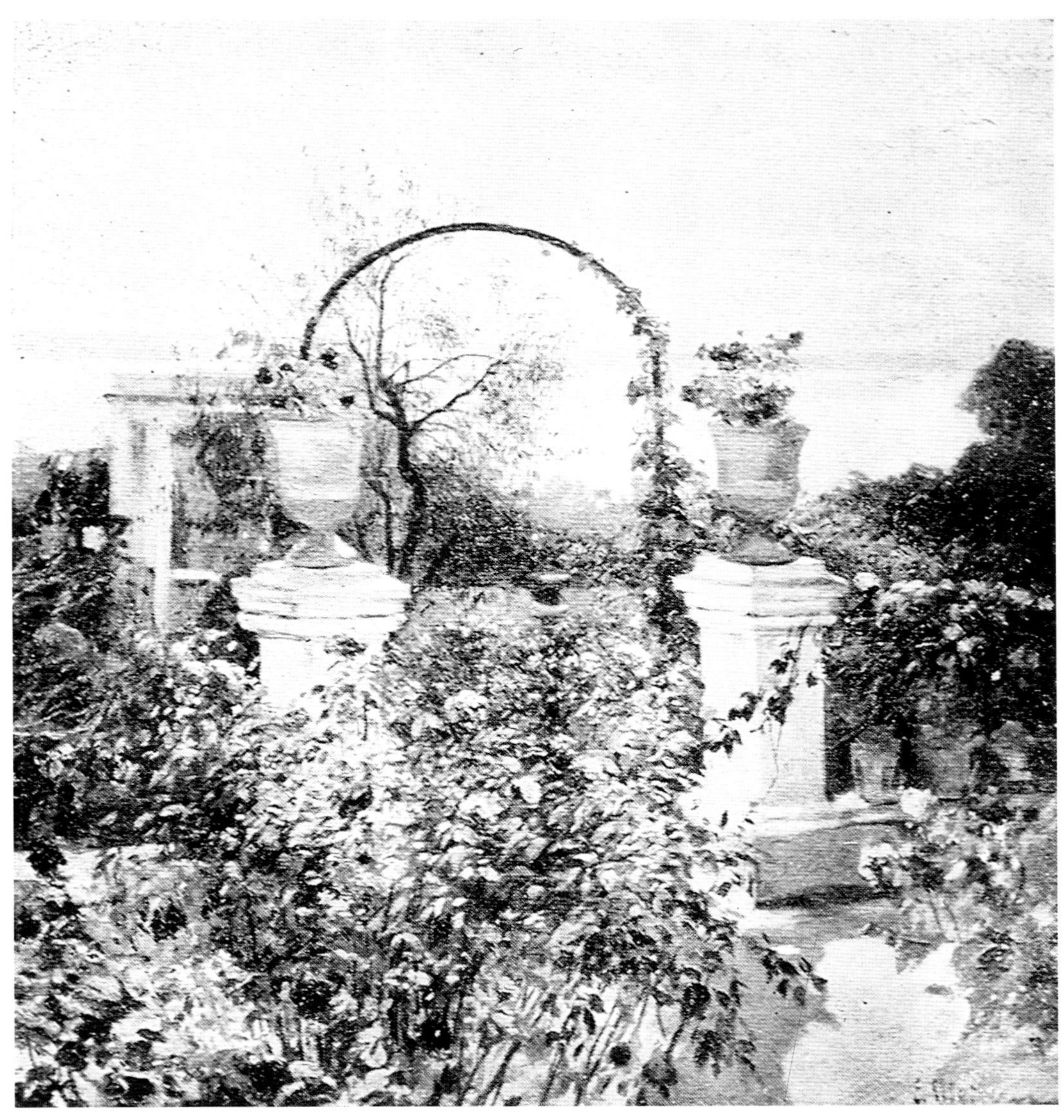

Eliseo Meifrén
"Desde mi casa" (From my House)
Italian Catalogue

1926

Curator:
Mariano Fortuny y Madrazo

Participating artists:
Juan Adsuara
Pedro Antonio
Octavio Bianqui y Sánchez
Santiago Bonome
Enrique Bráñez
José Capuz
Raimundo Castro Cires
Manuel Castro Gil
José Clará
José Cruz Herrera
Miguel Cruz Martín
Ángel Ferrant Vázquez
Ricardo Font Estors
José Garnelo Alda
Luis Gil de Vicario
Eugenio Hermoso Martínez
Moisés Huerta
Fernando Labrada
Francisco Llorens Díaz
Eduardo Martínez Vázquez
Francisco Mateos
Eliseo Meifrén
Manuel Menéndez y Domínguez
Julio Moisés
Gabriel Morcillo Raya
José Moreno Carbonero
Antonio Muñoz Degrain
Eduardo Navarro
Vicente Navarro Romero
Fructuoso Orduña
Leandro Oroz Lacalle
José Ortells López
Juan Palacios
Ceferino Palencia y Álvarez Tubau
Bernardino de Pantorba
José Pedraza Ostos
Ignacio Pinazo
José Planes
Francisco Pons Arnau
Gregorio Prieto
César Prieto Martínez
Julio Prieto Nespereira
Carlos dal Re
Francisco Reyes Pérez
José Ramón Zaragoza
Marceliano Santamaría
Vicente Santos Sáinz
Enrique Simonet
Joaquín Sorolla
Pedro Torre-Isunza
Daniel Vázquez Díaz
Ricardo Verdugo Landi
Carlos Verger Fioretti
Julio Vicent Mengual
Valentín de Zubiaurre

1928

Curator:
Mariano Fortuny y Madrazo

Participating artists:
Juan Adsuara
Fernando Álvarez de Sotomayor
Gustavo Bacarisas (solo exhibition)
Manuel Beneditc
José Benlliure
Gonzalo Bilbao
Santiago Bonome
Francisco Broch y Llop
Tomás Campuzano
Manuel Castro Gil
José Clará
Juan Espina
Francisco Esteve Botey
Rogelio de Egusquiza
Mariano Fortuny y Madrazo
Eugenio Hermoso
Miguel Hernández Nájera
Fernando Labrada
Francisco Llorens
Eliseo Meifrén
Gabriel Morcillo
Fructuoso Orduña
Leandro Oroz
Antonio Ortiz Echagüe (solo exhibition)
Nicolás Raurich
Marceliano Santamaría
José G. Solana (solo exhibition)
Joaquín Sunyer
Quintín de Torre
Daniel Vázquez Díaz
Ricardo Verdugo Landi
Julio Vicent
Valentín de Zubiaurre

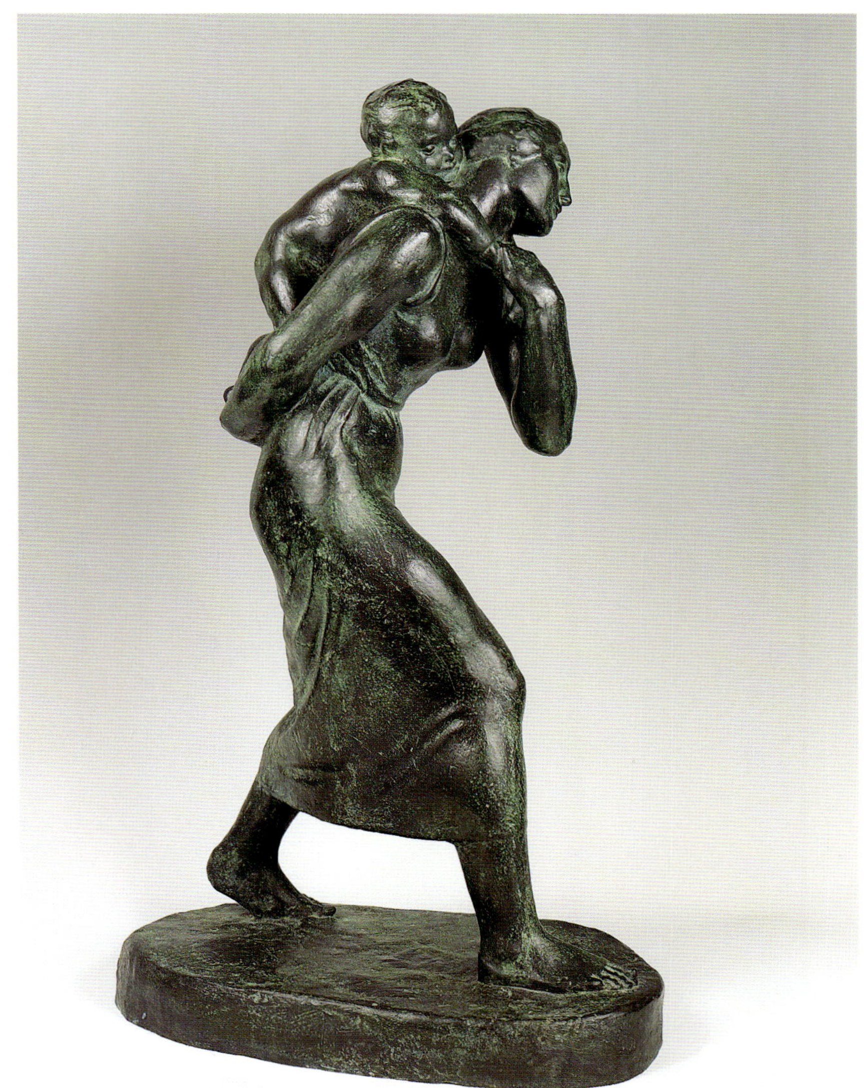

Juan Adsuara
"La carga" (The Load)
Private collection. Photograph made available by the Castellón Fine Arts Museum

1930

Curator:
Mariano Fortuny y Madrazo

Participating artists:
Juan Adsuara
Pedro Antonio
Ricardo Baroja Nessi
Luis Benedito Vives
José Benlliure
Mariano Benlliure
Gonzalo Bilbao
Ismael Blat
Enrique Bráñez de Hoyos
Guido Caprotti
Enrique Casanovas Roi
Pedro Casas Abarca
Manuel Castro Gil
José Clará
Lorenzo Coullaut Valera
Eduardo Chicharro Aguera
José Dunyach
Juan Espina y Capo
Francisco Esteve Botey
Julio Moisés Fernández
Mariano Fortuny y Madrazo
Enrique Galwey García
José Garnelo Alda
Alfonso Grosso Sánchez
Francisco Guinart Candelich
Ernesto Gutiérrez Hernández
Eugenio Hermoso
Miguel Hernández Nájera
Fernando Labrada
José María López Mezquita
Francisco Llorens
Gustavo de Maeztu
Federico Mares Denlovol
Aniceto Marinas García
Enrique Martínez Cubells y Ruiz
Luis Masriera
Eliseo Meifrén Roig
Eduardo Navarro
Vicente Navarro Romero
Antonio Ollé Pinell
Leandro Oroz
José Pedraza Ostos
Enrique Pérez Comendador
José Pinazo
Nicanor Piñole y Rodríguez
Cecilio Plá
José Planes
Francisco Pons Arnau
Julio Prieto Nespereira
Nicolás Raurich
Santiago Rusiñol
Elías Salaverría
Marceliano Santamaría
José G. Solana
Francisco Soria Aedo
Quintín de Torre
Salvador Tuset
Ricardo Verdugo Landi
Julio Vicent Mengual
Valentín de Zubiaurre
Ramón de Zubiaurre

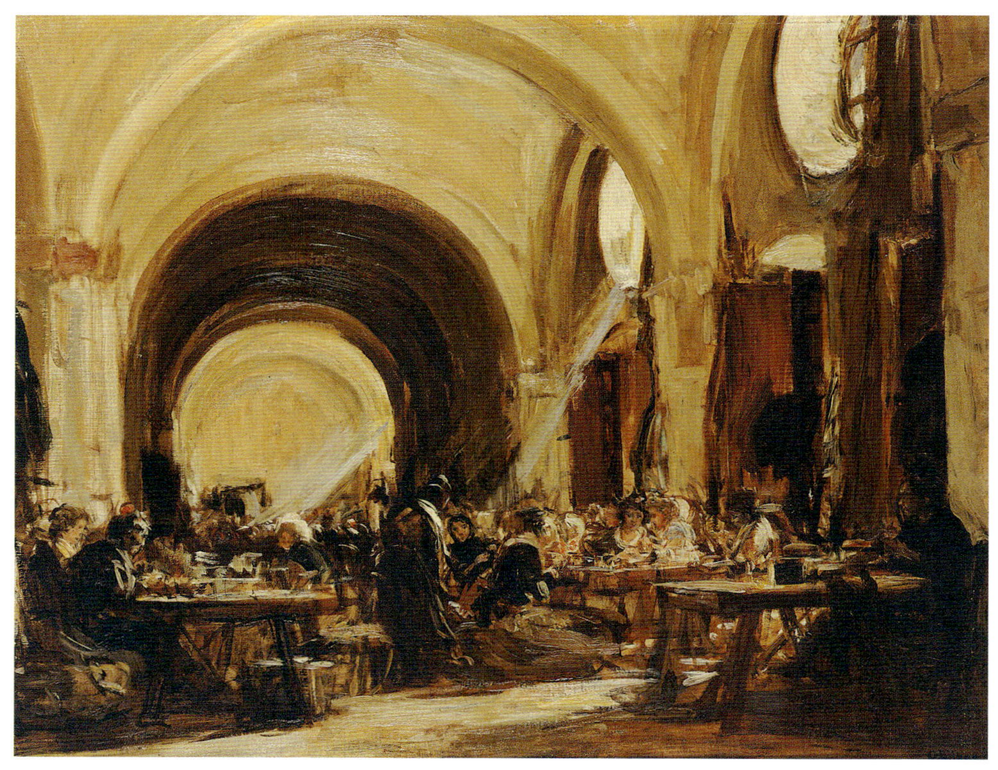

Gonzalo Bilbao
"Estudio Interior de fábricas de tabaco de Sevilla" (Inside the Seville Cigarette Factory)
Seville Museum of Fine Arts

1932

Curatorship:
Organising Committee presided by Ricardo de Orueta y Duarte
Vice-Chairman:
José Francés

Participating artists
José Aguiar
Emiliano Barral
Manuel Benedito
Alejandro Cabanyes
Manuel Colmeiro
Aurelio García Lesmes
Hipólito Hidalgo de Caviedes
Luis López Juan
Victorio Macho (solo exhibition)
Eduardo Martínez Vázquez
Joaquín Mir
Julio Moisés
Gabriel Morcillo
Antonio Muñoz Degrain (solo exhibition)
Timoteo Pérez Rubio
Cristóbal Ruiz
José G. Solana (solo exhibition)
Arturo Souto
Joaquín Sunyer
Joaquín Valverde
Evaristo Valle
Daniel Vázquez Díaz
Rosario de Velasco
J. Vila-Puig

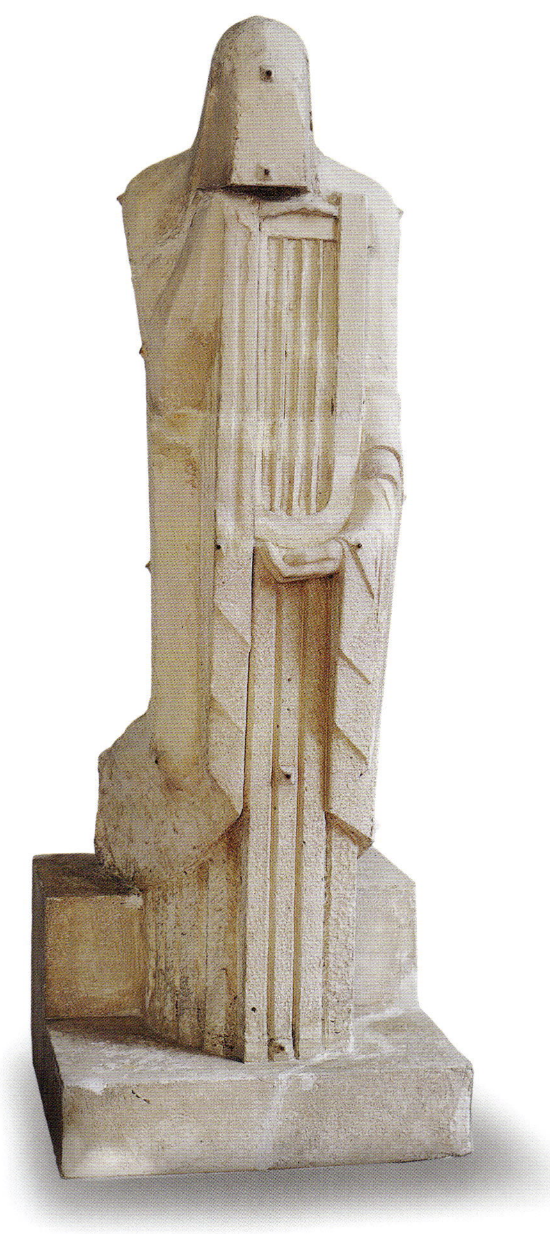

Victorio Macho
"Parca para la tumba de Tomás Morales" (*Parcae* for the Tomb of Tomás Morales)
Toledo Royal Foundation–Victorio Macho Museum, Toledo

1934

Curator:
M. López Mezquita

Participating artists:
Juan Adsuara
José Aguiar
Aurelio Arteta
Agustín Ballester
Manuel Benedito
Mariano Benlliure
Francisco Berges
José Bermejo
Gonzalo Bilbao
Enrique Bráñez
José Bueno
José Capuz (solo exhibition)
Manuel Castro Gil
José Clará
Juan Colom
Eduardo Chicharro
Roberto Fernández Valbuena
Mariano Fortuny
Mariano Fortuny y Madrazo
Francisco de Goya
Ernesto Gutiérrez
Eugenio Hermoso
Manuel Hugué
Francisco Labarta
Fernando Labrada
Vicente López
José María López Mezquita
Francisco Llorens
Federico Madrazo
Raimundo Madrazo
Enrique Martínez Cubells
Joaquín Mir (solo exhibition)
Julio Moisés Fernández
José Ortells
Pedro Pascual
Rafael Pellicer
Enrique Pérez Comendador
Francisco Pérez Mateos
Juan Bautista Porcar
Julio Prieto
José María Rodríguez Acosta
Eduardo Rosales
Marceliano Santamaría
José G. Solana
Joaquín Sorolla
Rafael Tejeo
Salvador Tuset
Joaquín Valverde
Daniel Vázquez Díaz
Rosario de Velasco
José de Zamora
Alberto Ziegler
Ramón de Zubiaurre
Valentín de Zubiaurre

*We have included in this list the artists on show at the International 19th-Century Portraits Exhibition in the Palazzo Centrale

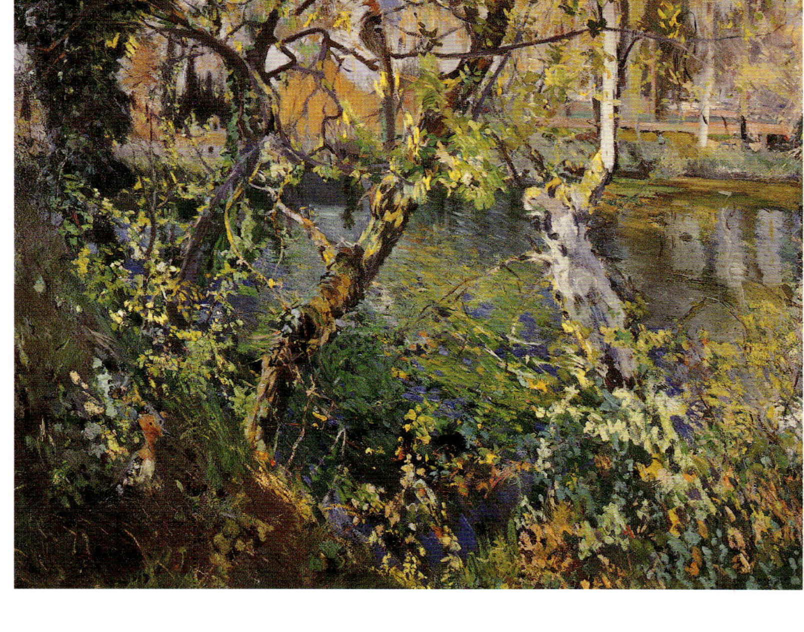

Joaquín Mir
"Aguas de Meguda" (Meguda Waters)

1936

Curator:
José López-Rey y Arrojo

Participating artists:
Juan Adsuara
Eva Aggerholm
Javier Alexandri
Fernando Álvarez de Sotomayor
José Amat
Emiliano Barral
Manuel Benedito
Mariano Benlliure
Gonzalo Bilbao
Fernando Briones
José Caballero y Caballero
Alejandro Cabanyes
Agapito Casas Abarca
Pedro Casas Abarca
Enrique Casanovas
Eduardo Chicharro
José Clará (solo exhibition)
Pedro Creixams
Jaime Durán
Apeles Fenosa
César Fernández Ardavín
Mariano Fortuny y Madrazo
José Frau
Margarita de Frau
Francisco Galí Fabra
Honorio García Condoy
José Garnelo
Balbino Giner
José Luis González Bernal
Emilio Grau Sala
Eugenio Hermoso
Hipólito Hidalgo de Caviedes
Manuel Hugué
Manuel Humbert
Francisco Labarta
Fernando Labrada
Genaro Lahuerta
Martin Llauradó
Rafael Llimona
Francisco Llorens
Maruja Mallo
Ernesto Maragall
Enrique Martínez Cubells y Ruiz
Eliseo Meifrén
Jaime Mercadé
Joaquín Mir
Jesús Molina
José Mongrell
Juan Antonio Morales Ruiz
José Moreno Carbonero
José Moreno Villa
Luis Muntané
Enrique Ochoa
Godofredo Ortega Muñoz
Benjamín Palencia
Ivo Pascual
Manuel Pascual
Enrique Pérez Comendador
Nicanor Piñole
José Planas-Doria
Juan Bautista Porcar
Gregorio Prieto
Pedro Pruna
Buenaventura Puig Perucho
Enrique Ricart
José María Rodríguez Acosta
Cristóbal Ruiz
Marceliano Santamaría
Ernesto Santasusagna
Ángeles Santos
Juan Serra
José G. Solana
Arturo Souto
Joaquín Sunyer
Julián Tellaeche
Gregorio Toledo
José Ucelay
Pedro de Valencia
Daniel Vázquez Díaz
Rosario de Velasco
Antonio Vila Arrufat
Juan Vila Puig
Valentín de Zubiaurre

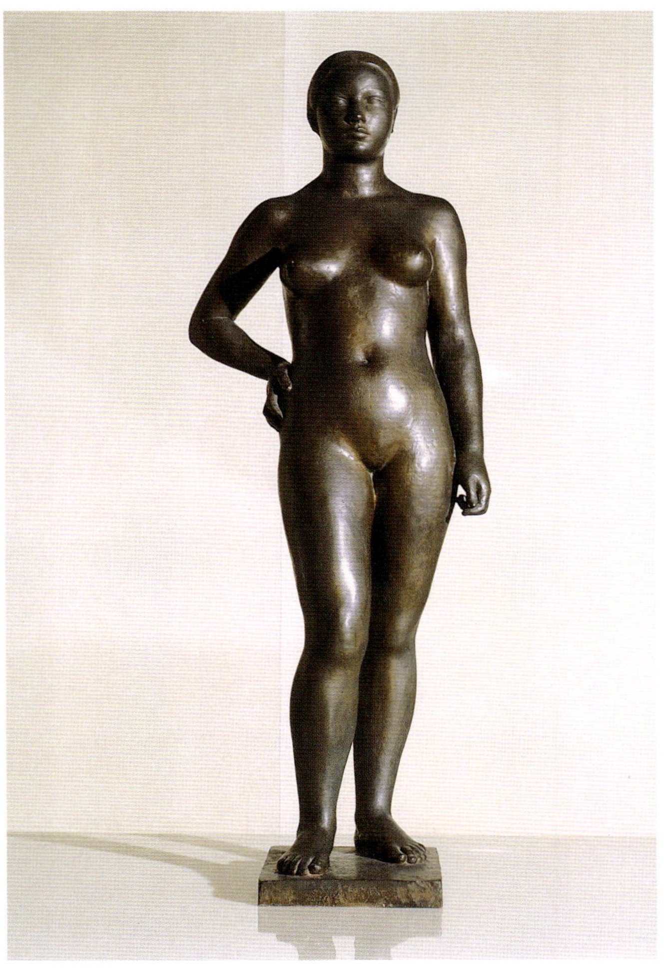

José Clará
"Juventud" (Youth)
National Art Museum of Catalonia

1938

Chief Curator:
Eugenio d'Ors

Participating artists:
José Aguiar
Fernando Álvarez de Sotomayor
Gustavo de Maeztu Udituey
Mariano Fortuny y Madrazo
Antonio Lino
Pablo Mañé (sic)
Enrique Pérez Comendador
Pedro Pruna
José de Togores
Quintín de Torre
Ignacio Zuloaga

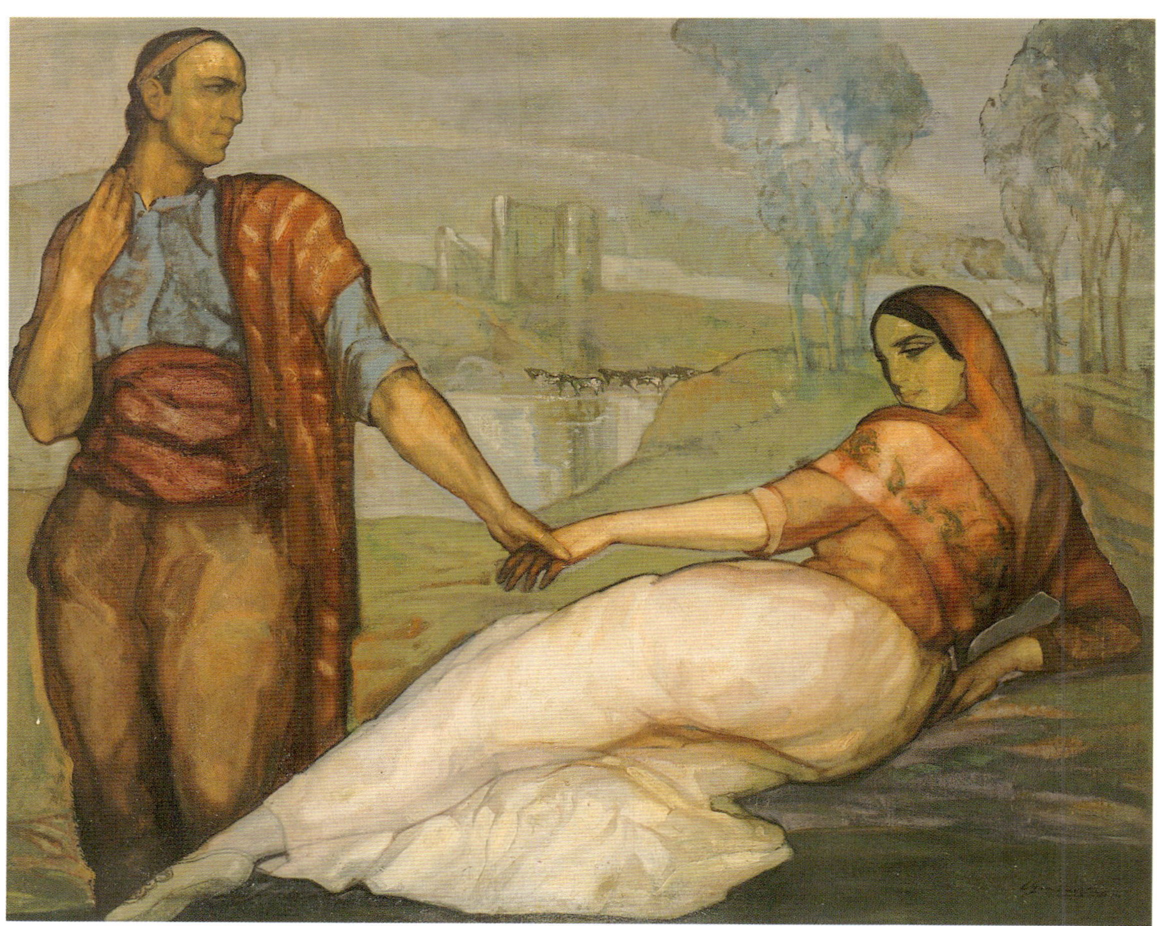

Gustavo de Maeztu
"Los novios de Voz Mediana" (The Newlyweds of Voz Mediana)
Gustavo de Maeztu Museum

1940

Curator:
Enrique Pérez Comendador

Participating artists:
Juan Adsuara
José Aguiar
José Amat Pagés
José Amerigo Salazar
Ramón Barnadas Fábrega
Luis Benedito
Mariano Benlliure
Julio Beovide
L. Berdejo Elipe
Guido Caprotti
Domingo Carles Rosich
José Clará
Juan Colom
Teresa Condeminas
Juan Cristóbal
Eduardo Chicharro
Mariano Fortuny y Madrazo
José Frau
Margarita de Frau
Alfonso Grosso
Eugenio Hermoso (solo exhibition)
Francisco Labarta
Fernando Labrada
José María Labrador
Genaro Lahuerta
Magdalena Leroux
Rafael Llimona Benet
Francisco Llorens
José María Mallol Suazo
Enrique Martínez Cubells
Santiago Martínez
Julio Moisés Fernández
Evaristo Mora Roselló
Luis Muntané Muns
Vicente Navarro
Luis Olasagasti Muns
Fructuoso Orduña
Benjamín Palencia
Enrique Pérez Comendador
Juan Bautista Porcar
Enrique Porta Mestre
Pedro Pruna
Darío de Regoyos (solo exhibition)
Marisa Roesset
Carlos Sáenz de Tejada
Elías Salaverría
Augusto Sánchez Cid
Mariano Sancho
Ernesto Santasusagna
José G. Solana
Pedro Torre-Isunza
Quintín de Torre
Pedro de Valencia
Joaquín Valverde
Joaquín Vaquero
Daniel Vázquez Díaz
Rosario de Velasco
Antonio Vila Arrufat
Ramón de Zubiaurre
Valentín de Zubiaurre
Ignacio Zuloaga

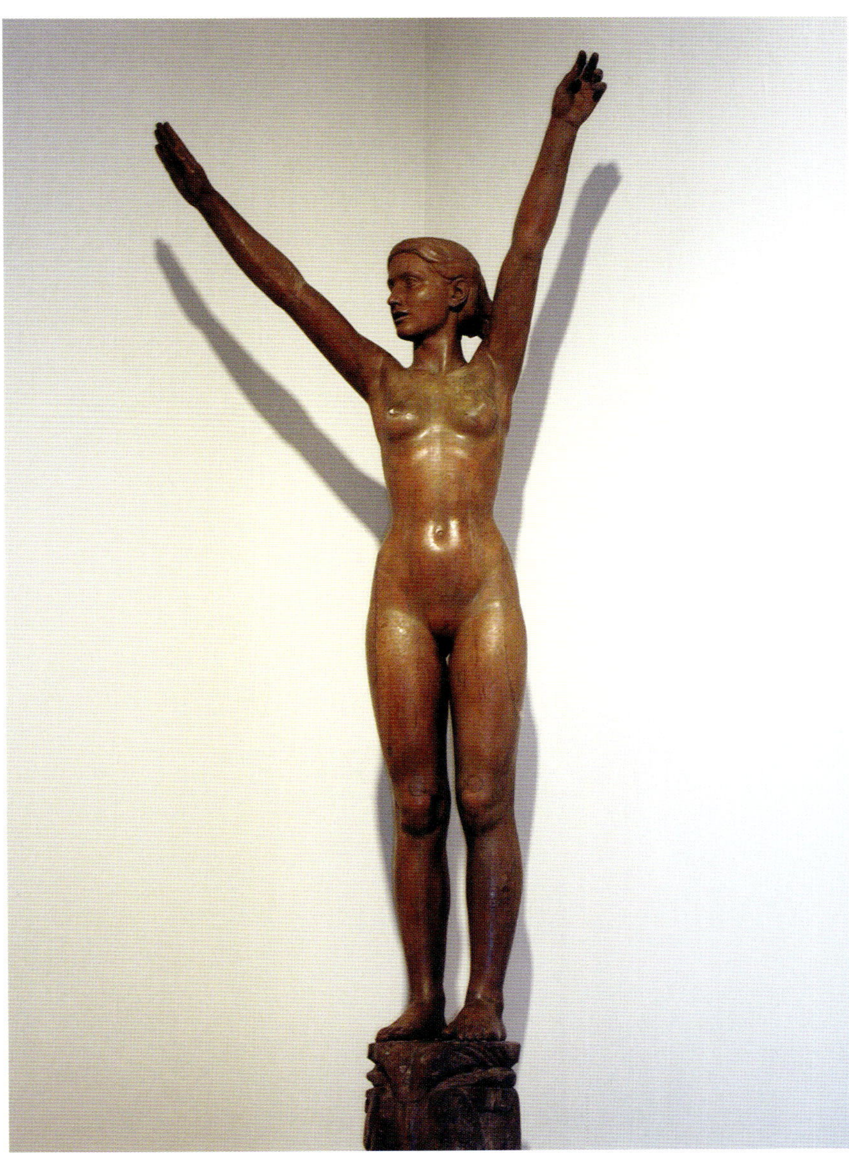

Enrique Pérez Comendador
"Alba" (Dawn)
Pérez Comendador-Leroux Museum

1942

Curator:
Enrique Lafuente Ferrari

Participating artists:
José Aguiar
José Amat Pagés
Luis Benedito
Manuel Benedito Vives
Luis Berdejo Elipe
José Bermejo Sobera
Aureliano de Beruete
Ismael Blat
Enrique Bráñez
Alejandro de Cabanyes
Antonio Casamor
Manuel Castro Gil
Eduardo Chicharro
José Clará
Rafael Durancamps
Francisco Esteve Botey
Mariano Fortuny y Madrazo
José Frau
Alfonso Grosso
Eugenio Hermoso Martínez
Manuel Hugué
José María Labrador Arjona
Bonifacio Lázaro Lozano
Magdalena Leroux
Francisco Llorens
Federico Marés
Francisco Marsá
Enrique Martínez Cubells
Julia Minguillón
Julio Moisés
Gabriel Morcillo
Luis Mosquera
Francisco Núñez Losada
Antonio Ollé Pinell
Rafael Pellicer
Francisco Pons Arnau
Buenaventura Puig Perucho
Miguel Renom de Garate
Enrique Ricart
José Rodríguez Jaldón
Carlos Sáenz de Tejada
Marceliano Santamaría
Ernesto Santasusagna
José G. Solana
José Suárez Peregrín
Gregorio Toledo
Joaquín Valverde
Joaquín Vaquero
Daniel Vázquez Díaz
Rosario de Velasco
Antonio Vila Arrufat
Juan Vila Puig
Valentín de Zubiaurre
Ignacio Zuloaga

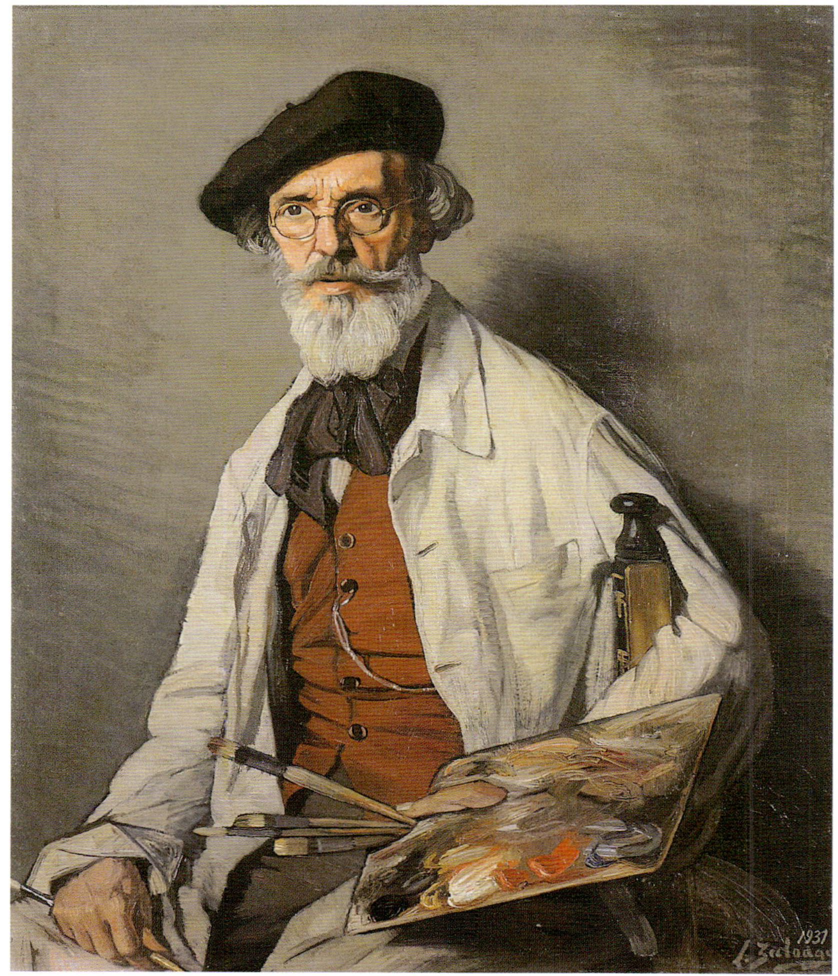

Ignacio Zuloaga
"El pintor Uranga" (Painter Uranga)
Reina Sofía National Art Centre Museum, Madrid

1950

Curator:
Enrique Pérez Comendador

Participating artists:
José Aguiar
Juan Adsuara
Luis Alegre Núñez
Fernando Álvarez de Sotomayor
José Amat
Francisco Arias
Juan de Ávalos
Manuel Benedito Vives
José Benet
Pedro Bueno
José Capuz
Domingo Carles
Enrique Casanova
José Clará
Antonio de la Cruz Collado
Fernando Cruz Solís
Eduardo Chicharro Briones
Andrés Conejo
Salvador Dalí
Álvaro Delgado
Carlos Ferreira de la Torre
Mariano Fortuny
Mariano Fortuny y Madrazo
Menchu Gal
Luis García Ochoa
Pablo Gargallo
Antonio Gómez Cano
Alfonso Grosso
José Guerrero
Francisco Gutiérrez Cossío
Genaro Lahuerta
Carlos Pascual de Lara
Manuel A. Laviada
Magdalena Leroux
Manuel López Villaseñor
Francisco Lozano
Federico Madrazo
Raimundo Madrazo
Ricardo Madrazo
José María Mallol Suazo
Cirilo Martínez Novillo
Julio Moisés
Ramón V. Molezún
Jesús Molina García
Juan Antonio Morales
Pedro Mozos
Benjamín Mustieles Navarro
Fructuoso Orduña
Carmelo Pastor Pla
José Planes
Francisco Núñez Losada
Benjamín Palencia
Victoriano Pardo Galindo
Andrés Parlade
Rafael Pellicer
Enrique Pérez Comendador
Juan Bautista Porcar
Gregorio Prieto
José Puigdengolas
Agustín Redondela
Ernesto Santasusagna
Juan Miguel Sánchez
Agustín Sánchez Cid
Rafael Sanz Rodríguez
Agustín Segura Iglesias
Enrique Segura Iglesias
José G. Solana
Gregorio Toledo
A. Valdivieso
Pedro de Valencia
Joaquín Valverde
Joaquín Vaquero Palacios
Juan Luis Vasallo
Daniel Vázquez Díaz
Eduardo Vicente
Antonio Vila Arrufat
Miguel Villa
Rafael Zabaleta
Valentín de Zubiaurre

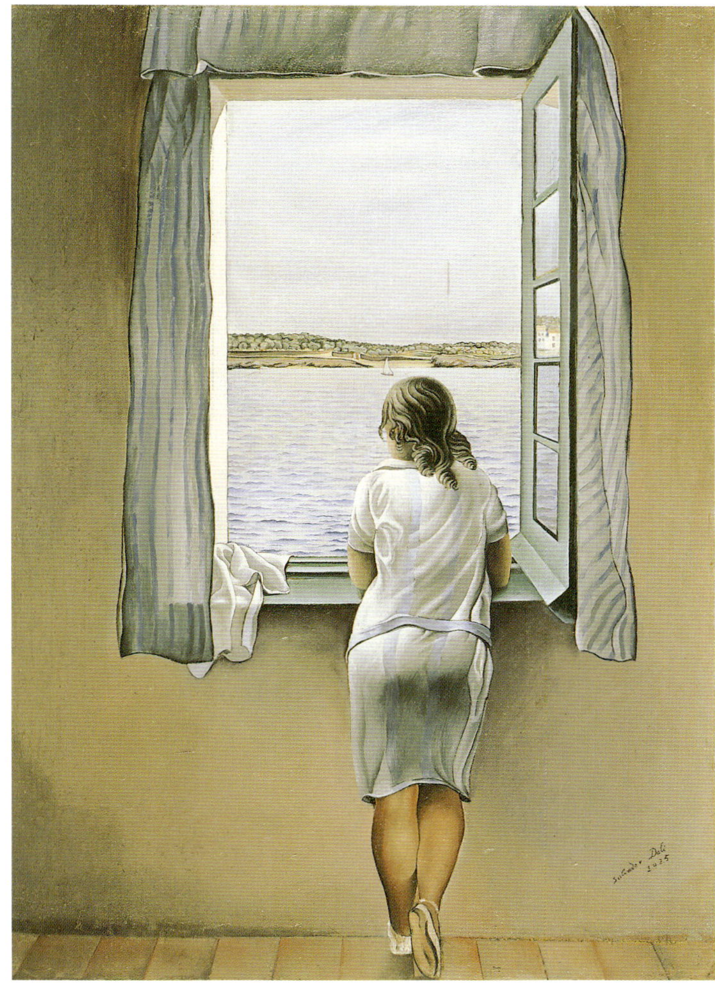

Salvador Dalí
"Muchacha en la ventana" (Girl at a Window)
Reina Sofía National Art Centre Museum, Madrid

1952

Curator:
Enrique Lafuente Ferrari

Participating artists:
José Caballero
Manuel Capdevila
Andrés Conejo
Francisco G. Cossío
Fernando Cruz Solís
Mateo Hernández
Luis García Ochoa
Francisco de Goya (show organised by the Spanish Government in collaboration with the Biennale)
Antonio Guijarro
José Guinovart
José Hurtuna Guiralt
Francisco Lozano
Martín Llauradó
Manuel Maldonado
Cristino Mallo
José María Mallol Suazo
Juan Antonio Morales
Benjamín Palencia
José Planes
Gregorio Prieto
Ramón Rogent
Eduardo Serra Güell
Alfredo Sisquella
Antoni Tàpies
Gregorio Toledo
Joaquín Vaquero Palacios
Joaquín Vaquero Turcios
Daniel Vázquez Díaz
Antonio Vila Arrufat
Miguel Villa
Rafael Zabaleta

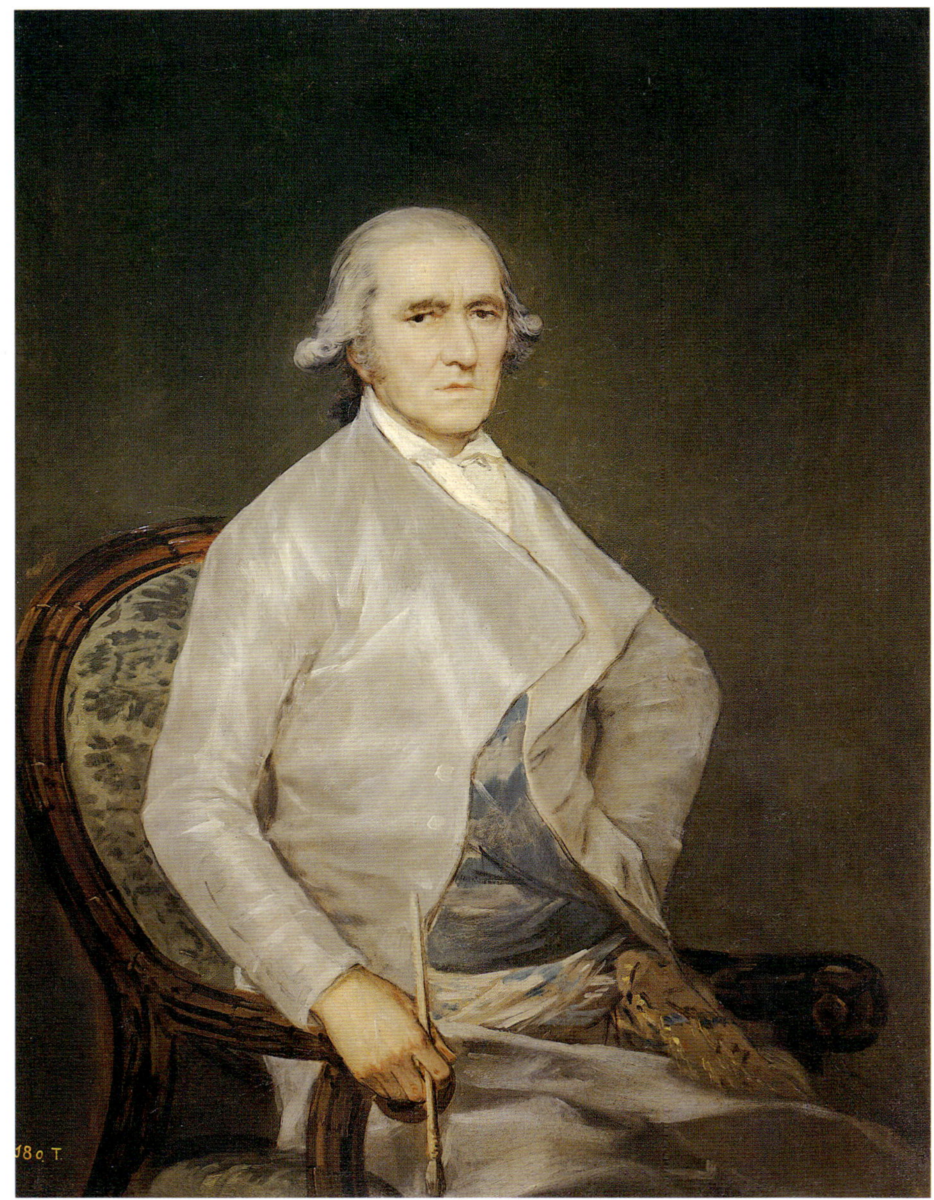

Francisco de Goya
"El pintor Francisco Bayeu" (Painter Francisco Bayeu)

1954

Curator:
Juan de Contreras López de Ayala, Marqués de Lozoya

Participating artists:
Francisco Arias
Manuel Baeza
Néstor Basterretxea
Juan Brotat
José Caballero
Francisco G. Cossío
Salvador Dalí
Francisco Farreras
Juana Concepción Francés
Luis García Ochoa
Antonio Gómez Cano
Antonio Guijarro
Francisco Lozano
Cristino Mallo
Cirilo Martínez Novillo
Joan Miró (solo exhibition)
Pedro Mozos
Isidro Nonell
Julio Antonio Ortiz
Miguel Ortiz
Godofredo Ortega Muñoz
Máximo de Pablo
Victoriano Pardo Galindo
Rafael Pena
José Planes
Demetrio Salgado
José Luis Sánchez
José Santianez
Antoni Tàpies
Santiago Uranga
Joaquín Vaquero
Eduardo Vicente

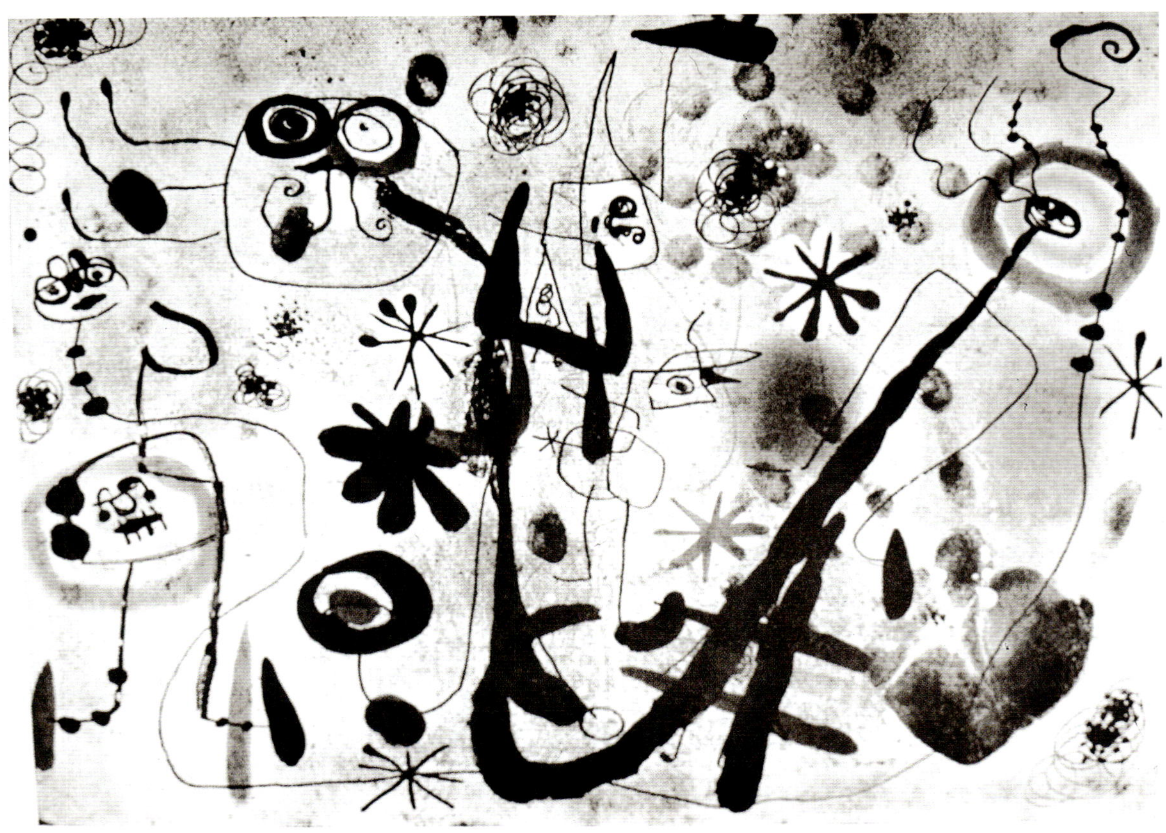

Joan Miró
"La mano" (The Hand)
Spanish Catalogue

1956

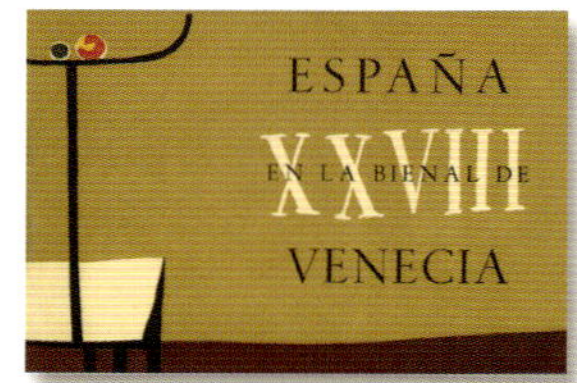

Curator:
Juan de Contreras López de Ayala, Marqués de Lozoya

Deputy curator:
Joaquín Vaquero Palacios

Participating artists:
Francisco Arias Álvarez
José Beulas Recasens
José Caballero
Manuel Caneja
Antonio Cano Correa
Rafael Canogar
Manuel Capdevila
Modesto Ciruelos González
Fernando Cruz Solís
Echauz Buisan
Juan de Echevarría (solo exhibition)
Will Faber
Luis Feito
Carlos Ferreira de la Torre
Pedro Flores
Amadeo Gabino Úbeda
Menchu Gal
Joaquín García Donaire
Pablo Gargallo (solo exhibition)
Antonio Guijarrro Gutiérrez
José María de Labra Suazo
Ramón Lapayese
Manuel López Villaseñor
Francisco Lozano
Ricardo Macarrón
Manuel Maldonado Rodríguez
Cristino Mallo
Manuel Mampaso Bueno
César Manrique
Manuel Millares
José Antonio Molina Sánchez
José Mompou
Pedro Mozos
Benjamín Palencia
Victoriano Pardo Galindo
Carmelo Pastor Pla
Enrique Planasdurá
José Planes
Rafael Reyes Torrent
José Luis Sánchez
Eudaldo Serra Güell
Antonio Saura
Antoni Tàpies
Juan José Tharrats
José María de Ucelay
Santiago de Uranga
Joaquín Vaquero Palacios
Joaquín Vaquero Turcios
Eduardo Vicente
Miguel Villa Bassols
Rafael Zabaleta

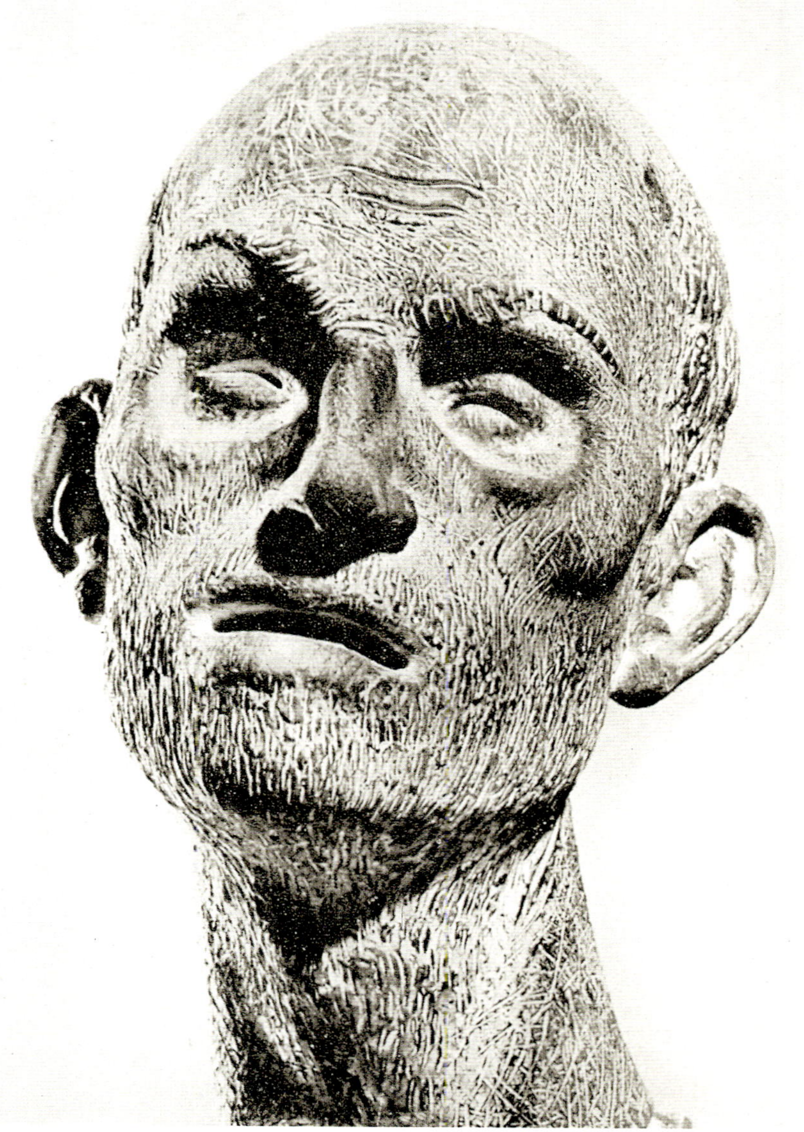

Fernando Cruz Solís
"Ciego" (Blind)
Spanish Catalogue

1958

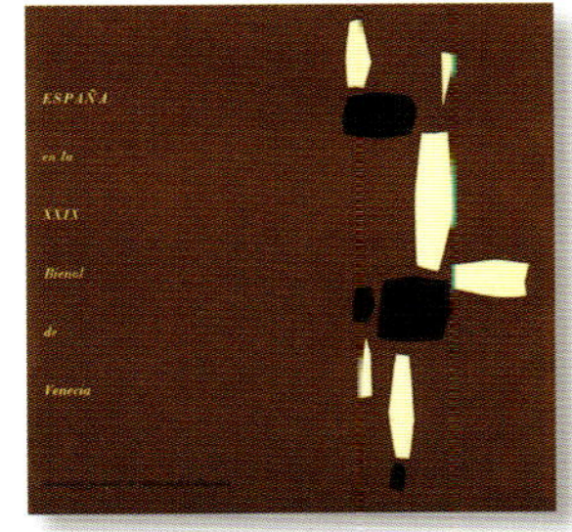

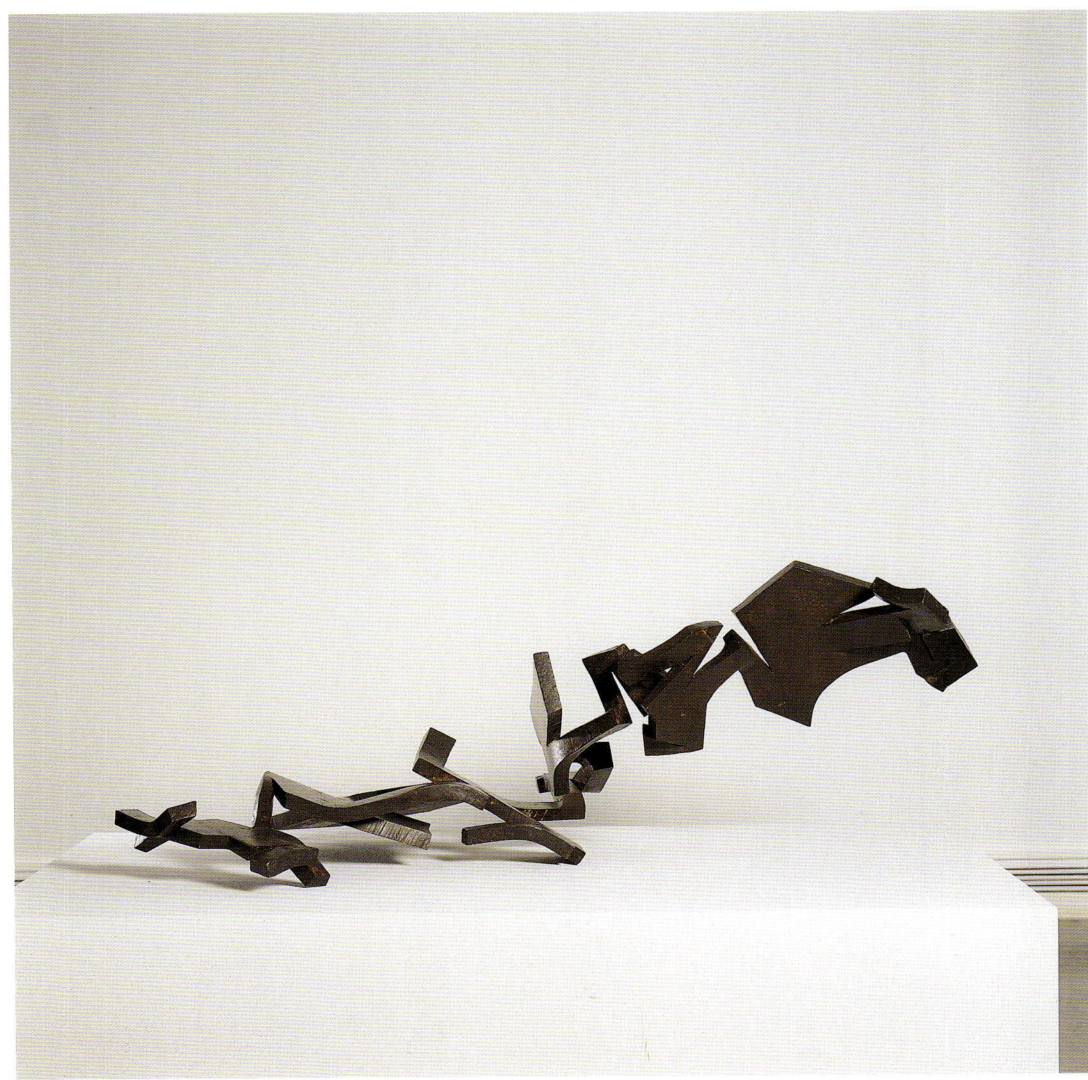

Curator:
Luis González Robles

Participating artists:
Rafael Canogar
Francisco G. Cossío
Modesto Cuixart
Eduardo Chillida
Francisco Farreras
Luis Feito
José Guinovart
Manuel Mampaso
Manuel Millares
Godofredo Ortega Muñoz
Enrique Planascurá
Antonio Povedano
Manuel Rivera
Antonio Saura
Antonio Suárez
Antoni Tàpies
Juan José Tharrats
Joaquín Vaquero Turcios
Vicente Vela

Eduardo Chillida
"Irakundi"
Chillida-Leku Museum

1960

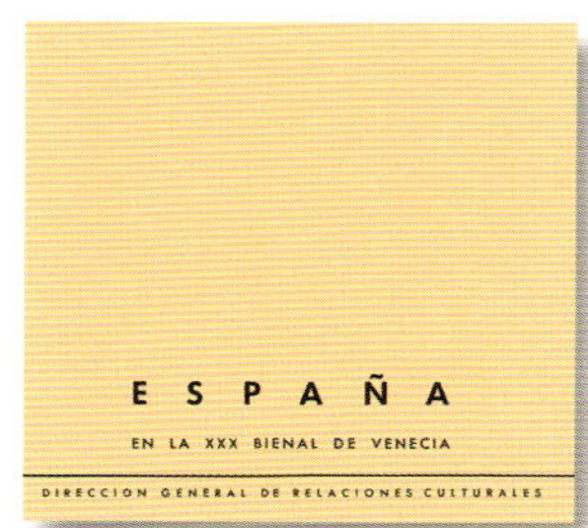

Curator:
Luis González Robles

Participating artists:
Marcos Aleu
Eduardo Alcoy
María Droc
Francisco Farreras
Luis Feito
Ángel Ferrant
Juan Fluviá
Juana Francés
José Luis García
Juan Hernández Pijuán
Antonio Lago Rivera
César Manrique
Alfonso Mier
Monjalés
Lucio Muñoz
Francisco Nieva
Carlos Planell
Julio Ramis
Joaquín Ramo
Gerardo Rueda
Eusebio Sempere
Salvador Soria
Juan José Tharrats
Salvador Victoria
Juan Vilacasas
José Vento
Rafael Zabaleta

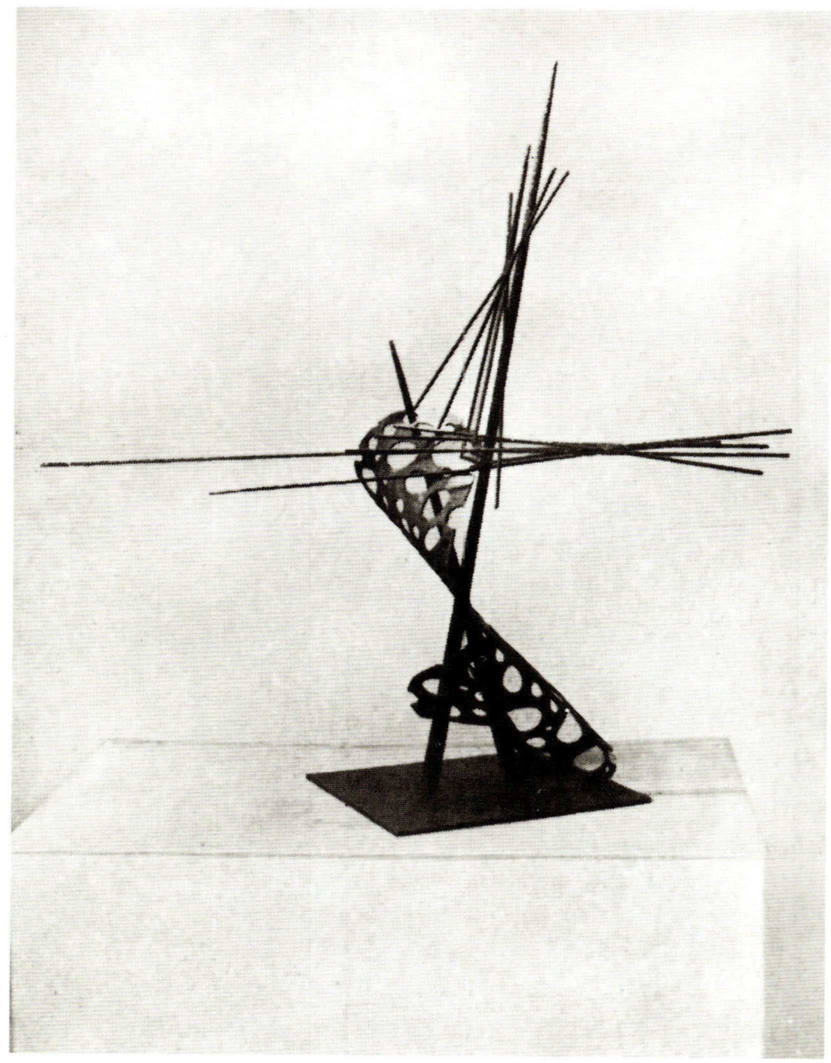

Ángel Ferrant
Spanish Catalogue

1962

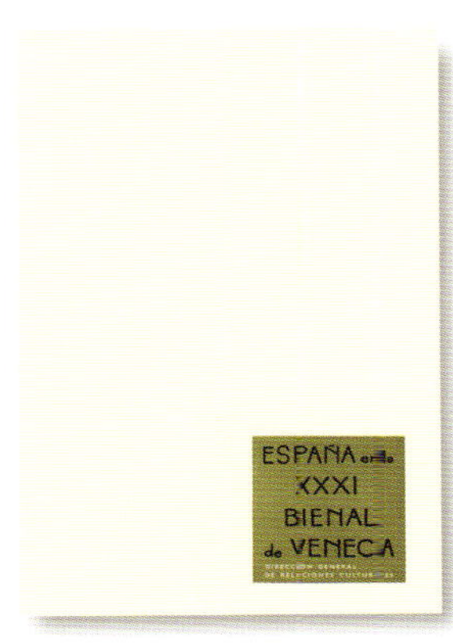

Curator:
Luis González Robles

Participating artists:
Agustín Albalat
Arcadio Blasco
Rafael Canogar
José Alfonso Curi
Federico de Echevarría
Juan Genovés
Enrique Gran
José Guevara
José Guinovart
Julián R. Martín de Vidales
Ángel Medina
Manuel H. Mompó
Jesús Núñez
Eduardo Sanz
Pablo Serrano
Antonio Suárez
Gustavo Torner
Senén Ubiña
Vicente Vela
Cristino de Vera
Fernando Zobel

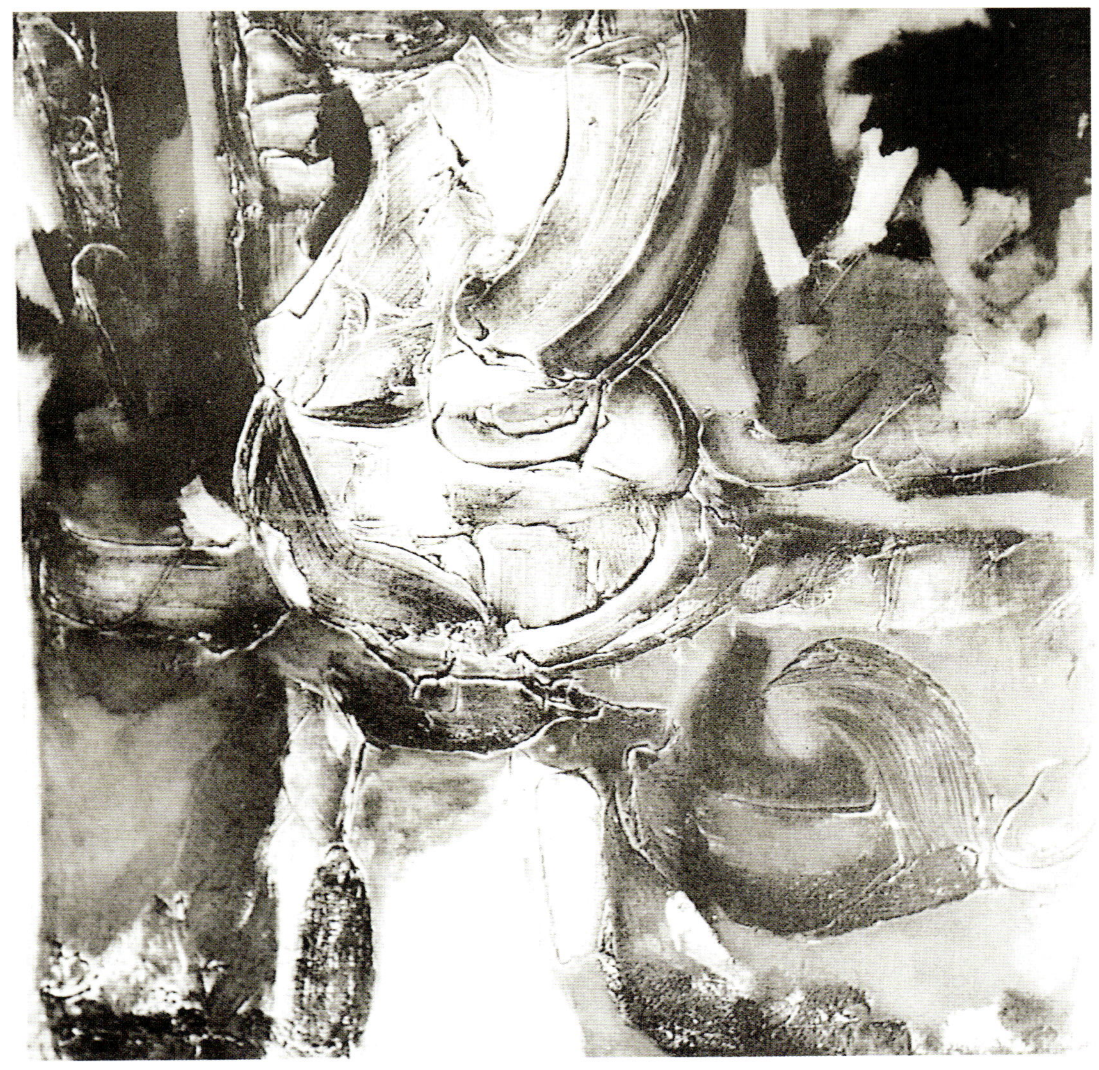

Antonio Suárez
"Pintura" (Painting)
Spanish Catalogue

1964

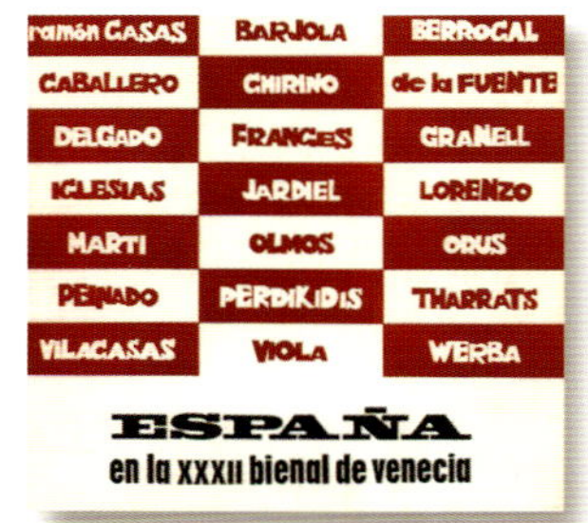

Curator:
Luis González Robles

Participating artists:
Juan Barjola
Miguel Berrocal
José Caballero
Ramón Casas (solo exhibition)
Martín Chirino
Álvaro Delgado
Juana Francés
Victoria de la Fuente
Eugenio Granell
José María Iglesias
José Jardiel
Antonio Lorenzo
Marcelo Martí
César Olmos
José Orus
Francisco Peinado
Dimitri Perdikidis
Juan José Tharrats
Juan Vilacasas
Manuel Viola
Nadia Werba

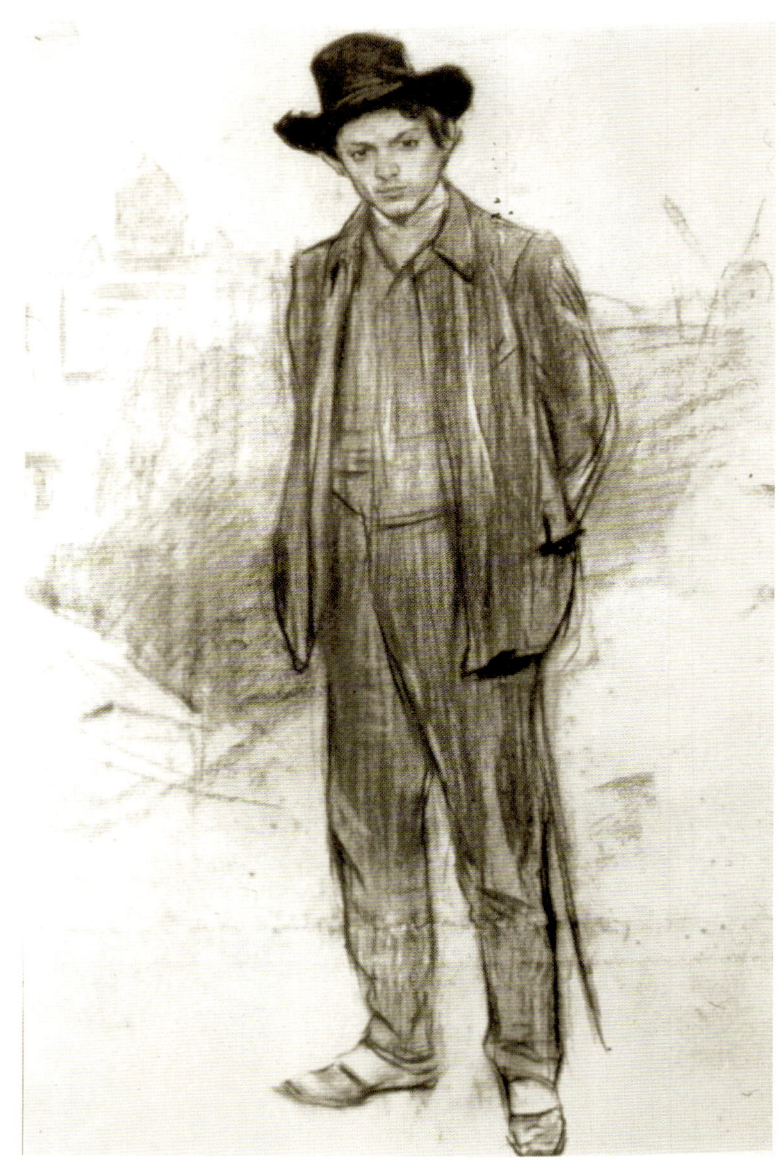

Ramón Casas
"Retrato de Picasso" (Portrait of Picasso)
Italian Catalogue

1966

Curator:
Luis González Robles

Participating artists:
Andreu Alfaro
María Droc
Federico de Echevarría
Juana Francés
Amadeo Gabino
José Luis Galicia
Pedro A. Garcia Ramos
José Luis García Severo
Juan Genovés
Juan Giralt
Manuel Gómez Raba
Francisco Hernández
José María Iglesias
Antonio Lorenzo
Julián Martín de Vidales
Manuel Méndez
Remigio Mendiburu
Jesús Núñez
Francisco Peinado
Dimitri Perdikidis
Joaquín Rubio Camín
Eduardo Sanz
Salvador Soria
Vicente Vela
Ignacio de Yraola

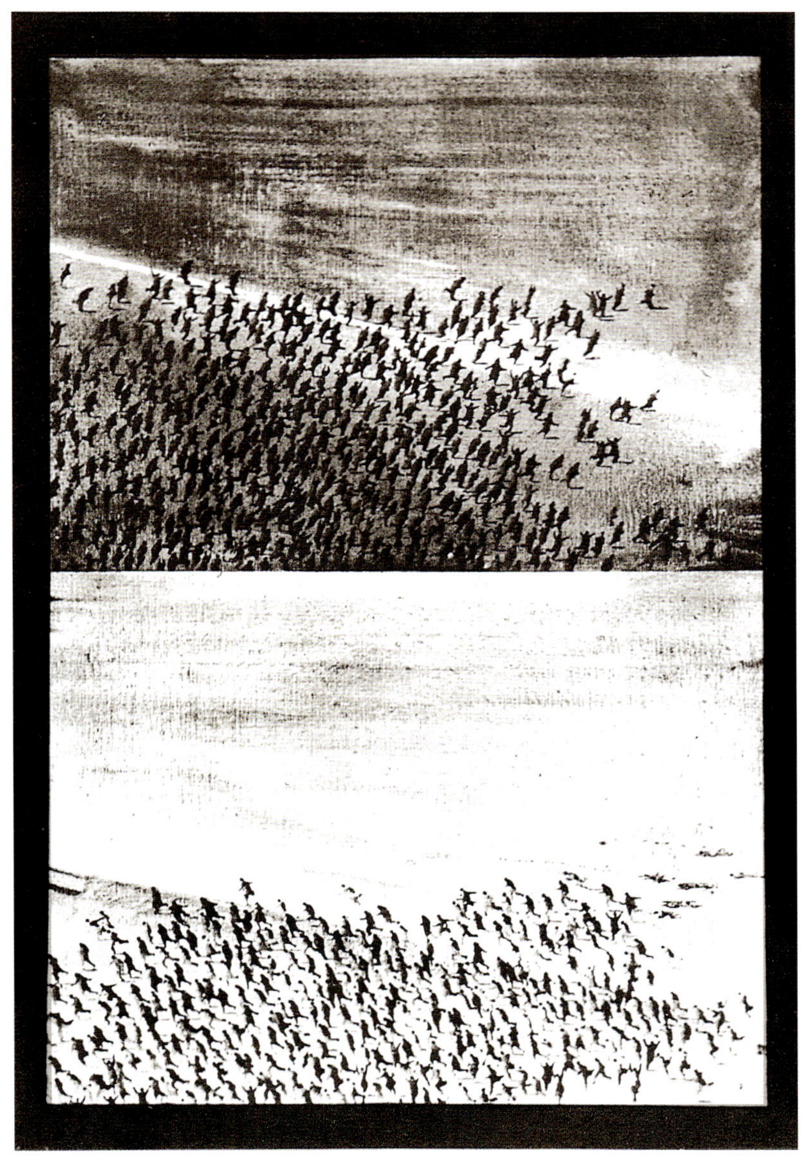

Juan Genovés
"Avance y retroceso" (Progress and Regression)
Spanish Catalogue

XXXIV Biennale

1968

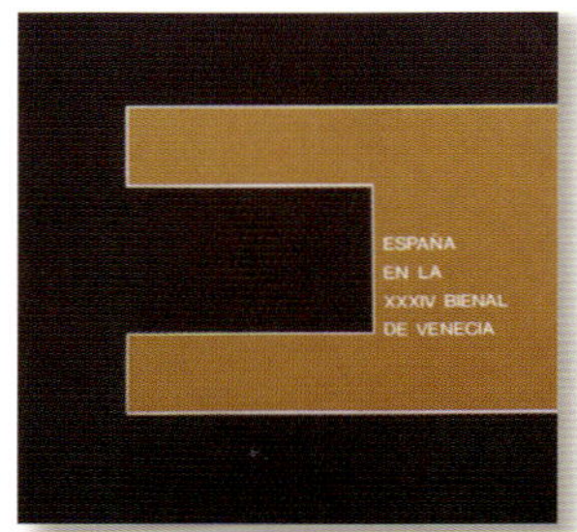

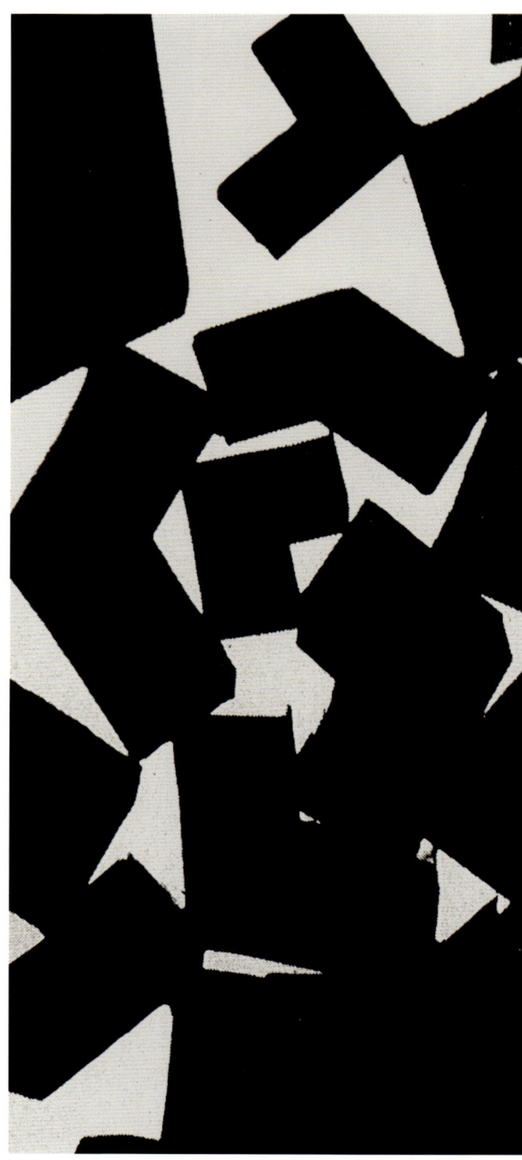

Curator:
Luis González Robles

Participating artists:
Amador
Anzo
Salvador Aulestia
Antonio Bueno
Rafael Canogar
Agustín de Celis
Luis Feito
Trinidad Fernández
Pedro García Ramos
Enrique Gran
Feliciano Hernández
Julián Martín de Vidales
Manuel H. Mompó
Ceferino Moreno
Reinaldo Paluzzi
Joaquín Rubio Camín
Luis Sáez
Julián Santamaría
Eduardo Sanz
José María Subirachs
Senén Ubiña
Salvador Victoria
Juan Vilacasas

XXXV Biennale

1970

Curator:
Luis González Robles

Participating artists:
Doroteo Arnaiz
Ignacio Berriobeña
Arcadio Blasco
Francisco Cruz de Castro
José Dámaso
Alfonso Fraile
Juana Francés
Manuel Gómez Raba
Luis Gordillo
Francisco Hernández
Juan Hernández Pijuán
Ángel Orcajo
Gastón Orellana
Juan Romero
Eduardo Úrculo
José Vento
Darío Villalba

1972

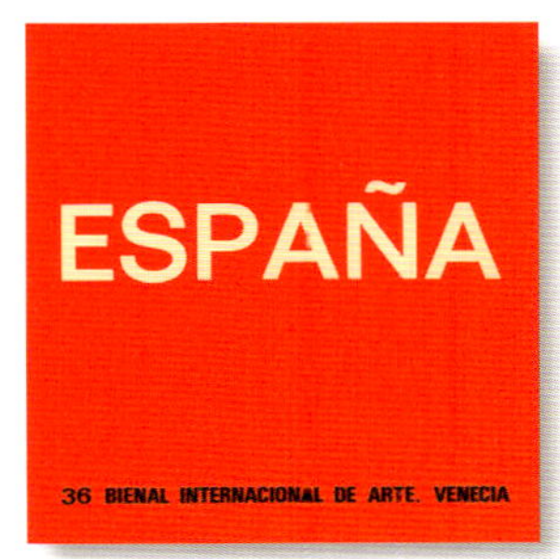

Curator:
Ceferino Moreno

Participating artists:
Francisco Echauz
José Luis Gómez Perales
José María Iglesias
José María de Labra
Luis Lugán
Joaquín Mouliaa
Jordi Pericot
Amador Rodríguez
Salvador Victoria

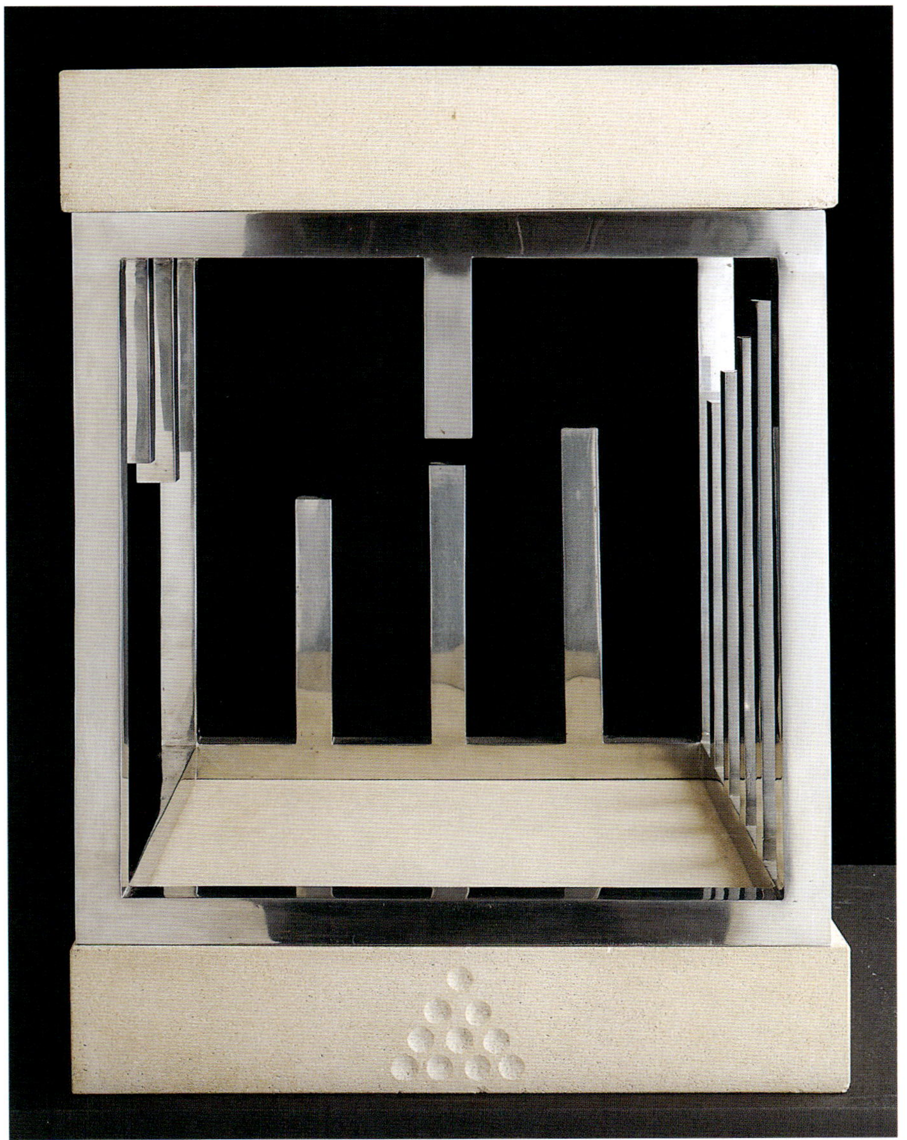

Amador Rodríguez
"Tetraktys"
Asturias Fine Arts Museum

1976

The unofficial exhibition entitled "Spain: The Artistic Avant-Garde and Social Reality, 1936-1976" was held this year.

Curatorship:
The organisation was entrusted to the so-called Committee of Ten, although it was basically the responsibility of Valeriano Bozal and Tomàs Llorens. The committee comprised Antoni Tàpies, Antonio Saura, Oriol Bohigas, Agustín Ibarrola, and the members of the Equipo Crónica: Manuel Valdés and Rafael Solbes, Alberto Corazón and the aforementioned Valeriano Bozal and Tomàs Llorens. Manuel García performed the duties of secretary. Participating for purposes of consultation and specific organisational matters were: Inmaculada Julián, Víctor Pérez Escolano, Josep Renau and José Miguel Gómez. In the definitive catalogue of the Biennale, this list of collaborators was enlarged to include Antonio González Cordón, Vicente Lleó Cañal, Fernando Martín Martín, Ludolfo Paramio and Ignacio de Solá-Morales. Later the name of Simón Marchán appeared in the catalogue of the exhibition at the Joan Miró Foundation. The task of final readying of the spaces for the exhibition was carried out by Martorell, Bohigas and Mackay-Barcelona. Eduardo Arroyo helped to set up the committee, although he did not form part of it.

Participating artists:

I. Images of the Civil War
Selection of anonymous posters, M. Adam, V. Aguado, Am Gil, Arago, Arribas, Arteta, Artigas, Ballester, Badia Vilato, Bardasano, Bartoli, Beltrán, Cabedo, Castelao, Clavé, Dag, Díaz Balino, Dibujantes CNT, Durban, Espert, Fontseré, Fors, Friedfeld, Giralt Miracle, Goñi, Goves, Juan y S., Martí Bas, Millà, Moneny, Mupal, G.M., R. Obiols, Olivé, Oliver, Parilla, Peinador, Petit Guillen, Puyol, Rabal, Raga, Reinoso, Renau, Repa Liehas, Rodríguez Luna, Sim, Solana, Souto, Subirats, Thomas, Tona, E. Vicente, H.V., Wila, L.Y.

II. 1937 Pavilion
Alexander Calder, Julio González, Pablo Picasso, Joan Miró.

III. Defeat and Exile
Enrique Castelo, Óscar Domínguez, Luis Fernández, Julio González, Pablo Picasso, Joan Miró, Josep Renau, Alberto Sánchez.
1. The Recovery of the Avant-Garde: 1939-1954. Ángel Ferrant, "Dau al Set": Tàpies.
2. Between Testimony and Freedom: 1954-1964.
  2.1. First Approximations: Manuel Millares, Lucio Muñoz, Antonio Saura.
  2.2. El Paso: Manuel Millares, Antonio Saura.
  2.3. Testimony of Violence: Josep Guinovart, Millares, Lucio Muñoz.
  2.4. Utopian Spaces: Andreu Alfaro, Equipo 57, Jorge Oteiza (although this artist removed his works exhibited in this section as they belonged to private collections), Eusebio Sempere.
  2.5. Archeology of Practical Reason: Tàpies.
3. Areas of Realism: 1959-1964.
  3.1. Lives, Myths, figures: Antonio Saura.
  3.2. Popular Images: Francisco Álvarez, José Luis Delgado, Agustín Ibarrola, Arturo Martínez, Monjalés, José Ortega, Manuel Ortiz Valiente, Ricard Zamorano.
  3.3. Phantoms, Nightmares (and other) Anecdotes: Eduardo Arroyo, Jorge Castillo, Juan Genovés, José Hernández, Modesto Roldán.
4. The Political Objective is Narrowed (limits of meaning): 1964-1972.
  4.1. Emblematic Games: Andreu Alfaro, Joan Brossa, Juan Genovés, Josep Guinovart, Albert Ràfols Casamada, Antoni Tàpies.
  4.2. Iconographic Systems (limits of reference): Eduardo Arroyo, Jorge Castillo, Equipo Crónica, "Estampa Popular de Valencia" (Popular Images of Valencia), Manuel Millares.

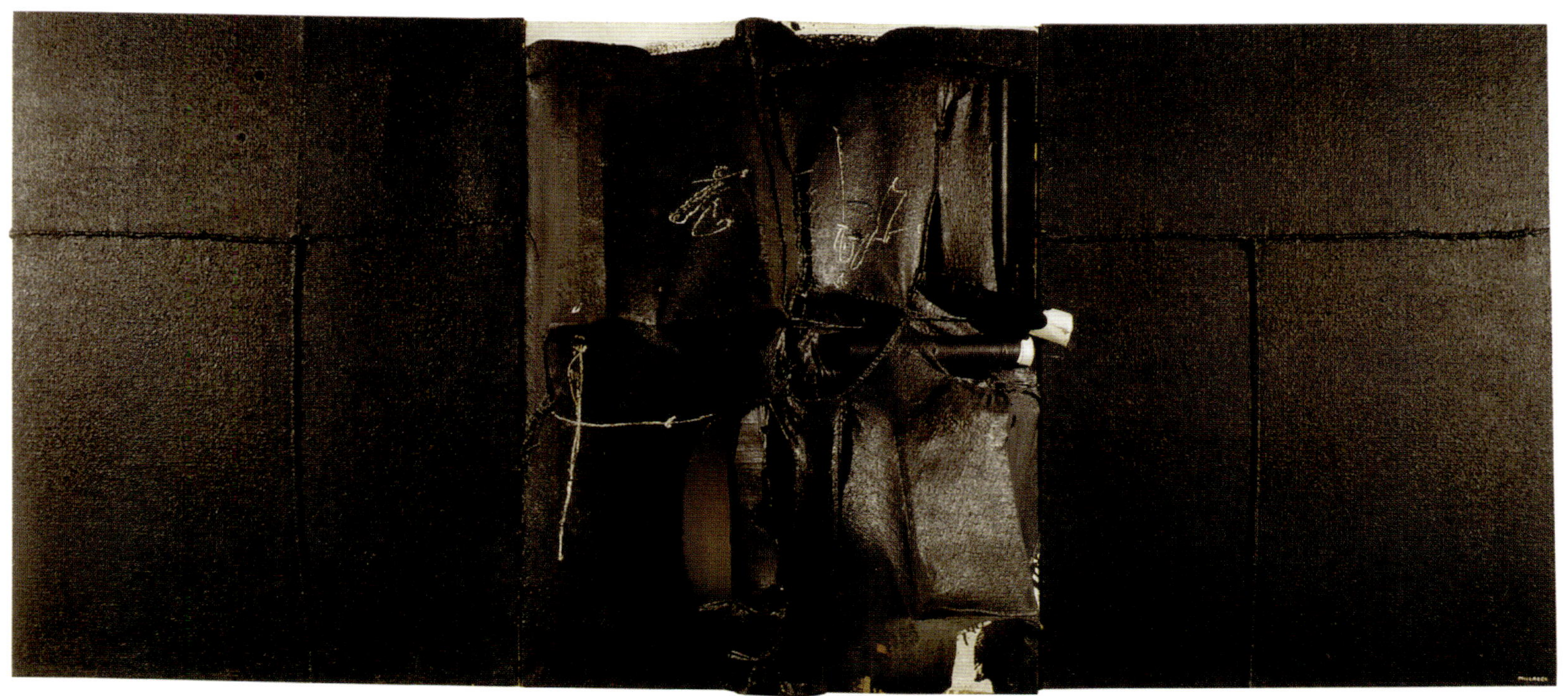

5. Painting, Criticism, Meaning: 1967-1976.

5.1. El asalto a la pintura: la vida cotidiana (The Attack on Painting: Daily Life): Luis Gordillo, Josep Guinovart.

5.2. El asalto a la vida cotidiana: la pintura (The Attack on Daily Life: Painting): Tàpies.

5.3. Dialéctica proceso-código (Process-Code Dialectics): José M. Broto, Xavier Grau, Carlos León, Albert Ràfols Casamada, José Rubio, Gil Tena, Jordi Teixidor.

5.4. Reductions: Grup de Treball (Treball Group): Antoni Muntadas and Francesc Torres.

5.5. Role Games: Eduardo Arroyo, Equipo Crónica.

Hors texte: Andreu Alfaro, Eduardo Arroyo, Alberto Corazón, Equipo Crónica, Juan Genovés, Agustín Ibarrola, Monjalés, Lucio Muñoz, José Ortega, Julián Pacheco (withdrew), Antonio Saura, Eusebio Sempere, Antoni Tàpies.

Manuel Millares
"Tríptico a Miguel Hernández" (Triptych to Miguel Hernández)
Catalogue *Millares: Luto de oriente y occidente* (Mourning for East and West) (Programme: Spanish Art Abroad)

XXXVIII Biennale

1978

Curators:
José María Ballester
Deputy curators:
Vicente Aguilera Cerni
Antonio Bonet Correa
Francesc Vicens

Participating artists:
Nacho Criado
José Antonio Fernández Ordóñez
Julio Martínez Calzón
Josefina Miralles
Juan Navarro Baldeweg
Pilar Palomer
José María Yturralde

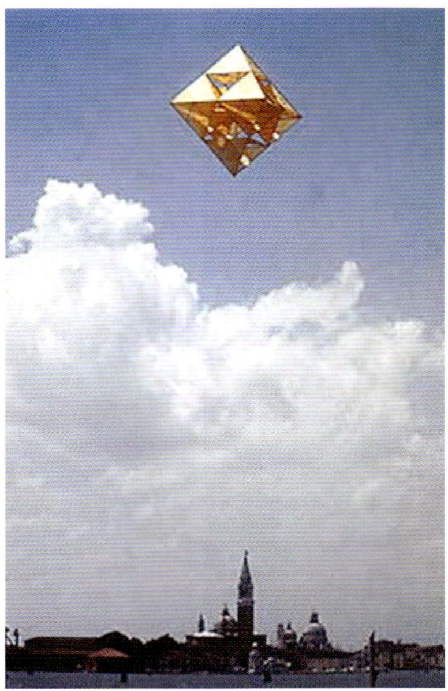

Jose María Yturralde
"Estructura volante. Octaedro"
(Flying Structure: Octahedron)
Photograph made available by the artist

XXXIX Biennale

1980

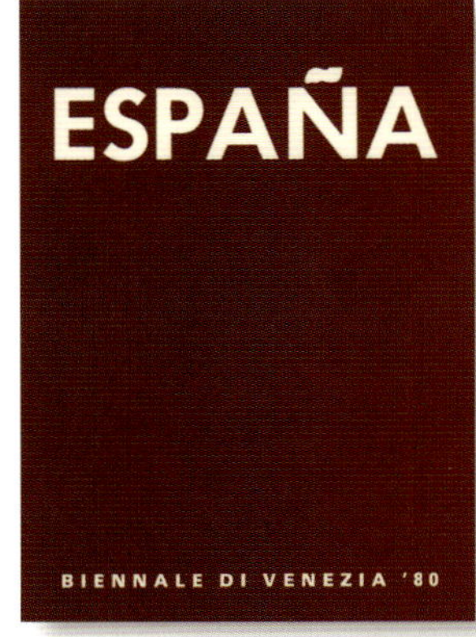

Curators:
Ceferino Moreno

Participating artists:
Javier Aleixandre
Eduardo Arranz Bravo
Rafael Bartolozzi
Luis Delacámara
Juan Gomila
Juan Martínez
José Luis Pascual

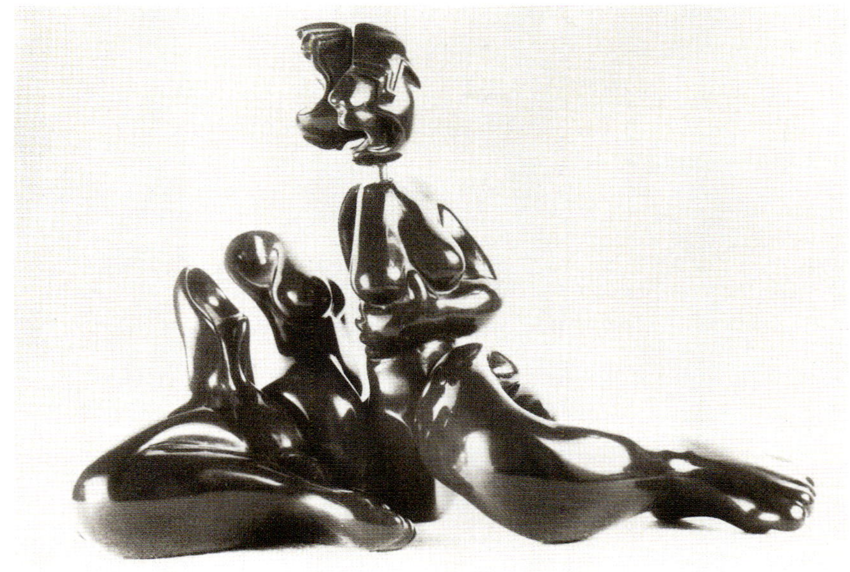

Javier Aleixandre
"Punto límite" (Limit Point)
Spanish Catalogue

1982

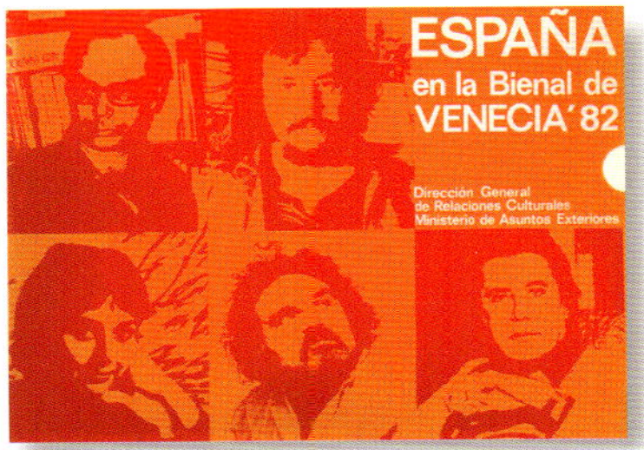

Curator:
Luis González Robles

Participating artists:
José Abad
Eugenio Chicano
Francisco Cruz de Castro
Josep Guinovart
Rosa Torres

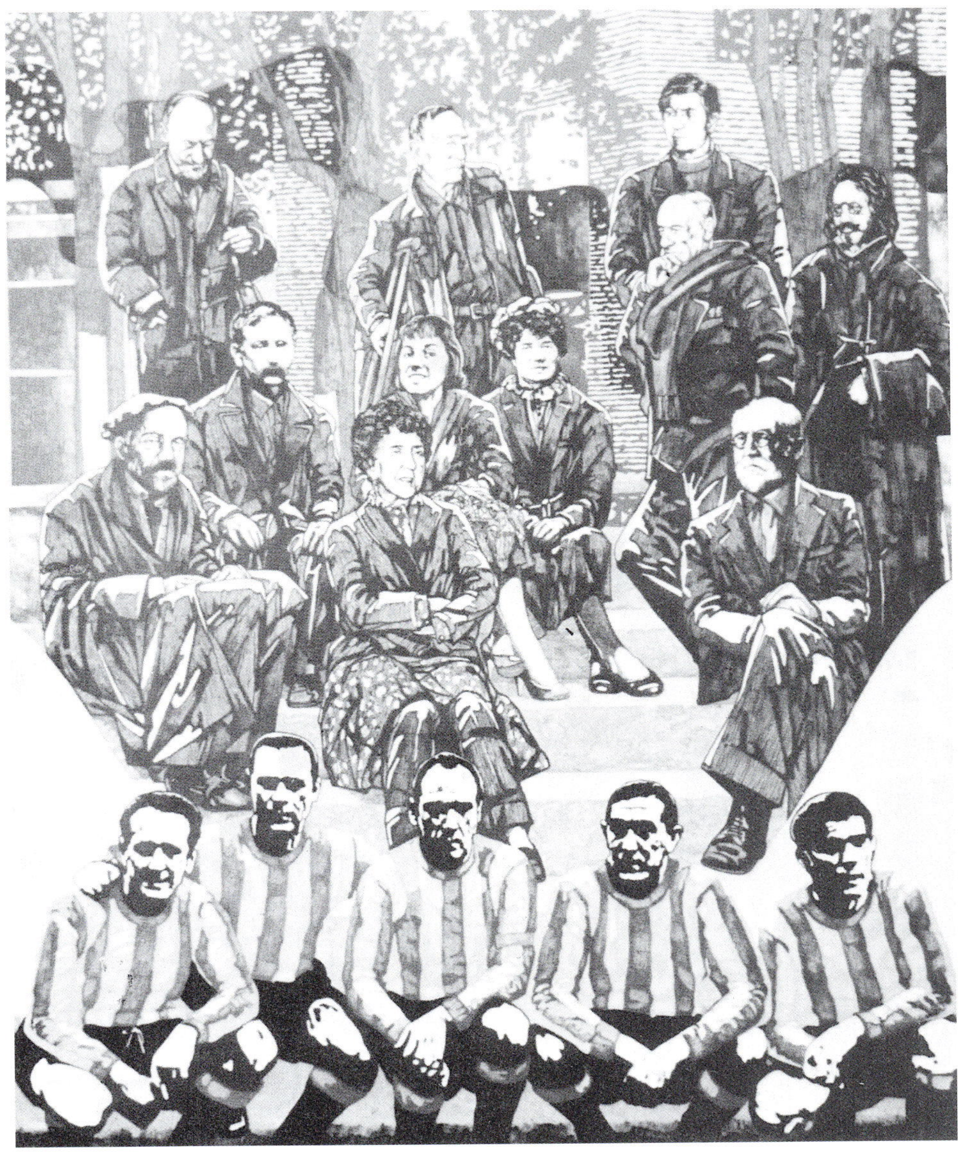

Eugenio Chicano
"Viridiana"
Spanish Catalogue

1984

Curator:
Luis González Robles

Participating artist:
Antoni Clavé

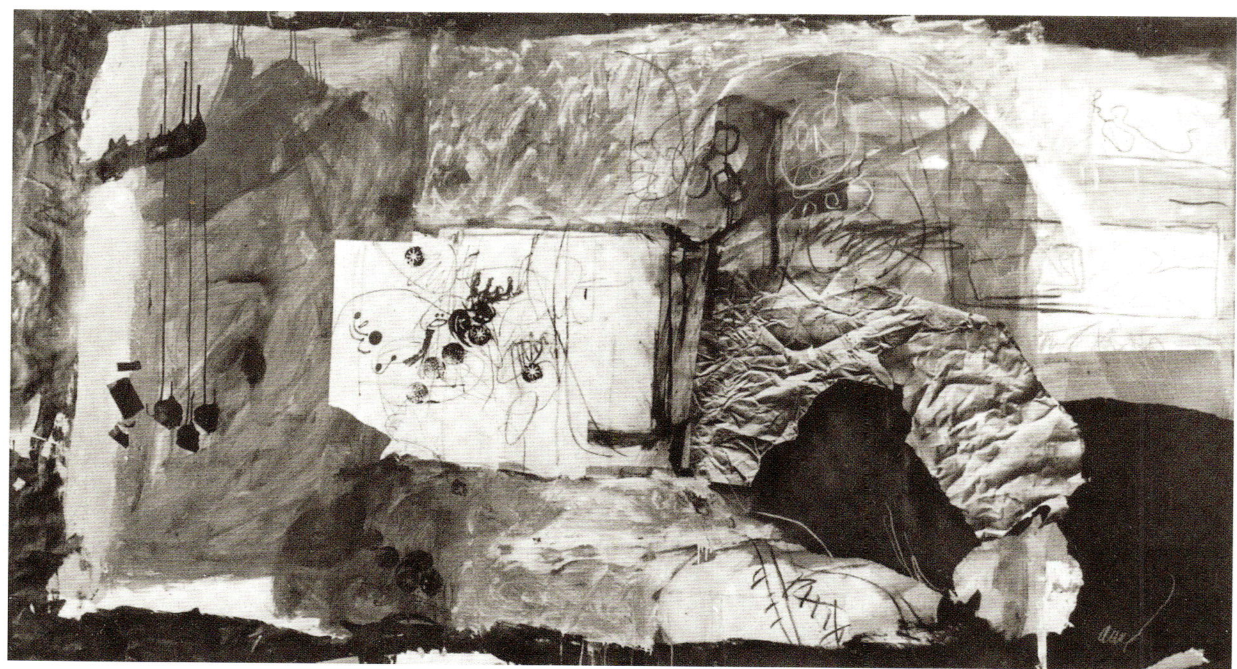

Antoni Clavé
"Estrellas" (Stars)
Italian Catalogue

1986

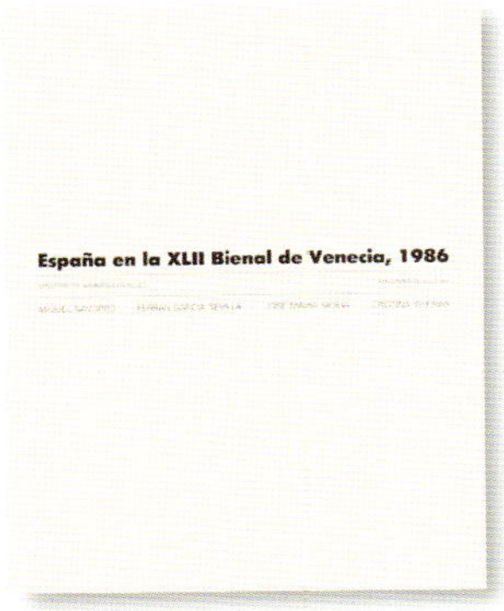

Curator:
Ana Vázquez de Parga

Participating artists:
Ferrán García Sevilla
Cristina Iglesias
Miquel Navarro
José María Sicilia

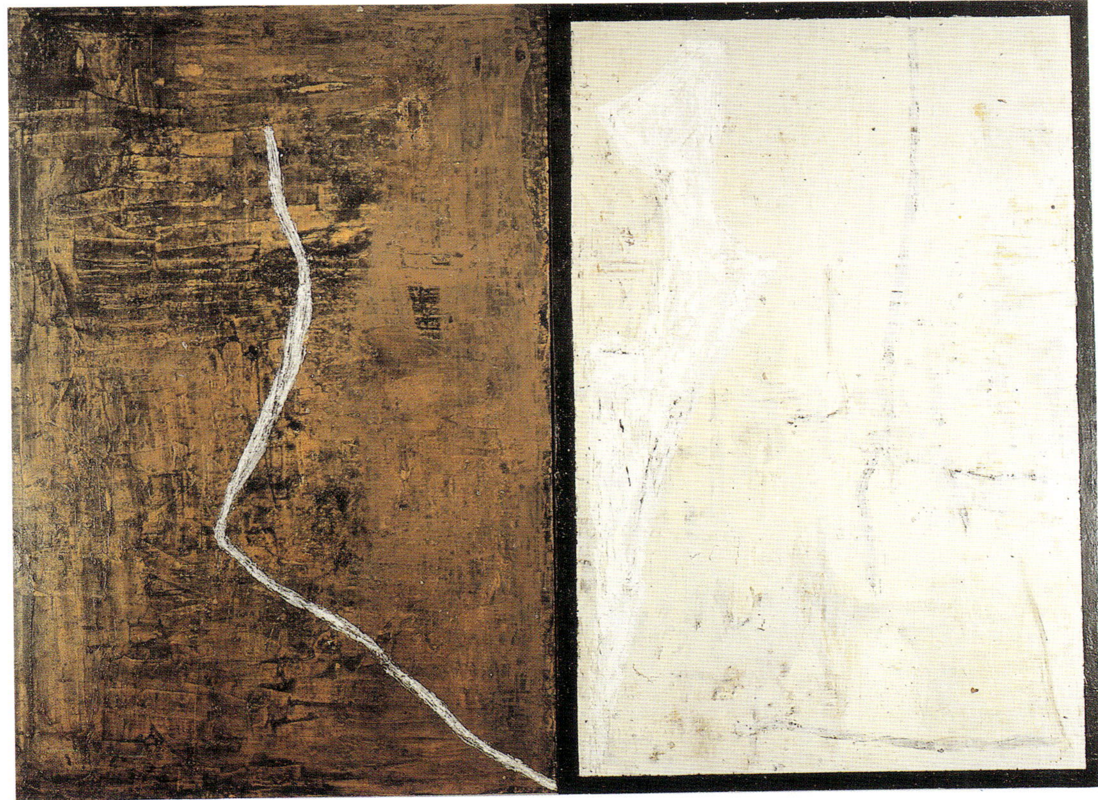

José María Sicilia
"Black and White Flower"
Spanish Catalogue

1988

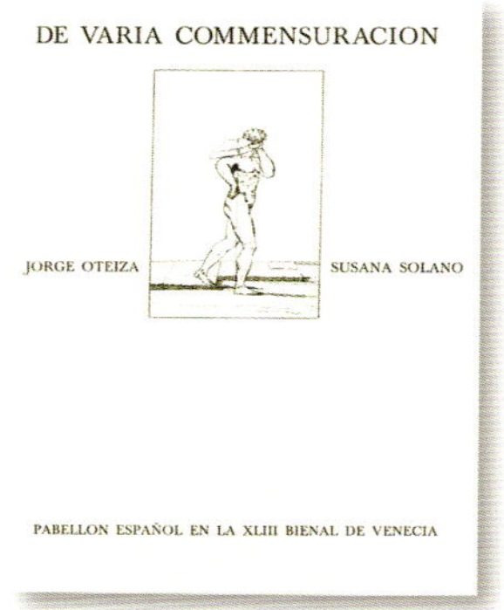
DE VARIA COMMENSURACION

JORGE OTEIZA SUSANA SOLANO

PABELLON ESPAÑOL EN LA XLIII BIENAL DE VENECIA

Curator:
María Corral

Participating artists:
Jorge Oteiza
Susana Solano

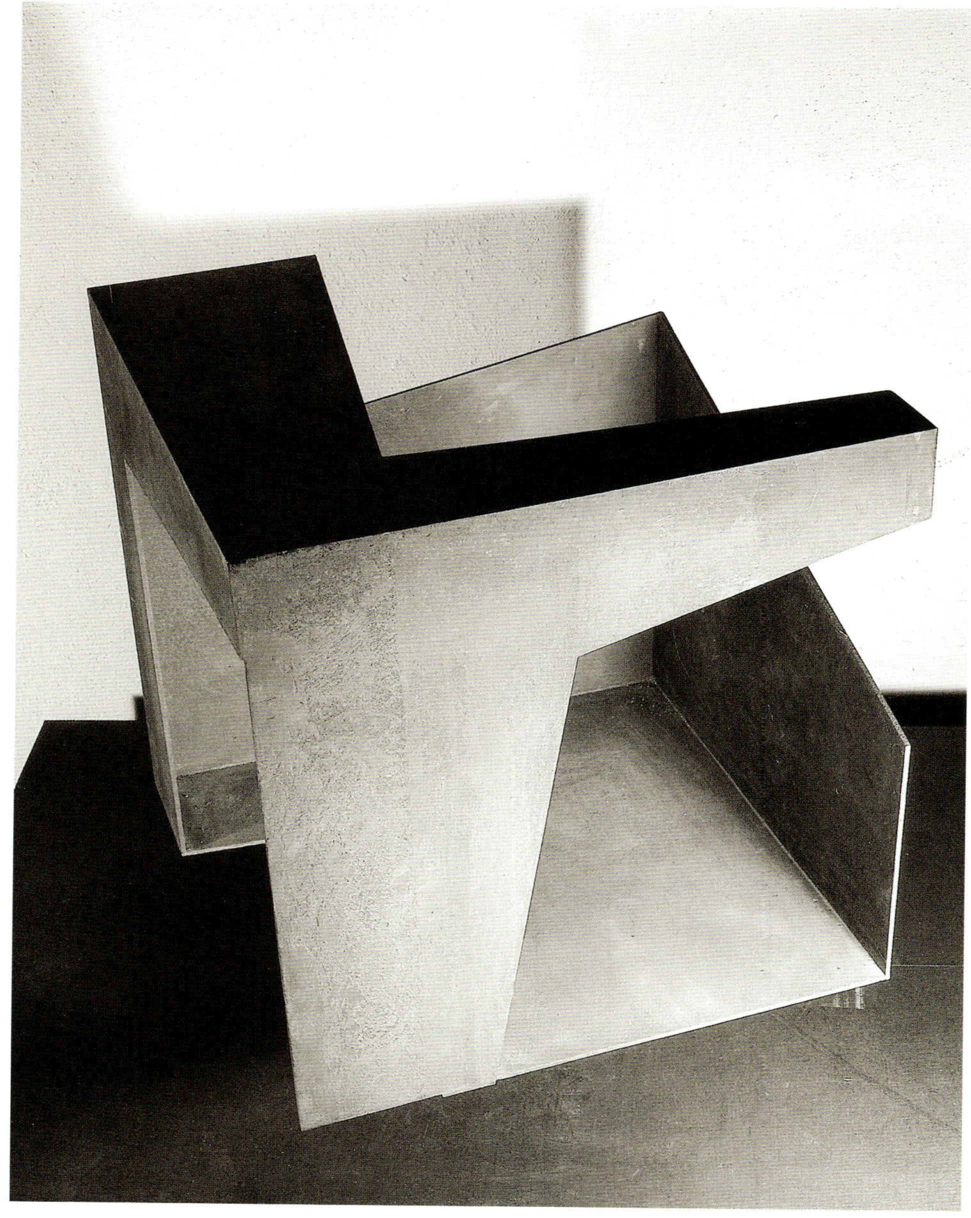

Jorge Oteiza
"Caja vacía" (Empty Box)
Spanish Catalogue

1990

Curator:
Maria Lluïsa Borràs

Participating artist:
Antoni Miralda

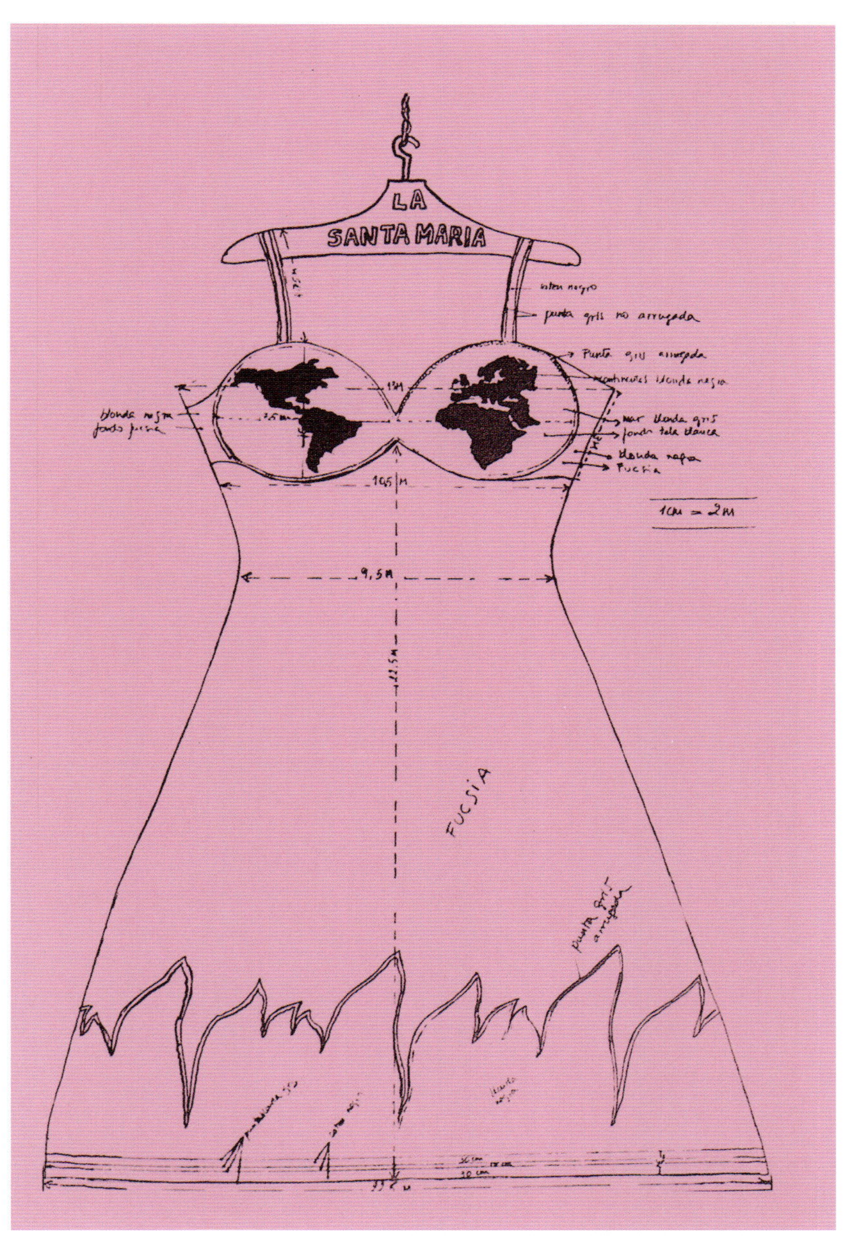

Antoni Miralda
"Proyecto Honeymoon" (Project Honeymoon)
Picture from the magazine *Lápiz*, 1990, no. 68

1993

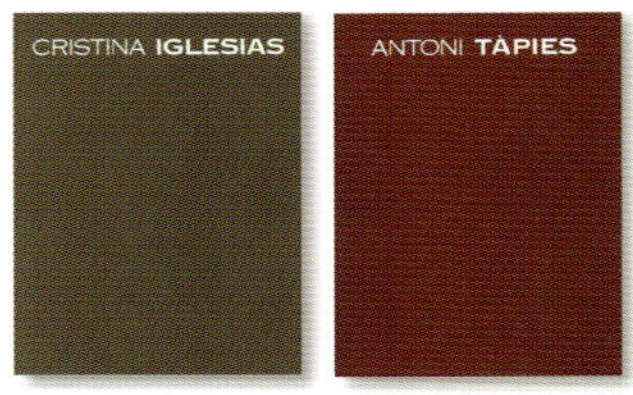

Curator:
Aurora García

Participating artists:
Cristina Iglesias
Antoni Tàpies

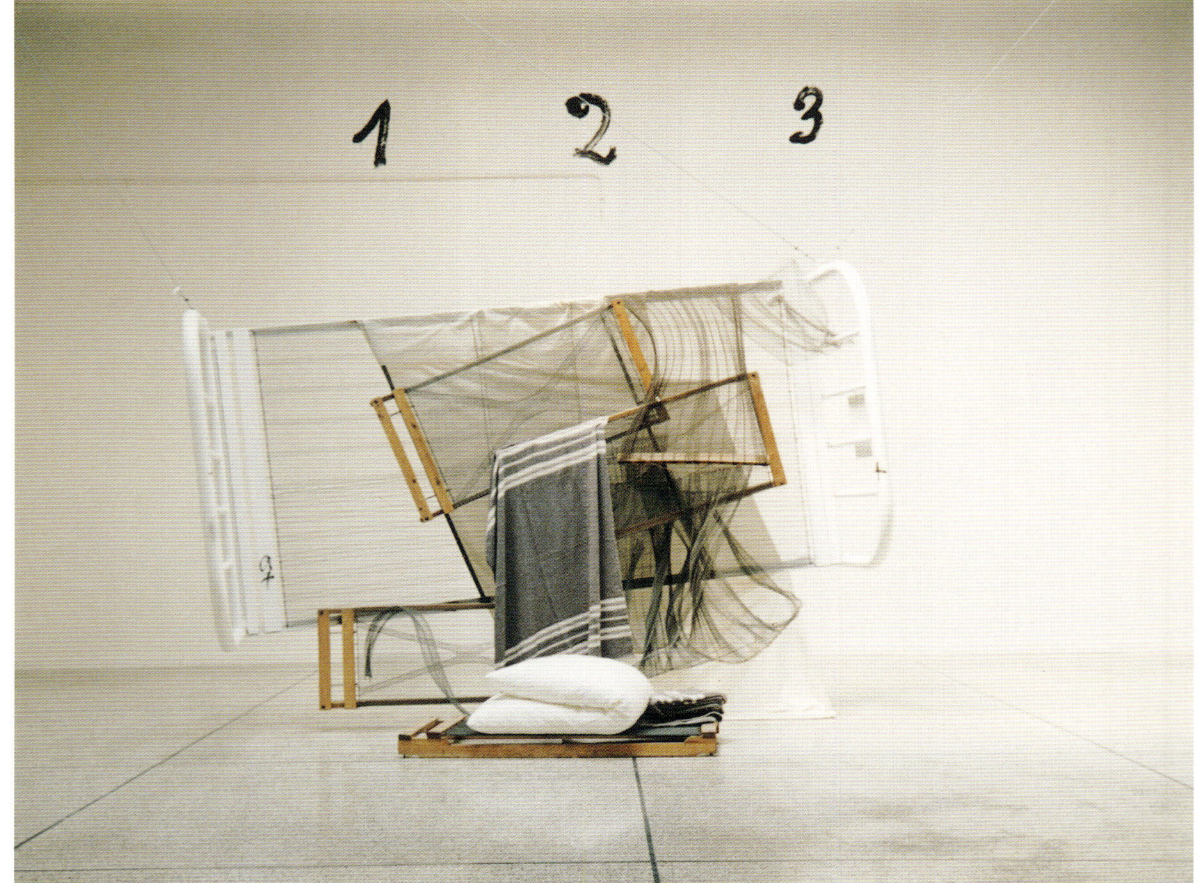

Antoni Tàpies
"Rinzen" (Sudden Awakening – detail)
Spanish Catalogue

1995

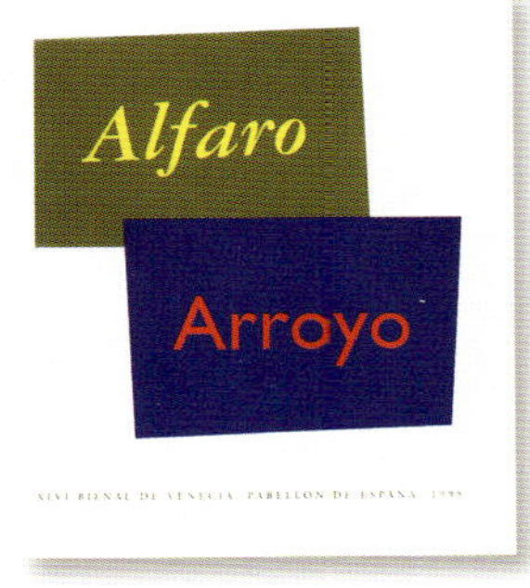

Curator:
Fernando Huici

Participating artists:
Andreu Alfaro
Eduardo Arroyo

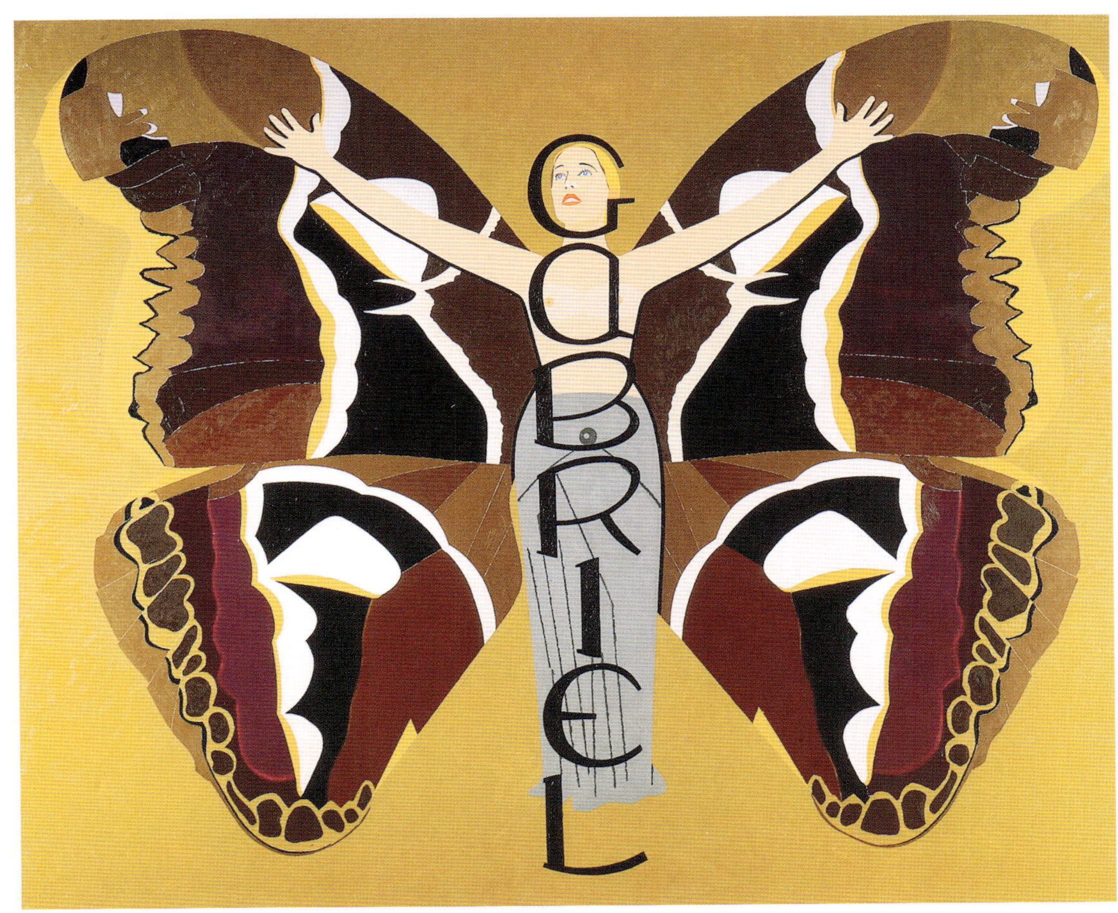

Eduardo Arroyo
"El arcángel San Gabriel" (The Archangel Gabriel)
Spanish Catalogue

1997

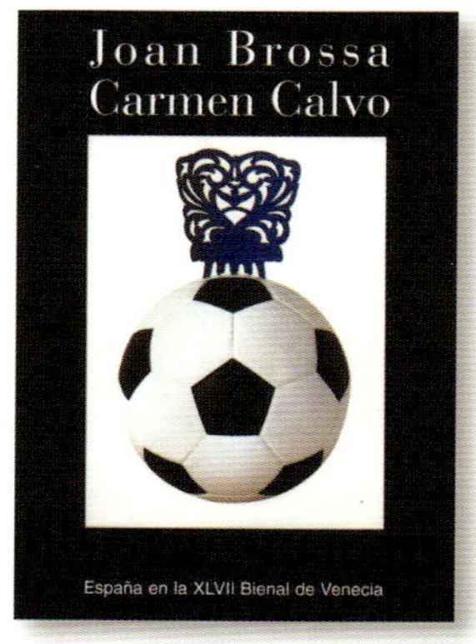

Curator:
Victoria Combalía

Participating artists:
Joan Brossa
Carmen Calvo

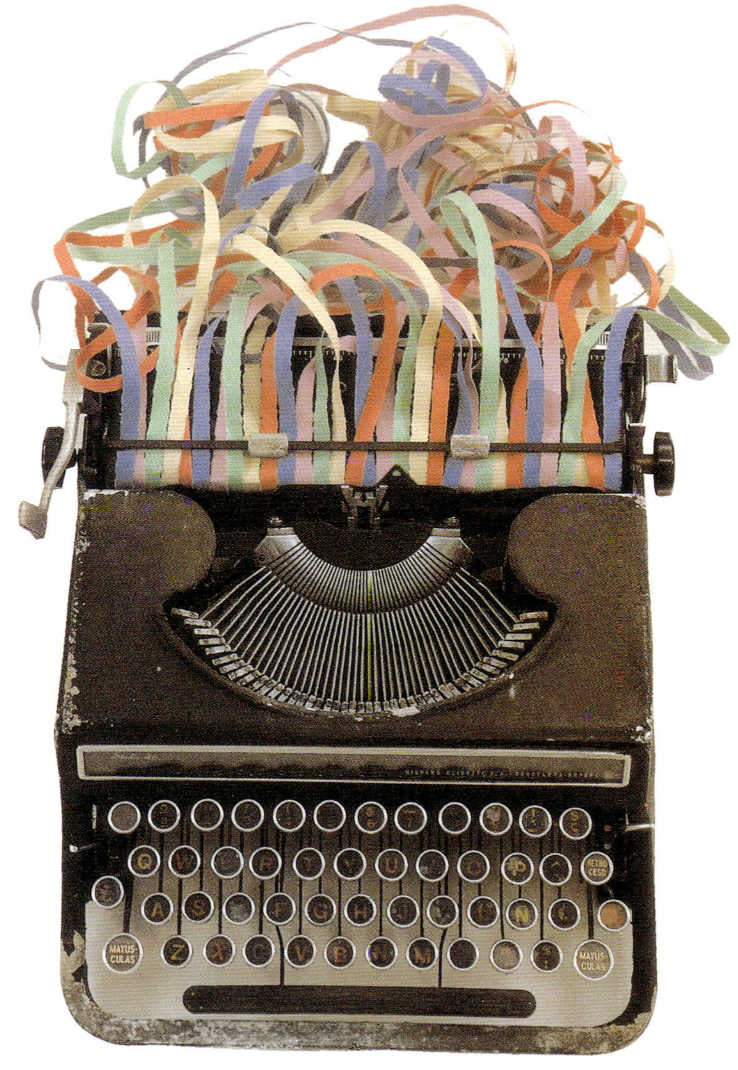

Joan Brossa
"Contes" (Stories)
Spanish Catalogue

1999

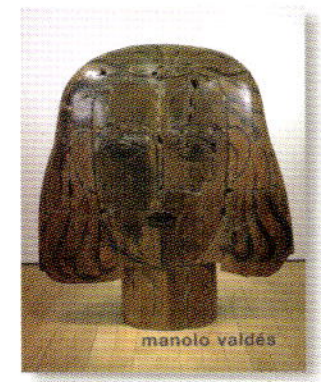

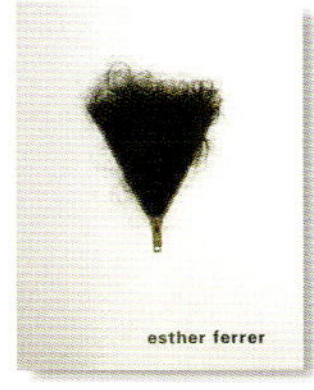

Curator:
David Pérez

Participating artists:
Esther Ferrer
Manolo Valdés
collaboration of Carles Santos

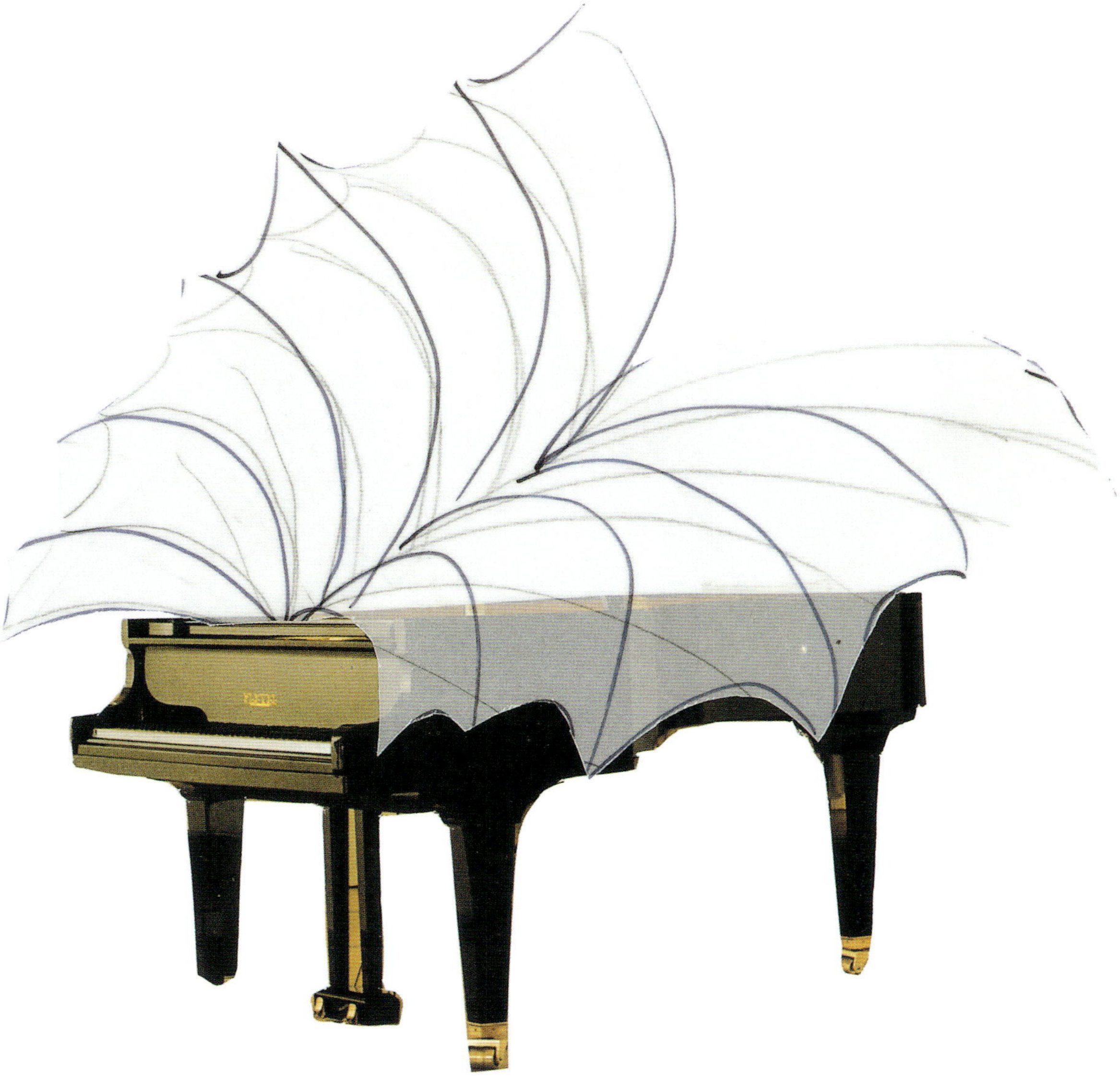

Esther Ferrer
"Piano con alas" (Piano with Wings)
Spanish Catalogue

2001

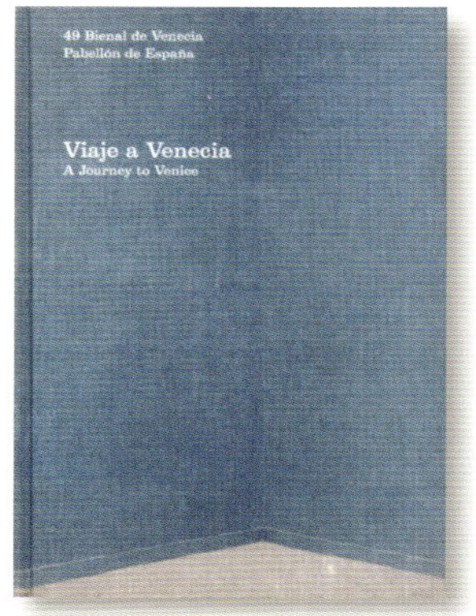

Curator:
Estrella de Diego

Participating artists:
Ana Laura Aláez
Javier Pérez

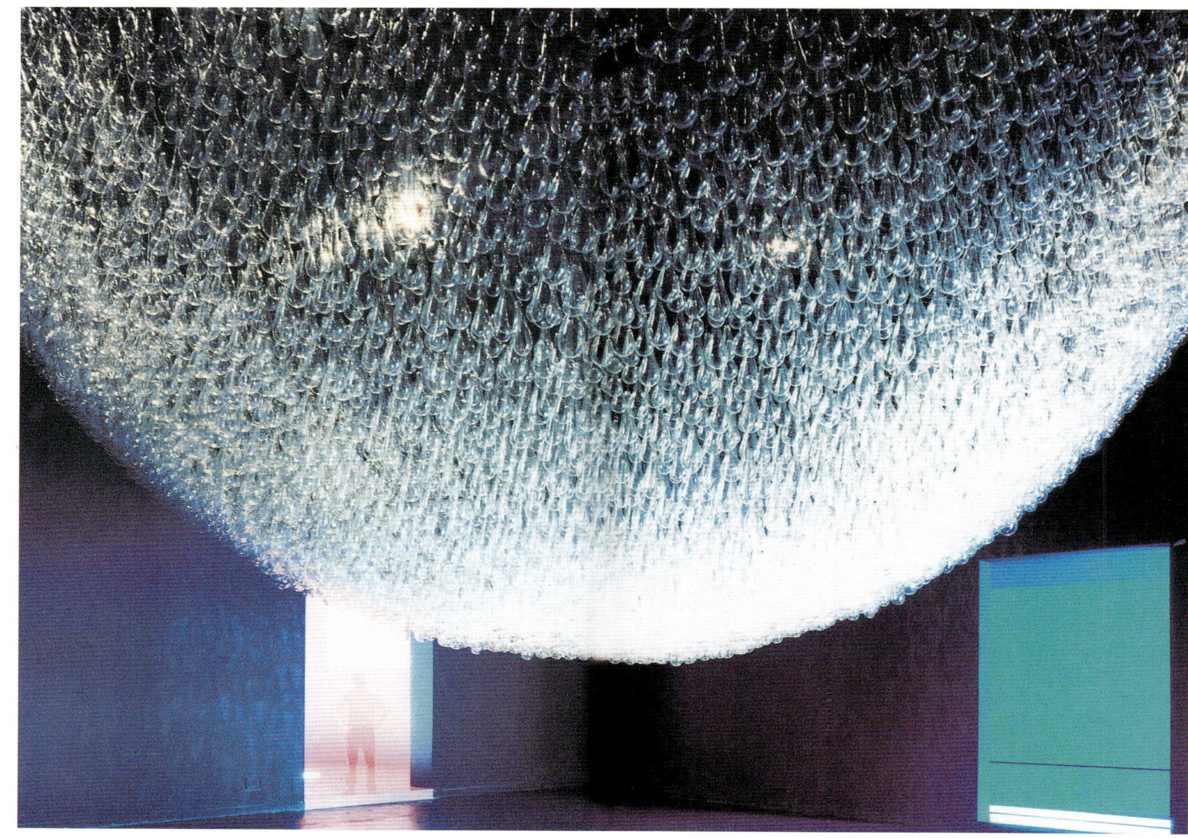

Javier Pérez
Spanish Catalogue

2003

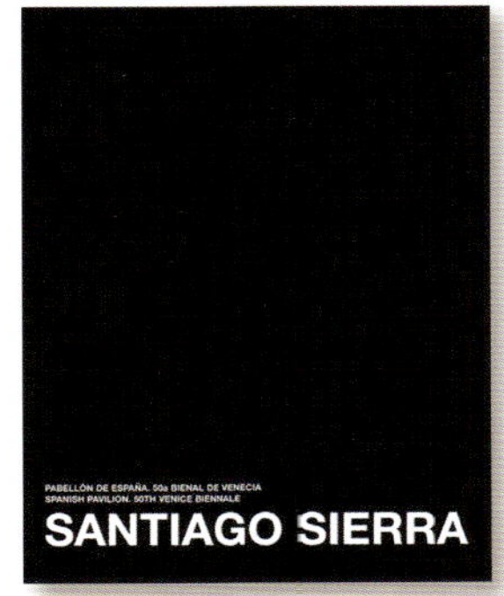

Curator:
Rosa Martínez

Participating artist:
Santiago Sierra

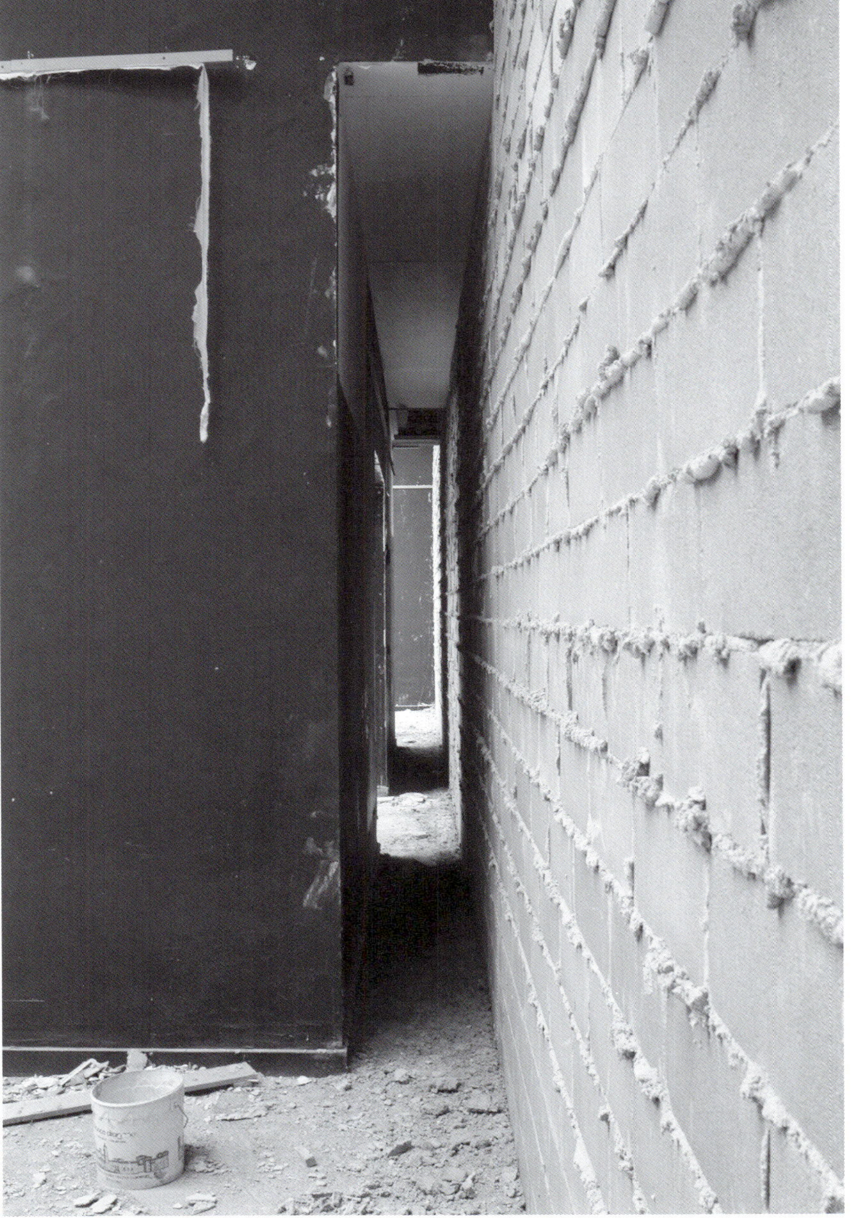

Santiago Sierra
"Muro cerrando un espacio" (Wall Enclosing a Space)
Spanish Catalogue

Personal Recollections

The "Red" Biennale.
Conversations with Tomàs Llorens

In 1976 the Venice Biennale had a facelift. The Left was gaining ground in Italy and those circumstances marked the most important manifestation of art in Europe. To the shock of some and the satisfaction of others, contemporary art regained political significance. No Venice Biennale has been talked about as much as that one; none has been so insulted or so applauded; none attracted as many visitors or has remained for ever in the collective memory as much as the one which went down in history, the "red" Biennale. And if this is true for all the countries which competed in it, it is especially so for Spain. This was because for the first time in forty years, the Spain which turned up for the great art fair was a democratic Spain. Tomàs Llorens, a young critic and history of art teacher, who was teaching in the UK and had declared himself a Marxist, like so many intellectuals of that time, was called upon by the Biennale's director, Carlo Ripa di Meana to prepare the Spanish entry. An unofficial entry, of course, and consequently, a task which was as difficult as it was risky. It was a challenge which Llorens talks about today, from his office as curator of the Thyssen-Bornemisza Museum, with a mixture of passion and distance.

There has never been so much controversy surrounding the Spanish entry in a Biennale. How would you describe today the exhibition you were principally in charge of?
A total flop.

I suppose that's just one way of putting it....
For me and for all the team's collaborators it was a huge intellectual task. But it was very poorly understood both in Spain and abroad. In that sense I mean it was a failure.

Perhaps you didn't take the trouble to explain your project....
We explained it a thousand times: by letter, verbally, in articles, at press conferences, in documents which were handed out at the Biennale itself....

But they didn't understand it.
I don't think so. The political circumstances were not right for a project like ours, and I realised that too. Our project was doomed to fail.

Could you explain once again what it consisted of?
Our project tried to make a theory out of contemporary art in Spain under Franco. The starting point was: there has been a dictatorship for forty years and in spite of the repression, the fact is that there are avant-garde movements. And the question was to determine the historical nature of these vanguard movements, where we place them. I think the argument we were proposing was fairly simple: avant-garde is a project which always pursues social change, and avant-garde art, in one way or another, pursues political change. So, how come this vanguard movement has emerged within a dictatorial, stagnant regime? And we replied: because the idea of newness is tolerated by the regime up to the specific point at which the vanguard is absorbed and integrated. So a second avant-garde wave arises, which tries to break through beyond that level, until that second level is also integrated, and so on. And so, in the end, the idea of vanguard ends up just evaporating away.

That was your controversial thesis....
Yes. To sum up, it would be that an avant-garde movement is always relative, it is always a forward escape.

In any type of society?
We realised that this was happening in capitalist society, and therefore the notion of avant-garde itself, in a society like ours, was what we were questioning.

When you say "we" do you mean your team?
Yes. Valeriano Bozal, Alberto Corazón and the two members of the Equipo Crónica: Manuel Valdés and Rafael Solbes. We all got an invitation to participate in the 1976 Venice Biennale during the summer of 1975. It was later called the Red Biennale. At that time there was a Christian Democratic Government in Italy but with a strong contingent from the Italian Communist party and major involvement of the trade unions and left-wing parties.

Was there a substantial difference between that Biennale and the preceding ones?
Of course. One of the principles of the Red Biennale was to reduce the autonomy of the national pavilions, in order to give a greater role to the artists and intellectuals, i.e. the productive

sector of art instead of the ministries of foreign affairs of each country. They also tried to be very strict about giving a slogan to each Biennale. In 1976 the slogan was "The environment." And a censorship committee was set up in order, if necessary, to reject anybody who didn't stick to the proposed slogan.

Did you think that new direction for the Biennale was a good idea?
Yes, though I didn't identify with it much. Organisational issues didn't really interest me much. I was there as an art historian, which is what I am; a philosopher who works in the area of aesthetics.

And who perhaps viewed these matters with a certain detachment....
Exactly. The fact is that we decided by common agreement to present a review of Spanish art from the end of the Civil War up to that year, 1976, forty years in total.

And with Franco still in power....
You mustn't forget that. And the project we presented was completely independent, quite separate from any Spain might present at the Biennale.

I think that's one of the questions which is never clear when we talk about this subject....
Exactly. It's never clear, and yet it's fundamental in order to understand the nature of our project. We didn't at any point feel we had the mission to represent Spain nationally, Franco's Spain. We had an order directly from the Biennale Council to stage an exhibition on an historical theme: The Avant-Garde in Art and Social Representation. The subject had a political aspect which we were very interested in....

Does it still interest you now?
It still interests me because the theoretical principles from which I designed that project I still hold to a great extent.

And while you who were chosen by the Biennale worked on the project, what was happening with the official Spanish pavilion?
The Biennale authorities decided to close the Spanish pavilion for political reasons, precisely because Spain was not a democratic regime. So, there was only going to be one Spanish project: ours.

Once again, Franco was still alive....
Yes, of course. When we outlined our project, it was July 1975. In September we received the letter telling us we had been accepted, and then a committee was set up in with, apart from the people I've already mentioned, Antonio Saura, Tàpies, Agustín Ibarrola and Oriol Bohigas. At the end of September I went back to the UK where I lived and we met up. As an architect, Oriol took charge of the design of the exhibition and Valeriano and I handled the content, following the painting and sculpture project which I had proposed. And in October we set to work. I had never done an exhibition and for me it was something very special and very important, and we put a lot of positive energy and enthusiasm into it.

You said that you started work in October and....
And at that moment we had to down tools because the Biennale Council received a series of protest letters from Spanish artists and critics who disagreed with our project, and with the committee.... Then Franco died and the Biennale stopped everything for a few months. They didn't know what was going to happen in Spain. They feared the worst.

In the meantime, if I'm not mistaken, what happened is that opposition strengthened against the project you represented.
That's right, and very intensely. There was a letter from Aguilera Cerni directed to the president of the Biennale, which was also signed by José María Moreno Galván, Alberti, who lived in Rome, and Julio Carlo Argán.... It was a sector of the Communist Party with a lot of authority in its group, very much respected and worthy of respect.

But at first sight, it's not clear what the basis of their protest was....
They were protesting because they preferred more of a tactical project, a project of national reconciliation, while the project I was proposing did not bear in mind tactical political considerations.

But it was equally political. And organised by the Left.
It was political at a theoretical level, in that it had a Marxist basis. But let's remember that Marxism is a school of philosophy.

But it is still strange that you were rejected by those who were closest to you, as if what you had presented were a defence of capitalist society.
Quite the opposite. We felt that Spain was above all a capitalist society and the object of our criticism was capitalist society.... We also thought

–and I still do– that the avant-garde movement had gradually become an academic neo-vanguard, lacking in content and utopian substance. But that criticism was not understood at the time.

Because it was too intellectual or too advanced?

Possibly. The notion of post-modernity had still not been formulated, and ours was an argument which attempted to explain the development of Spanish art from 1939 to 1976 as an exemplary case in an historic process that was the process of all modern art of the 20th century.

Why exemplary?

Because precisely the Civil War had meant turning over a new leaf and starting again, and therefore a beginning of the modernisation of Spanish culture from the most radical conservative positions. It was as if we were going back to the beginnings of modernity, and in a brief period of forty years we had turned the full circle. That is what I was basically trying to do. Others in the team thought that sounded good, but they didn't take my reasoning on board completely, nor did they have to.

So, your project was not understood. And do you think it would be understood now?

Even less so, although for different reasons. We are far from that moment. Today we live in the awareness that modernity is over and then it was still alive. And above all, we had a Marxist culture then, which we shared, and there were concepts like the process of history, or the agents of that process, which we dealt with and which today people don't understand because they haven't even heard of them.

Yes. It's not easy to explain to young people today that mix of art and politics which we experienced....

It's very difficult. The notion of politics has changed, the way of understanding politics has rejected totalising concepts. The very concept of totality is taboo; everything that reeks of totality is automatically rejected without trying to understand it. It's not in fashion and therefore is very difficult to understand.

The oddest thing is that they didn't understood you then, as those who rejected your project were also on the Left.

The Left rarely has any ambitions in the area of theory and at that moment it didn't have any either. We dared to talk of the crisis of the avant-garde movement, and to criticise it from a leftist position was a sin; it was Stalinist, and from 1960 onwards Stalinism was a sin for Marxists, therefore they shunned those concepts, that is as regards its spreading internationally. As regards publicising our project in Spain, we had two problems. Since we were forced to be very selective in the choice of artists, those who were left out complained. "We were also against Franco," they said, and the debate then went off in that direction. Secondly, we were introducing a criticism of capitalist society which at that moment was totally unsuitable. In fact, it really still is. Let's not forget that Spain after Franco is based on two dogmas: "national reconstruction," which was a slogan proposed by Santiago Carrillo in the fifties, and which means that everything which comes within the rhetoric of the embrace is good, and everything which forms part of the rhetoric of analysis and division is bad. And ours, therefore, was bad. And the other dogma is: Spain is a country with a market economy and therefore is a capitalist country, and that is unquestionable. The strange outcome was that our project was an intellectual project belonging to the Left, and the only attacks we received were precisely from there.

Perhaps what they didn't accept was that the political regime didn't have a determining influence over the development of art.

That argument seemed to us to be superficial and false.

And a bit populist, perhaps?

Certainly. And we were radically anti-populist Marxists. What I must say is that Ripa di Meana was magnificent and backed us all the way against the accusations of the Italian communists.

But really, what were they accusing you of?

Of being left-wing provacateurs, the same accusation they levelled at Eduardo Arroyo, who was linked to our group from the beginning as a bridge between Carlo Ripa di Meana, the Biennale Council and ourselves. From Madrid Arroyo was seen as an anti-communist left-wing provocateur and people remembered he had exhibited a painting of *La Pasionaria* when Franco signed the first U.S. agreement for the first bases. At that time the PCE (Spanish Communist Party) was in Moscow and, as the Soviet Communist party was in favour of avoiding confrontation with the United States, the PCE gave the order to stifle any type of anti-American protest. Arroyo then did a painting in which Dolores Ibarruri appeared as Stalin's waitress, presenting him with the American bases on a dish.

Yes. I remember that painting annoyed a lot of people....

Even a lot of honest people in the Party, people who had languished in prison for twenty years; Simón Sánchez Montero, for instance, radicals, true martyrs of the Franco period. Isaac exclaimed to me, "But how can you possibly insult Dolores in that way! He's an anti-communist and a provoker...!"

Tricky situations....

Well, yes. Because while on the one hand people were criticising us that way, on the other we were accused of being Stalinist Marxists ourselves.

In spite of everything, so many years later, that story makes you feel a bit nostalgic. It doesn't seem such a bad thing that at some time art should serve as a banner.

That's true. In Franco's Spain art was a banner, something which was not always as bad as it might seem because it helped create brilliant works. I am thinking of Blas de Otero's poetry, for instance, which was a banner and was marvellous. And on some occasions the films of Carlos Saura, and Bardem's films sometimes, and Tàpies' best paintings, or the works of the Equipo Crónica which are so good precisely for their political content.

Let's go back to the Red Biennale and to those who were in disagreement with you and presented their own project....

The alternative project was set up by Moreno Galván and Aguilera Cerni. It consisted of purely and simply taking two hundred artists to Venice. In other words: as the Venice Biennale wants to give this opportunity to democratic Spain, democratic Spain is going to be there with its two hundred artists, each one with the work he or she wants. That was the project.

And how did you react?

We tried to explain that we had nothing against his project, but that it wasn't the project that the Biennale had commissioned us to undertake. We repeatedly insisted that we didn't claim to represent Spanish art. Finally, a representative of the Artists' Assembly headed by Canogar and Genovés –I don't remember who– came to Venice to kick up a fuss at the opening, but we met him and persuaded him not to do so.

Did you get to the point of feeling that everyone was against you?

No, because many artists, critics and intellectuals respected our project and they either joined it or they didn't. At least they didn't make that sort of facile populist criticism that the others made; a criticism which, little by little, melted away.

The director of the Biennale must have been wondering which horse to back?

He considered everything but turned down the alternative project. Then, what he did do was give a place to other trends at that very important time. For instance, the group of Basque artists distanced themselves from our project because they didn't want to have anything to do with Spain. In spite of my direct negotiations with them, in the end they sent an envoy to Venice, in a very militant attitude. The Biennale Council received him and called an assembly meeting attended by us, on the one hand, them on the other, and the representatives of the Biennale Council. The Basque representative spoke in Basque, with an interpreter, and in the end they were given a pavilion and hoisted the *Ikurriña* (Basque flag).

And the Catalonians...?

There was less resistance in Catalonia because we had a lot of friends and Tàpies was involved in the project right from the start. Cirici Pellicer criticised us because we were talking on behalf of Spain and he considered that Catalonian art was not Spanish, but in general there was no active opposition as a front.

And after so many trials and tribulations, when you look back, what do you see?

On the one hand, there was the Biennale itself, which was a total success. It was visited by 700,000 people, double the number of any Biennale before or after. And then there was our exhibition, which was not understood. The international critics didn't understand anything because they had in mind this cliché that said: "Well, this is a political exhibition to represent the Spain in which Franco has just died and to spur on democratic Spain." That's how the critics saw it and logically they ignored us. As for the Italian critics, there were two positions. The old guard looked for polemics but understood us well. But the new young critics who were going to take over after the Red Biennale were only interested in the New York avant-garde, and from their point of view we were a bunch of undesirables.

And in Spain....

Here the debate dragged on for some time. In key areas of the media the Left called us controversial but acted with moderation; and the Right called us Marxists and therefore bad. We made an effort to prolong the debate. Valeriano Bozal and I wrote some articles but.. well, they were times of "national reconciliation" and that's all there is to it.

If you had landed the job for this Biennale, would you maintain your position?

The main position, yes, as regards criticism of the notion of avant-garde, but I would have to introduce variants to include everything that's happened from 1976 up till now. What would best stand the test of time would be the selection of works. Without a doubt I'd still take sixty per cent of them. And I'd also add a few names which I didn't include then.

And as regards the Biennale itself, do you think it still makes sense?

It's in decline but that's nothing new; the Red Biennale was already an attempt to revitalise it. Before that it had an absolutely brilliant period with a great historical role: to recover the spirit of modernity and classify it after the Second World War, when Italy became a democracy and the Biennale, which is its artistic window of communication with the outside world, tried to become a great window opening up to the 20th century. But that entered a crisis, like all modernity, and that crisis dragged on right through the sixties. In the seventies there was an attempt at regeneration from a position of left-wing political commitment, and the Venice Biennale is part of that context. Then it gradually became an institution again which is very much at the beck and call of the market.

There's no hope for it then?

The most interesting art today is produced by those who are outside the system, and for that reason the function of the Biennale should be to make itself the milieu where these resistance movements could be effective, as it's in Venice where, in spite of everything, the little which may remain of resistance in art today continues to surface.

• Enriqueta Antolín

My Memory of the Venice Biennale

Venice was resplendent. In the *Giardini*, curators, artists and workmen were finishing off their work. The pavilions were almost ready for the opening, which was imminent and, as usual, people were trying to keep their nerves under control. Our pavilion, Spain, had been erected a few days before that. We were apparently relaxed, however there was a certain amount of fear floating in the air; it was the first time I had acted as a curator in Venice and the artists exhibiting were practically unknown, and unexpected to boot, with a way of doing things that was different from what had been usual in previous presentations of Spanish art. Even before opening, the rumour that Spain was going to be the big surprise had circulated among the curators of the different countries. But we were the ones who were surprised at the unaccustomed to-ing and fro-ing, the murmurs, the smiles, and some disagreeable behaviour. We were happy and longing to get going. We were staking a lot but were equally confident of what we had to offer. The president of the Biennale had invited all the curators to a lunch, a prelude to the meeting of the jury which was to present the awards –awards which, we all knew had already been earmarked between the big players, much to the displeasure of the rest of us. During the lunch I noticed, somewhat to my amazement, that every time I exchanged glances with a smiling face, well disposed towards me, it was a curator from "the East". The frowns, on the other hand, came from the big players, particularly France, Britain and Germany; the strong ones and sure winners. With signs of impatience, the French curator, while still at the table, launched forth the candidature of a dreadful sculptor who, incredible as it may seem, was presented to us as the grand, uncontested winner, and whose name I prefer not to remember. There was a general silence, with a certain amount of consternation. At the end of the lunch, over coffee, the Russian curator came up to me and said, "Without a doubt you're the person who's going to put the cat among the pigeons, the one who's going to surprise everyone. What more do you want?" "Thanks," I said. "I've already got what I want. I've come to have lunch." A loud guffaw and then, "I have orders to abstain, but there are many friends who will follow my advice. That minor sculptor you people have brought..." The formal meeting began. Everyone had their candidate. Nearly all of them had a stack of books and catalogues to help them hammer home the virtues of their respective candidates. In front of me I had only my hands crossed, a writing pad, a pen and a glass of water. The Grand Prize went to the then unknown minor sculptor. His name was Eduardo Chillida.

That is how I remember my debut as Spanish curator of the Venice Biennale. That moment was preceded by a great deal of work during those months, major arguments, untiring visits, and quite a lot of doubts, all thrown in with a fair amount of concern, as I was worried that the risk of stirring the waters of national art would not be compensated for by success, although, the truth be told, what we were most worried about was being given a cold reception.

We had successfully held the Latin-American Biennales in Madrid and Barcelona and the large-scale complicated one in Cuba. Perhaps spurred by that result, the Ministry of Foreign Affairs entrusted us, as the exhibition department of the Instituto de Cultura Hispánica, with the task of handling the Spanish pavilion at the Alexandria Biennale, which was really my baptism in this complicated business of Biennales. There Álvaro Delgado received an important award. One fine day, Ambassador Villacieros, who at that time was the head of cultural relations, had called me to tell me what I least expected: "González Robles, I want you to handle the selection of the Spanish artists for the Venice Biennale". "With all its consequences?" I asked. "Just as you see fit" was the reply. And those were all the instructions or orders I got then, and all those years I was curator. No-one at the ministry or at any other institution ever told me who I should take and who not. I always followed my own judgement and what I believed was best for Spanish art to win. I suppose that, seen with the wisdom of hindsight, the different groups of artists chosen may have had some common denominator when all is said and done, although you aim to avoid your own personal tastes having too much influence. They always do anyway, but my aim was always to chose artists who my intuition told me would best fit in. For that reason I didn't take the same people to Venice as the ones who went to Sâo Paulo. Chillida won in Venice and Oteiza in Sâo Paulo, for instance. Tàpies stood out in Venice, Cuixart in Sâo Paulo.

Of course from time to time I have received calls and recommendations. But I have never suffered from the least government pressure. It was artists, galleries, critics and friends; all had something to say and I listened to all of them but, in the end, my final choice gradually took shape as a result of my visits to studios, exhibitions, and my interest in getting a complete view of what was afoot in the centres of opinion, and in knowing which road would lead us to the awards. There were also some curious pieces of advice. For example, after the triumph and big surprise over the new Spanish art at the Venice Biennale, one of the artists, now a major influence all over the world, who achieved great personal success and was courted by the world's leading galleries, was coming back with me in the car after the excitement of Venice was over. He spent the whole of the journey back giving me advice; "You mustn't look for any more new artists, no more brilliant, earth-shattering young talents. You've got to call the people who always used to go; the